The Collected Poems

by Sylvia Plath

poetry

THE COLOSSUS
ARIEL
CROSSING THE WATER
WINTER TREES

fiction

THE BELL JAR

The Collected Poems

Sylvia Plath

Edited by Ted Hughes

1817

HARPER & ROW, PUBLISHERS, New York

Cambridge, Philadelphia, San Francisco,
London, Mexico City, São Paulo, Sydney

"Rhyme," "Black Pine Tree in an Orange Light," "Incommunicado," and "Morning in the Hospital Solarium" originally appeared in *The American Poetry Review*.

"Waking in Winter," "Barren Woman," "Perseus," and "Song for a Summer's Day" originally appeared in *The New York Times Book Review*.

FIRST U.S. EDITION

Library of Congress Cataloging in Publication Data

Plath, Sylvia.
  The collected poems.
  Includes index.
  I. Hughes, Ted, 1930-   II. Title.
PS3566.L27A17 1981   811'.54   75-25057
                        AACR2
ISBN 0-06-013369-4   81 82 83 84 85 10 9 8 7 6 5 4 3 2 1
ISBN 0-06-090900-5 (pbk.)   81 82 83 84 85 10 9 8 7 6 5 4 3 2 1

Contents

Contents

Contents

Contents

Contents

Contents

Contents

Juvenilia

A Selection of Fifty Early Poems

Contents

Introduction

By the time of her death, on 11 February 1963, Sylvia Plath had written a large bulk of poetry. To my knowledge, she never scrapped any of her poetic efforts. With one or two exceptions, she brought every piece she worked on to some final form acceptable to her, rejecting at most the odd verse, or a false head or a false tail. Her attitude to her verse was artisan-like: if she couldn't get a table out of the material, she was quite happy to get a chair, or even a toy. The end product for her was not so much a successful poem, as something that had temporarily exhausted her ingenuity. So this book contains not merely what verse she saved, but—after 1956—all she wrote.

From quite early she began to assemble her poems into a prospective collection, which at various times she presented—always hopeful—to publishers and to the judging committees of contests. The collection evolved through the years in a natural way, shedding old poems and growing new ones, until by the time the contract for *The Colossus* was signed with Heinemann, in London, on 11 February 1960, this first book had gone through several titles and several changes of substance. 'I had a vision in the dark art lecture room today of *the* title of my book of poems,' she wrote in early 1958. 'It came to me suddenly with great clarity that *The Earthenware Head* was the right title, the only title.' She goes on to say, 'Somehow this new title spells for me the release from the old crystal-brittle and sugar-faceted voice of *Circus in Three Rings* and *Two Lovers and a Beachcomber*' (the two immediately preceding titles). Two months later she had replaced *The Earthenware Head*, briefly, with *The Everlasting Monday*. A fortnight later the title had become *Full Fathom Five*, 'after what I consider one of my best and most curiously moving poems, about my father-sea god-muse . . . "[The Lady and] The Earthenware Head" is out: once, in England, my "best poem": too fancy, glassy, patchy and rigid—it embarrasses me now— with its ten elaborate epithets for head in five verses.'

During the next year *Full Fathom Five* was replaced by *The Bull of Bendylaw*, but then in May 1959 she wrote: 'Changed title of poetry book in an inspiration to *The Devil of the Stairs* . . . this title encompasses my book and "explains" the poems of despair, which is as deceitful as hope is.' This title lasted until October, when she was at Yaddo, and now on a different kind of inspiration she noted: 'Wrote two poems that pleased me. One a poem to Nicholas' (she expected a son, and titled the poem 'The Manor Garden') 'and one the old father-worship subject' (which she titled 'The Colossus'). 'But different. Weirder. I see a picture, a weather, in these poems. Took "Medallion" out of the early book and made up my mind to start a second book, regardless. The main thing is to get rid of the idea that what I write now is for the old book. That soggy book. So I have three poems for the new, temporarily called *The Colossus and other poems*.'

This decision to start a new book 'regardless', and get rid of all that she'd written up to then, coincided with the first real breakthrough in her writing, as it is now possible to see. The actual inner process of this quite sudden development is interestingly recorded, in a metaphorical way, in 'Poem for a Birthday', which she was thinking about on 22 October 1959 (cf. note on No. 119). On 4 November she wrote: 'Miraculously I wrote seven poems in my "Poem for a Birthday" sequence, and the two little ones before it, "The Manor Garden" and "The Colossus", I find colorful and amusing. But the manuscript of my [old] book seems dead to me. So far off, so far gone. It has almost no chance of finding a publisher: just sent it out to the seventh. . . . There is nothing for it but to try to publish it in England.' A few days later she noted: 'I wrote a good poem this week on our walk Sunday to the burnt-out spa, a second-book poem. How it consoles me, the idea of a second book with these new poems: "The Manor Garden", "The Colossus", the seven birthday poems and perhaps "Medallion", if I don't stick it in my present book.' But then she realized: 'If I were accepted by a publisher . . . I would feel a need to throw all my new poems in, to bolster the book.'

This last is exactly what happened. With time running out at Yaddo, which had suddenly become so fruitful for her, followed by the upheaval of returning to England in December, she was able to add very little to her 'second' book. So it was this combination of the old poems, which she had inwardly rejected, and the few new ones that seemed to her so different, that James Michie told her—in January 1960—Heinemann would like to publish, under the title of *The Colossus*.

Once that contract had been signed, she started again, though with a noticeable difference. As before, a poem was always 'a book poem' or 'not a book poem', but now she seemed more relaxed about it, and made no attempt to find an anxious mothering title for the growing brood, over the next two years, until she was overtaken by the inspiration that produced the poems of the last six months of her life.

Some time around Christmas 1962, she gathered most of what are now known as the 'Ariel' poems in a black spring binder, and arranged them in a careful sequence. (At the time, she pointed out that it began with the word

'Love' and ended with the word 'Spring'. The exact order of her text is given in the Notes, p. 295.) This collection of hers excluded almost everything she had written between *The Colossus* and July 1962—or two and a half years' work. She had her usual trouble with a title. On the title-page of her manuscript *The Rival* is replaced by *A Birthday Present* which is replaced by *Daddy*. It was only a short time before she died that she altered the title again, to *Ariel*.

The *Ariel* eventually published in 1965 was a somewhat different volume from the one she had planned. It incorporated most of the dozen or so poems she had gone on to write in 1963, though she herself, recognizing the different inspiration of these new pieces, regarded them as the beginnings of a third book. It omitted some of the more personally aggressive poems from 1962, and might have omitted one or two more if she had not already published them herself in magazines—so that by 1965 they were widely known. The collection that appeared was my eventual compromise between publishing a large bulk of her work—including much of the post-*Colossus* but pre-*Ariel* verse—and introducing her late work more cautiously, printing perhaps only twenty poems to begin with. (Several advisers had felt that the violent contradictory feelings expressed in those pieces might prove hard for the reading public to take. In one sense, as it turned out, this apprehension showed some insight.)

A further collection, *Crossing the Water* (1971), contained most of the poems written between the two earlier books; and the same year the final collection, *Winter Trees*, was published, containing eighteen uncollected poems of the late period together with her verse play for radio, *Three Women*, which had been written in early 1962.

The aim of the present complete edition, which contains a numbered sequence of the 224 poems written after 1956 together with a further 50 poems chosen from her pre-1956 work, is to bring Sylvia Plath's poetry together in one volume, including the various uncollected and unpublished pieces, and to set everything in as true a chronological order as is possible, so that the whole progress and achievement of this unusual poet will become accessible to readers.

The manuscripts on which this collection is based fall roughly into three phases, and each has presented slightly different problems to the editor.

The first phase might be called her juvenilia and the first slight problem here was to decide where it ended. A logical division occurs, conveniently, at the end of 1955, just after the end of her twenty-third year. The 220 or more poems written before this are of interest mainly to specialists. Sylvia Plath had set these pieces (many of them from her early teens) firmly behind her and would certainly never have republished them herself. Nevertheless, quite a few seem worth preserving for the general reader. At their best, they are as distinctive and as finished as anything she wrote later. They can be intensely artificial, but they are always lit with her unique excitement. And that sense of a deep mathematical inevitability in the sound and texture of her lines was well developed quite early. One can see here, too, how exclusively her writing depended on a supercharged system of inner symbols and images, an enclosed cosmic circus. If that could have been projected visually, the substance and patterning of these poems would have made very curious mandalas. As poems, they are always inspired high jinks, but frequently quite a bit more. And even at their weakest they help chart the full acceleration towards her final take-off.

The greater part of these early poems survive in final typed copies; some others have been recovered from magazines, and still others, not in the typescript and not appearing in any magazine, have turned up in letters and elsewhere. Presumably there may be more, still hidden. The chronological order of the work of this period is often impossible to determine, except in its broadest outlines. A date can sometimes be fixed from a letter or from the date of magazine publication, but she occasionally took poems up again— sometimes years later—and reworked them.

From this whole pre-1956 period, I have selected what seem to be the best, some fifty pieces, and these are printed—as nearly as possible in the order of their writing—at the back of the book, as an appendix. Also given there is a complete list, alphabetically by title, of all the pre-1956 poems that survive, with dates where these can be assigned.

The second phase of Sylvia Plath's writing falls between early 1956 and late 1960. Early 1956 presents itself as a watershed, because from later this year come the earliest poems of her first collection, *The Colossus*. And from this time I worked closely with her and watched the poems being written, so I am reasonably sure that everything is here. Searching over the years, we have failed to unearth any others. Final typescripts exist for all of them. The chronological order, also, is less in doubt here, though the problem does still linger. Her evolution as a poet went rapidly through successive moults of style, as she realized her true matter and voice. Each fresh phase tended to bring out a group of poems bearing a general family likeness, and is usually associated in my memory with a particular time and place. At each move we made, she seemed to shed a style.

So the sequence of the groups of poems through this period is fairly certain. But I am rarely sure now which poem comes before which in any particular group. In among them, the odd poem will pop up that looks like a leftover from long before. Occasionally, she anticipated herself and

Introduction

produced a poem ('Two Lovers and a Beachcomber by the Real Sea', for instance, in the pre-1956 selection, or 'The Stones' from her 1959 'Poem for a Birthday') which now seems to belong quite a bit later. In several cases I can fix poems precisely to a date and place. (She was writing 'Miss Drake Proceeds to Supper' on a parapet over the Seine on 21 June 1956.) Then again, in one or two cases the dates she left on the manuscripts contradict what seem to me very definite memories. So I have nowhere attempted to affix a date where none appears on the manuscript. Fortunately, after 1956 she kept a full record of the dates on which she sent her poems off to magazines, and she usually did this as soon as possible after writing them, which sets one limit to my approximations of order.

The third and final phase of her work, from the editorial point of view, dates from about September 1960. Around that time, she started the habit of dating the final typescript of each poem. On the two or three occasions when she modified a poem later, she dated the revision as well. From early 1962 she began to save all her handwritten drafts (which up to that time she had systematically destroyed as she went along), and provisional final versions among these are usually dated as well. So throughout this period the calendar sequence is correct, and the only occasional doubt concerns the order of composition among poems written on the same day.

I have resisted the temptation to reproduce the drafts of these last poems in variorum completeness. These drafts are arguably an important part of Sylvia Plath's complete works. Some of the handwritten pages are aswarm with startling, beautiful phrases and lines, crowding all over the place, many of them in no way less remarkable than the ones she eventually picked out to make her final poem. But printing them all would have made a huge volume.

A poem 'for two voices', never produced or published, is given in the notes to the poem 'Ouija' (No. 62), where it is relevant. Some cancelled but quite large fragments or sections of poems are also given in the Notes, and the poet's literal rendering of Rilke's 'A Prophet'. The Notes provide brief biographical information for each of the years 1956–1963, and the background on certain poems. A concordance sets out the contents of each of the four published volumes in terms of the chronological numbering adopted in this complete edition.

Thanks and acknowledgements are due to Judith Kroll, who went over the manuscripts and did much to establish many of the final texts in their detail, and to the Lilly Library, Indiana University, Bloomington, for access to the Sylvia Plath Archive of juvenilia.

August 1980   TED HUGHES

POEMS
1956-1963

1956

1 Conversation Among the Ruins

Through portico of my elegant house you stalk
With your wild furies, disturbing garlands of fruit
And the fabulous lutes and peacocks, rending the net
Of all decorum which holds the whirlwind back.
Now, rich order of walls is fallen; rooks croak
Above the appalling ruin; in bleak light
Of your stormy eye, magic takes flight
Like a daunted witch, quitting castle when real days break.

Fractured pillars frame prospects of rock;
While you stand heroic in coat and tie, I sit
Composed in Grecian tunic and psyche-knot,
Rooted to your black look, the play turned tragic:
With such blight wrought on our bankrupt estate,
What ceremony of words can patch the havoc?

2 Winter Landscape, with Rooks

Water in the millrace, through a sluice of stone,
  plunges headlong into that black pond
where, absurd and out-of-season, a single swan
  floats chaste as snow, taunting the clouded mind
which hungers to haul the white reflection down.

The austere sun descends above the fen,
  an orange cyclops-eye, scorning to look
longer on this landscape of chagrin;
  feathered dark in thought, I stalk like a rook,
brooding as the winter night comes on.

1956

Last summer's reeds are all engraved in ice
　as is your image in my eye; dry frost
glazes the window of my hurt; what solace
　can be struck from rock to make heart's waste
grow green again? Who'd walk in this bleak place?

3

Pursuit

Dans le fond des forêts votre image me suit.
RACINE

There is a panther stalks me down:
　One day I'll have my death of him;
　His greed has set the woods aflame,
He prowls more lordly than the sun.
Most soft, most suavely glides that step,
　Advancing always at my back;
　From gaunt hemlock, rooks croak havoc:
The hunt is on, and sprung the trap.
Flayed by thorns I trek the rocks,
　Haggard through the hot white noon.
　Along red network of his veins
What fires run, what craving wakes?

Insatiate, he ransacks the land
　Condemned by our ancestral fault,
　Crying: blood, let blood be spilt;
Meat must glut his mouth's raw wound.
Keen the rending teeth and sweet
　The singeing fury of his fur;
　His kisses parch, each paw's a briar,
Doom consummates that appetite.
In the wake of this fierce cat,
　Kindled like torches for his joy,
　Charred and ravened women lie,
Become his starving body's bait.

Now hills hatch menace, spawning shade;
　Midnight cloaks the sultry grove;
　The black marauder, hauled by love

On fluent haunches, keeps my speed.
Behind snarled thickets of my eyes
  Lurks the lithe one; in dreams' ambush
  Bright those claws that mar the flesh
And hungry, hungry, those taut thighs.
His ardor snares me, lights the trees,
  And I run flaring in my skin;
  What lull, what cool can lap me in
When burns and brands that yellow gaze?

I hurl my heart to halt his pace,
  To quench his thirst I squander blood;
  He eats, and still his need seeks food,
Compels a total sacrifice.
His voice waylays me, spells a trance,
  The gutted forest falls to ash;
  Appalled by secret want, I rush
From such assault of radiance.
Entering the tower of my fears,
  I shut my doors on that dark guilt,
  I bolt the door, each door I bolt.
Blood quickens, gonging in my cars:

The panther's tread is on the stairs,
Coming up and up the stairs.

Bucolics

4

Mayday: two came to field in such wise:
'A daisied mead,' each said to each,
So were they one; so sought they couch,
Across barbed stile, through flocked brown cows.

'No pitchforked farmer, please,' she said;
'May cockcrow guard us safe,' said he;
By blackthorn thicket, flower spray
They pitched their coats, come to green bed.

Below: a fen where water stood;
Aslant: their hill of stinging nettle;
Then, honor-bound, mute grazing cattle;
Above: leaf-wraithed white air, white cloud.

All afternoon these lovers lay
Until the sun turned pale from warm,
Until sweet wind changed tune, blew harm:
Cruel nettles stung her ankles raw.

Rueful, most vexed, that tender skin
Should accept so fell a wound,
He stamped and cracked stalks to the ground
Which had caused his dear girl pain.

Now he goes from his rightful road
And, under honor, will depart;
While she stands burning, venom-girt,
In wait for sharper smart to fade.

Tale of a Tub

5

The photographic chamber of the eye
records bare painted walls, while an electric light
flays the chromium nerves of plumbing raw;
such poverty assaults the ego; caught
naked in the merely actual room,
the stranger in the lavatory mirror
puts on a public grin, repeats our name
but scrupulously reflects the usual terror.

Just how guilty are we when the ceiling
reveals no cracks that can be decoded? when washbowl
maintains it has no more holy calling
than physical ablution, and the towel
dryly disclaims that fierce troll faces lurk
in its explicit folds? or when the window,
blind with steam, will not admit the dark
which shrouds our prospects in ambiguous shadow?

1956

Twenty years ago, the familiar tub
bred an ample batch of omens; but now
water faucets spawn no danger; each crab
and octopus—scrabbling just beyond the view,
waiting for some accidental break
in ritual, to strike—is definitely gone;
the authentic sea denies them and will pluck
fantastic flesh down to the honest bone.

We take the plunge; under water our limbs
waver, faintly green, shuddering away
from the genuine color of skin; can our dreams
ever blur the intransigent lines which draw
the shape that shuts us in? absolute fact
intrudes even when the revolted eye
is closed; the tub exists behind our back:
its glittering surfaces are blank and true.

Yet always the ridiculous nude flanks urge
the fabrication of some cloth to cover
such starkness; accuracy must not stalk at large:
each day demands we create our whole world over,
disguising the constant horror in a coat
of many-colored fictions; we mask our past
in the green of eden, pretend future's shining fruit
can sprout from the navel of this present waste.

In this particular tub, two knees jut up
like icebergs, while minute brown hairs rise
on arms and legs in a fringe of kelp; green soap
navigates the tidal slosh of seas
breaking on legendary beaches; in faith
we shall board our imagined ship and wildly sail
among sacred islands of the mad till death
shatters the fabulous stars and makes us real.

Southern Sunrise

6

Color of lemon, mango, peach,
These storybook villas
Still dream behind
Shutters, their balconies
Fine as hand-
Made lace, or a leaf-and-flower pen-sketch.

Tilting with the winds,
On arrowy stems,
Pineapple-barked,
A green crescent of palms
Sends up its forked
Firework of fronds.

A quartz-clear dawn
Inch by bright inch
Gilds all our Avenue,
And out of the blue drench
Of Angels' Bay
Rises the round red watermelon sun.

Channel Crossing

7

On storm-struck deck, wind sirens caterwaul;
With each tilt, shock and shudder, our blunt ship
Cleaves forward into fury; dark as anger,
Waves wallop, assaulting the stubborn hull.
Flayed by spray, we take the challenge up,
Grip the rail, squint ahead, and wonder how much longer

Such force can last; but beyond, the neutral view
Shows, rank on rank, the hungry seas advancing.
Below, rocked havoc-sick, voyagers lie
Retching in bright orange basins; a refugee
Sprawls, hunched in black, among baggage, wincing
Under the strict mask of his agony.

1956

Far from the sweet stench of that perilous air
In which our comrades are betrayed, we freeze
And marvel at the smashing nonchalance
Of nature: what better way to test taut fiber
Than against this onslaught, these casual blasts of ice
That wrestle with us like angels; the mere chance

Of making harbor through this racketing flux
Taunts us to valor. Blue sailors sang that our journey
Would be full of sun, white gulls, and water drenched
With radiance, peacock-colored; instead, bleak rocks
Jutted early to mark our going, while sky
Curded over with clouds and chalk cliffs blanched

In sullen light of the inauspicious day.
Now, free, by hazard's quirk, from the common ill
Knocking our brothers down, we strike a stance
Most mock-heroic, to cloak our waking awe
At this rare rumpus which no man can control:
Meek and proud both fall; stark violence

Lays all walls waste; private estates are torn,
Ransacked in the public eye. We forsake
Our lone luck now, compelled by bond, by blood,
To keep some unsaid pact; perhaps concern
Is helpless here, quite extra, yet we must make
The gesture, bend and hold the prone man's head.

And so we sail toward cities, streets and homes
Of other men, where statues celebrate
Brave acts played out in peace, in war; all dangers
End: green shores appear; we assume our names,
Our luggage, as docks halt our brief epic; no debt
Survives arrival; we walk the plank with strangers.

Prospect

Among orange-tile rooftops
  and chimney pots
the fen fog slips,
  gray as rats,

while on spotted branch
  of the sycamore
two black rooks hunch
  and darkly glare,

watching for night,
  with absinthe eye
cocked on the lone, late,
  passer-by.

The Queen's Complaint

In ruck and quibble of courtfolk
This giant hulked, I tell you, on her scene
With hands like derricks,
Looks fierce and black as rooks;
Why, all the windows broke when he stalked in.

Her dainty acres he ramped through
And used her gentle doves with manners rude;
I do not know
What fury urged him slay
Her antelope who meant him naught but good.

She spoke most chiding in his ear
Till he some pity took upon her crying;
Of rich attire
He made her shoulders bare
And solaced her, but quit her at cock's crowing.

1956

A hundred heralds she sent out
To summon in her slight all doughty men
Whose force might fit
Shape of her sleep, her thought—
None of that greenhorn lot matched her bright crown.

So she is come to this rare pass
Whereby she treks in blood through sun and squall
And sings you thus:
'How sad, alas, it is
To see my people shrunk so small, so small.'

Ode for Ted

10

From under crunch of my man's boot
green oat-sprouts jut;
he names a lapwing, starts rabbits in a rout
legging it most nimble
to sprigged hedge of bramble,
stalks red fox, shrewd stoat.

Loam-humps, he says, moles shunt
up from delved worm-haunt;
blue fur, moles have; hefting chalk-hulled flint
he with rock splits open
knobbed quartz; flayed colors ripen
rich, brown, sudden in sunglint.

For his least look, scant acres yield:
each finger-furrowed field
heaves forth stalk, leaf, fruit-nubbed emerald;
bright grain sprung so rarely
he hauls to his will early;
at his hand's staunch hest, birds build.

Ringdoves roost well within his wood,
shirr songs to suit which mood
he saunters in; how but most glad

could be this adam's woman
when all earth his words do summon
leaps to laud such man's blood!

21 April 1956

11   # Firesong

Born green we were
to this flawed garden,
but in speckled thickets, warted as a toad,
spitefully skulks our warden,
fixing his snare
which hauls down buck, cock, trout, till all most fair
is tricked to falter in spilt blood.

Now our whole task's to hack
some angel-shape worth wearing
from his crabbed midden where all's wrought so awry
that no straight inquiring
could unlock
shrewd catch silting our each bright act back
to unmade mud cloaked by sour sky.

Sweet salts warped stem
of weeds we tackle towards way's rank ending;
scorched by red sun
we heft globed flint, racked in veins' barbed bindings;
brave love, dream
not of staunching such strict flame, but come,
lean to my wound; burn on, burn on.

12   # Song for a Summer's Day

Through fen and farmland walking
With my own country love
I saw slow flocked cows move

1956

White hulks on their day's cruising;
Sweet grass sprang for their grazing.

The air was bright for looking:
Most far in blue, aloft,
Clouds steered a burnished drift;
Larks' nip and tuck arising
Came in for my love's praising.

Sheen of the noon sun striking
Took my heart as if
It were a green-tipped leaf
Kindled by my love's pleasing
Into an ardent blazing.

And so, together, talking,
Through Sunday's honey-air
We walked (and still walk there—
Out of the sun's bruising)
Till the night mists came rising.

Two Sisters of Persephone

Two girls there are: within the house
One sits; the other, without.
Daylong a duet of shade and light
Plays between these.

In her dark wainscoted room
The first works problems on
A mathematical machine.
Dry ticks mark time

As she calculates each sum.
At this barren enterprise
Rat-shrewd go her squint eyes,
Root-pale her meager frame.

1956

Bronzed as earth, the second lies,
Hearing ticks blown gold
Like pollen on bright air. Lulled
Near a bed of poppies,

She sees how their red silk flare
Of petaled blood
Burns open to sun's blade.
On that green altar

Freely become sun's bride, the latter
Grows quick with seed.
Grass-couched in her labor's pride,
She bears a king. Turned bitter

And sallow as any lemon,
The other, wry virgin to the last,
Goes graveward with flesh laid waste,
Worm-husbanded, yet no woman.

Vanity Fair

14

Through frost-thick weather
This witch sidles, fingers crooked, as if
Caught in a hazardous medium that might
Merely by its continuing
Attach her to heaven.

At eye's envious corner
Crow's-feet copy veining on stained leaf;
Cold squint steals sky's color; while bruit
Of bells calls holy ones, her tongue
Backtalks at the raven

Cleaving furred air
Over her skull's midden; no knife
Rivals her whetted look, divining what conceit
Waylays simple girls, church-going,
And what heart's oven

Craves most to cook batter
Rich in strayings with every amorous oaf,
Ready, for a trinket,
To squander owl-hours on bracken bedding,
Flesh unshriven.

Against virgin prayer
This sorceress sets mirrors enough
To distract beauty's thought;
Lovesick at first fond song,
Each vain girl's driven

To believe beyond heart's flare
No fire is, nor in any book proof
Sun hoists soul up after lids fall shut;
So she wills all to the black king.
The worst sloven

Vies with best queen over
Right to blaze as satan's wife;
Housed in earth, those million brides shriek out.
Some burn short, some long,
Staked in pride's coven.

Strumpet Song

15

With white frost gone
And all green dreams not worth much,
After a lean day's work
Time comes round for that foul slut:
Mere bruit of her takes our street
Until every man,
Red, pale or dark,
Veers to her slouch.

Mark, I cry, that mouth
Made to do violence on,
That seamed face
Askew with blotch, dint, scar

Struck by each dour year.
Walks there not some such one man
As can spare breath
To patch with brand of love this rank grimace
Which out from black tarn, ditch and cup
Into my most chaste own eyes
Looks up.

16   Tinker Jack and the Tidy Wives

'Come lady, bring that pot
Gone black of polish
And whatever pan this mending master
Should trim back to shape.
I'll correct each mar
On silver dish,
And shine that kettle of copper
At your fireside
Bright as blood.

'Come lady, bring that face
Fallen from luster.
Time's soot in bleared eye
Can be made to glister
For small charge.
No form's gone so awry,
Crook-back or bandy-leg,
But Tinker Jack can forge
Beauty from hag.

'Whatever scath
Fierce fire's wrought
Jack will touch up
And fit for use.
What scar's been knocked
Into cracked heart
Jack shall repair.

'And if there be
Young wives still blithe,
Still fair,
Whose labor's not yet smoked
Their fine skin sere,
From their white heat
Before he part
Let Jack catch fire.'

Faun

17

Haunched like a faun, he hooed
From grove of moon-glint and fen-frost
Until all owls in the twigged forest
Flapped black to look and brood
On the call this man made.

No sound but a drunken coot
Lurching home along river bank.
Stars hung water-sunk, so a rank
Of double star-eyes lit
Boughs where those owls sat.

An arena of yellow eyes
Watched the changing shape he cut,
Saw hoof harden from foot, saw sprout
Goat-horns. Marked how god rose
And galloped woodward in that guise.

Street Song

18

By a mad miracle I go intact
Among the common rout
Thronging sidewalk, street,
And bickering shops;
Nobody blinks a lid, gapes,
Or cries that this raw flesh

Reeks of the butcher's cleaver,
Its heart and guts hung hooked
And bloodied as a cow's split frame
Parceled out by white-jacketed assassins.

Oh no, for I strut it clever
As a greenly escaped idiot,
Buying wine, bread,
Yellow-casqued chrysanthemums—
Arming myself with the most reasonable items
To ward off, at all cost, suspicions
Roused by thorned hands, feet, head,
And that great wound
Squandering red
From the flayed side.

Even as my each mangled nerve-end
Trills its hurt out
Above pitch of pedestrian ear,
So, perhaps I, knelled dumb by your absence,
Alone can hear
Sun's parched scream,
Every downfall and crash
Of gutted star,
And, more daft than any goose,
This cracked world's incessant gabble and hiss.

Letter to a Purist

19

That grandiose colossus who
Stood astride
The envious assaults of sea
(Essaying, wave by wave,
Tide by tide,
To undo him, perpetually),
Has nothing on you,
O my love,

O my great idiot, who
With one foot
Caught (as it were) in the muck-trap
Of skin and bone,
Dithers with the other way out
In preposterous provinces of the madcap
Cloud-cuckoo,
Agawp at the impeccable moon.

Soliloquy of the Solipsist

20

I?
I walk alone;
The midnight street
Spins itself from under my feet;
When my eyes shut
These dreaming houses all snuff out;
Through a whim of mine
Over gables the moon's celestial onion
Hangs high.

I
Make houses shrink
And trees diminish
By going far; my look's leash
Dangles the puppet-people
Who, unaware how they dwindle,
Laugh, kiss, get drunk,
Nor guess that if I choose to blink
They die.

I
When in good humor,
Give grass its green
Blazon sky blue, and endow the sun
With gold;
Yet, in my wintriest moods, I hold
Absolute power

To boycott color and forbid any flower
To be.

I
Know you appear,
Vivid at my side,
Denying you sprang out of my head,
Claiming you feel
Love fiery enough to prove flesh real,
Though it's quite clear
All your beauty, all your wit, is a gift, my dear,
From me.

Dialogue Between Ghost and Priest

21

In the rectory garden on his evening walk
Paced brisk Father Shawn. A cold day, a sodden one it was
In black November. After a sliding rain
Dew stood in chill sweat on each stalk,
Each thorn; spiring from wet earth, a blue haze
Hung caught in dark-webbed branches like a fabulous heron.

Hauled sudden from solitude,
Hair prickling on his head,
Father Shawn perceived a ghost
Shaping itself from that mist.

'How now,' Father Shawn crisply addressed the ghost
Wavering there, gauze-edged, smelling of woodsmoke,
'What manner of business are you on?
From your blue pallor, I'd say you inhabited the frozen waste
Of hell, and not the fiery part. Yet to judge by that dazzled look,
That noble mien, perhaps you've late quitted heaven?'

In voice furred with frost,
Ghost said to priest:
'Neither of those countries do I frequent:
Earth is my haunt.'

1956

'Come, come,' Father Shawn gave an impatient shrug,
'I don't ask you to spin some ridiculous fable
Of gilded harps or gnawing fire: simply tell
After your life's end, what just epilogue
God ordained to follow up your days. Is it such trouble
To satisfy the questions of a curious old fool?'

'In life, love gnawed my skin
To this white bone;
What love did then, love does now:
Gnaws me through.'

'What love,' asked Father Shawn, 'but too great love
Of flawed earth-flesh could cause this sorry pass?
Some damned condition you are in:
Thinking never to have left the world, you grieve
As though alive, shriveling in torment thus
To atone as shade for sin that lured blind man.'

'The day of doom
Is not yet come.
Until that time
A crock of dust is my dear home.'

'Fond phantom,' cried shocked Father Shawn,
'Can there be such stubbornness—
A soul grown feverish, clutching its dead body-tree
Like a last storm-crossed leaf? Best get you gone
To judgment in a higher court of grace.
Repent, depart, before God's trump-crack splits the sky.'

From that pale mist
Ghost swore to priest:
'There sits no higher court
Than man's red heart.'

The Glutton

22

He, hunger-stung, hard to slake,
So fitted is for my black luck
(With heat such as no man could have
And yet keep kind)
That all merit's in being meat
Seasoned how he'd most approve;
Blood's broth,
Filched by his hand,
Choice wassail makes, cooked hot,
Cupped quick to mouth;
Though prime parts cram each rich meal,
He'll not spare
Nor scant his want until
Sacked larder's gone bone-bare.

Monologue at 3 a.m.

23

Better that every fiber crack
and fury make head,
blood drenching vivid
couch, carpet, floor
and the snake-figured almanac
vouching you are
a million green counties from here,

than to sit mute, twitching so
under prickling stars,
with stare, with curse
blackening the time
goodbyes were said, trains let go,
and I, great magnanimous fool, thus wrenched from
my one kingdom.

24

Miss Drake Proceeds to Supper

No novice
In those elaborate rituals
Which allay the malice
Of knotted table and crooked chair,
The new woman in the ward
Wears purple, steps carefully
Among her secret combinations of eggshells
And breakable hummingbirds,
Footing sallow as a mouse
Between the cabbage-roses
Which are slowly opening their furred petals
To devour and drag her down
Into the carpet's design.

With bird-quick eye cocked askew
She can see in the nick of time
How perilous needles grain the floorboards
And outwit their brambled plan;
Now through her ambushed air,
Adazzle with bright shards
Of broken glass,
She edges with wary breath,
Fending off jag and tooth,
Until, turning sideways,
She lifts one webbed foot after the other
Into the still, sultry weather
Of the patients' dining room.

25

Recantation

'Tea leaves I've given up,
And that crooked line
On the queen's palm
Is no more my concern.
On my black pilgrimage
This moon-pocked crystal ball
Will break before it help;

Rather than croak out
What's to come,
My darling ravens are flown.

'Forswear those freezing tricks of sight
And all else I've taught
Against the flower in the blood:
Not wealth nor wisdom stands
Above the simple vein,
The straight mouth.
Go to your greenhorn youth
Before time ends
And do good
With your white hands.'

The Shrike

26

When night comes black
Such royal dreams beckon this man
As lift him apart
From his earth-wife's side
To wing, sleep-feathered,
The singular air,
While she, envious bride,
Cannot follow after, but lies
With her blank brown eyes starved wide,
Twisting curses in the tangled sheet
With taloned fingers,
Shaking in her skull's cage
The stuffed shape of her flown mate
Escaped among moon-plumaged strangers;
So hungered, she must wait in rage
Until bird-racketing dawn
When her shrike-face
Leans to peck open those locked lids, to eat
Crowns, palace, all
That nightlong stole her male,
And with red beak
Spike and suck out
Last blood-drop of that truant heart.

27 ## Alicante Lullaby

In Alicante they bowl the barrels
Bumblingly over the nubs of the cobbles
Past the yellow-paella eateries,
Below the ramshackle back-alley balconies,
  While the cocks and hens
  In the roofgardens
Scuttle repose with crowns and cackles.

Kumquat-colored trolleys ding as they trundle
Passengers under an indigo fizzle
Needling spumily down from the wires:
Alongside the sibilant harbor the lovers
  Hear loudspeakers boom
  From each neon-lit palm
Rumbas and sambas no ear-flaps can muffle.

O Cacophony, goddess of jazz and of quarrels,
Crack-throated mistress of bagpipes and cymbals,
Let be your *con brios*, your *capricciosos*,
Crescendos, cadenzas, prestos and *prestissimos*,
  My head on the pillow
  (*Piano, pianissimo*)
Lullayed by susurrous lyres and viols.

28 ## Dream with Clam-Diggers

This dream budded bright with leaves around the edges,
Its clear air winnowed by angels; she was come
Back to her early sea-town home
Scathed, stained after tedious pilgrimages.

Barefoot, she stood, in shock of that returning,
Beside a neighbor's house
With shingles burnished as glass,
Blinds lowered on that hot morning.

No change met her: garden terrace, all summer
Tanged by melting tar,
Sloped seaward to plunge in blue; fed by white fire,
The whole scene flared welcome to this roamer.

High against heaven, gulls went wheeling soundless
Over tidal-flats where three children played
Silent and shining on a green rock bedded in mud,
Their fabulous heyday endless.

With green rock gliding, a delicate schooner
Decked forth in cockle-shells,
They sailed till tide foamed round their ankles
And the fair ship sank, its crew knelled home for dinner.

Plucked back thus sudden to that far innocence,
She, in her shabby travel garb, began
Walking eager toward water, when there, one by one,
Clam-diggers rose up out of dark slime at her offense.

Grim as gargoyles from years spent squatting at sea's border
In wait amid snarled weed and wrack of wave
To trap this wayward girl at her first move of love,
Now with stake and pitchfork they advance, flint eyes fixed on murder.

29   ## Wreath for a Bridal

What though green leaves only witness
Such pact as is made once only; what matter
That owl voice sole 'yes', while cows utter
Low moos of approve; let sun surpliced in brightness
Stand stock still to laud these mated ones
Whose stark act all coming double luck joins.

Couched daylong in cloisters of stinging nettle
They lie, cut-grass assaulting each separate sense
With savor; coupled so, pure paragons of constance,
This pair seek single state from that dual battle.
Now speak some sacrament to parry scruple
For wedlock wrought within love's proper chapel.

Call here with flying colors all watchful birds
To people the twigged aisles; lead babel tongues
Of animals to choir: 'Look what thresh of wings
Wields guard of honor over these!' Starred with words
Let night bless that luck-rooted mead of clover
Where, bedded like angels, two burn one in fever.

From this holy day on, all pollen blown
Shall strew broadcast so rare a seed on wind
That every breath, thus teeming, set the land
Sprouting fruit, flowers, children most fair in legion
To slay spawn of dragon's teeth: speaking this promise,
Let flesh be knit, and each step hence go famous.

Epitaph for Fire and Flower

30

You might as well haul up
This wave's green peak on wire
To prevent fall, or anchor the fluent air
In quartz, as crack your skull to keep
These two most perishable lovers from the touch
That will kindle angels' envy, scorch and drop
Their fond hearts charred as any match.

Seek no stony camera-eye to fix
The passing dazzle of each face
In black and white, or put on ice
Mouth's instant flare for future looks;
Stars shoot their petals, and suns run to seed,
However you may sweat to hold such darling wrecks
Hived like honey in your head.

Now in the crux of their vows hang your ear,
Still as a shell: hear what an age of glass
These lovers prophesy to lock embrace
Secure in museum diamond for the stare
Of astounded generations; they wrestle
To conquer cinder's kingdom in the stroke of an hour
And hoard faith safe in a fossil.

But though they'd rivet sinews in rock
And have every weathercock kiss hang fire
As if to outflame a phoenix, the moment's spur
Drives nimble blood too quick
For a wish to tether: they ride nightlong
In their heartbeats' blazing wake until red cock
Plucks bare that comet's flowering.

Dawn snuffs out star's spent wick,
Even as love's dear fools cry evergreen,
And a languor of wax congeals the vein
No matter how fiercely lit; staunch contracts break
And recoil in the altering light: the radiant limb
Blows ash in each lover's eye; the ardent look
Blackens flesh to bone and devours them.

Fiesta Melons

31

In Benidorm there are melons,
Whole donkey-carts full

Of innumerable melons,
Ovals and balls,

Bright green and thumpable
Laced over with stripes

Of turtle-dark green.
Choose an egg-shape, a world-shape,

Bowl one homeward to taste
In the whitehot noon:

Cream-smooth honeydews,
Pink-pulped whoppers,

Bump-rinded cantaloupes
With orange cores.

Each wedge wears a studding
Of blanched seeds or black seeds

To strew like confetti
Under the feet of

This market of melon-eating
Fiesta-goers.

32   # The Goring

Arena dust rusted by four bulls' blood to a dull redness,
The afternoon at a bad end under the crowd's truculence,
The ritual death each time botched among dropped capes, ill-judged
        stabs,
The strongest will seemed a will toward ceremony. Obese, dark-
Faced in his rich yellows, tassels, pompons, braid, the picador

Rode out against the fifth bull to brace his pike and slowly bear
Down deep into the bent bull-neck. Cumbrous routine, not artwork.
Instinct for art began with the bull's horn lofting in the mob's
Hush a lumped man-shape. The whole act formal, fluent as a dance.
Blood faultlessly broached redeemed the sullied air, the earth's grossness.

33   # The Beggars

Nightfall, cold eye—neither disheartens
These goatish tragedians who
Hawk misfortune like figs and chickens

And, plaintiff against each day, decry
Nature's partial, haphazard thumb.
Under white wall and Moorish window

Grief's honest grimace, debased by time,
Caricatures itself and thrives
On the coins of pity. At random

A beggar stops among eggs and loaves,
Props a leg-stump upon a crutch,
Jiggles his tin cup at the goodwives.

By lack and loss these beggars encroach
On spirits tenderer than theirs,
Suffering-toughened beyond the fetch

Of finest conscience.
              Nightfall obscures
The bay's sheer, extravagant blue,
White house and almond grove. The beggars

Outlast their evilest star, wryly
And with a perfidious verve
Baffle the dark, the pitying eye.

Spider

Anansi, black busybody of the folktales,
You scuttle out on impulse
Blunt in self-interest
As a sledge hammer, as a man's bunched fist,
Yet of devils the cleverest
To get your carousals told:
You spun the cosmic web: you squint from center field.

Last summer I came upon your Spanish cousin,
Notable robber baron,
Behind a goatherd's hut:
Near his small stonehenge above the ants' route,
One-third ant-size, a leggy spot,
He tripped an ant with a rope
Scarcely visible. About and about the slope

Of his redoubt he ran his nimble filament,
Each time round winding that ant
Tighter to the cocoon
Already veiling the gray spool of stone

From which coils, caught ants waved legs in
Torpid warning, or lay still
And suffered their livelier fellows to struggle.

Then briskly scaled his altar tiered with tethered ants,
Nodding in a somnolence
Appalling to witness,
To the barbarous outlook, from there chose
His next martyr to the gross cause
Of concupiscence. Once more
With black alacrity bound round his prisoner.

The ants—a file of comers, a file of goers—
Persevered on a set course
No scruple could disrupt,
Obeying orders of instinct till swept
Off-stage and infamously wrapped
Up by a spry black deus
Ex machina. Nor did they seem deterred by this.

35   Spinster

Now this particular girl
During a ceremonious April walk
With her latest suitor
Found herself, of a sudden, intolerably struck
By the birds' irregular babel
And the leaves' litter.

By this tumult afflicted, she
Observed her lover's gestures unbalance the air,
His gait stray uneven
Through a rank wilderness of fern and flower.
She judged petals in disarray,
The whole season, sloven.

How she longed for winter then!—
Scrupulously austere in its order
Of white and black
Ice and rock, each sentiment within border,

49

And heart's frosty discipline
Exact as a snowflake.

But here—a burgeoning
Unruly enough to pitch her five queenly wits
Into vulgar motley—
A treason not to be borne. Let idiots
Reel giddy in bedlam spring:
She withdrew neatly.

And round her house she set
Such a barricade of barb and check
Against mutinous weather
As no mere insurgent man could hope to break
With curse, fist, threat
Or love, either.

Rhyme

36

I've got a stubborn goose whose gut's
Honeycombed with golden eggs,
Yet won't lay one.
She, addled in her goose-wit, struts
The barnyard like those taloned hags
Who ogle men

And crimp their wrinkles in a grin,
Jangling their great money bags.
While I eat grits
She fattens on the finest grain.
Now, as I hone my knife, she begs
Pardon, and that's

So humbly done, I'd turn this keen
Steel on myself before profit
By such a rogue's
Act, but—how those feathers shine!

Exit from a smoking slit
Her ruby dregs.

Departure

37

The figs on the fig tree in the yard are green;
Green, also, the grapes on the green vine
Shading the brickred porch tiles.
The money's run out.

How nature, sensing this, compounds her bitters.
Ungifted, ungrieved, our leavetaking.
The sun shines on unripe corn.
Cats play in the stalks.

Retrospect shall not soften such penury—
Sun's brass, the moon's steely patinas,
The leaden slag of the world—
But always expose

The scraggy rock spit shielding the town's blue bay
Against which the brunt of outer sea
Beats, is brutal endlessly.
Gull-fouled, a stone hut

Bares its low lintel to corroding weathers:
Across the jut of ochreous rock
Goats shamble, morose, rank-haired,
To lick the sea-salt.

Maudlin

38

Mud-mattressed under the sign of the hag
In a clench of blood, the sleep-talking virgin
Gibbets with her curse the moon's man,
Faggot-bearing Jack in his crackless egg:

Hatched with a claret hogshead to swig
He kings it, navel-knit to no groan,
But at the price of a pin-stitched skin
Fish-tailed girls purchase each white leg.

Resolve

Day of mist: day of tarnish

with hands
unserviceable, I wait
for the milk van

the one-eared cat
laps its gray paw

and the coal fire burns

outside, the little hedge leaves are
become quite yellow
a milk-film blurs
the empty bottles on the windowsill

no glory descends

two water drops poise
on the arched green
stem of my neighbor's rose bush

o bent bow of thorns

the cat unsheathes its claws
the world turns

today
today I will not
disenchant my twelve black-gowned examiners
or bunch my fist
in the wind's sneer.

Landowners

From my rented attic with no earth
To call my own except the air-motes,
I malign the leaden perspective
Of identical gray brick houses,
Orange roof-tiles, orange chimney pots,
And see that first house, as if between
Mirrors, engendering a spectral
Corridor of inane replicas,
Flimsily peopled.
                But landowners
Own their cabbage roots, a space of stars,
Indigenous peace. Such substance makes
My eyeful of reflections a ghost's
Eyeful, which, envious, would define
Death as striking root on one land-tract;
Life, its own vaporous wayfarings.

Ella Mason and Her Eleven Cats

Old Ella Mason keeps cats, eleven at last count,
In her ramshackle house off Somerset Terrace;
People make queries
On seeing our neighbor's cat-haunt,
Saying: 'Something's addled in a woman who accommodates
That many cats.'

Rum and red-faced as a water-melon, her voice
Long gone to wheeze and seed, Ella Mason
For no good reason
Plays hostess to Tabby, Tom and increase,
With cream and chicken-gut feasting the palates
Of finical cats.

Village stories go that in olden days
Ella flounced about, minx-thin and haughty,
A fashionable beauty,

Slaying the dandies with her emerald eyes;
Now, run to fat, she's a spinster whose door shuts
On all but cats.

Once we children sneaked over to spy Miss Mason
Napping in her kitchen paved with saucers.
On antimacassars
Table-top, cupboard shelf, cats lounged brazen,
One gruff-timbred purr rolling from furred throats:
Such stentorian cats!

With poke and giggle, ready to skedaddle,
We peered agog through the cobwebbed door
Straight into yellow glare
Of guardian cats crouched round their idol,
While Ella drowsed whiskered with sleek face, sly wits:
Sphinx-queen of cats.

'Look! there she goes, Cat-Lady Mason!'
We snickered as she shambled down Somerset Terrace
To market for her dearies,
More mammoth and blowsy with every season;
'Miss Ella's got loony from keeping in cahoots
With eleven cats.'

But now turned kinder with time, we mark Miss Mason
Blinking green-eyed and solitary
At girls who marry—
Demure ones, lithe ones, needing no lesson
That vain jades sulk single down bridal nights,
Accurst as wild-cats.

Crystal Gazer

Gerd sits spindle-shanked in her dark tent,
Lean face gone tawn with seasons,
Skin worn down to the knucklebones
At her tough trade; without time's taint
The burnished ball hangs fire in her hands, a lens
Fusing time's three horizons.

Two enter to tap her sight, a green pair
Fresh leaved out in vows: 'Come tell
How we shall do together,
Well or ill.' Gerd slants a look at each: most dear,
Each to the other; fit fiber for stern weather.
Slowly she spins the ball:

'I see two stalwart apple trees
Coupled by branches intertwined
And, springing all about,
Staunch saplings; to this house, thriving days
Will bring crop's increase, and harvest fruit
Follow on kind wind.'

'No hardship then?' he asks. 'We'll take
Whatever trial's to come, so say true.'
His bride echoes his word. At that,
Gerd whirls the ball ablaze: 'Rough storm,' she grants, 'may wreak
Some havoc on tender limb, and yet
Strengthen that orchard thereby.'

Their small price paid, these wedded ones
Walk forth into sun-moneyed air, quickened
To savor their span of flourishing.
Aloof, squatting mummy-wise, Gerd scans
That clairvoyant quartz which once, at her own wishing,
Exacted her first simple sight for this strict second.

Then, a free-gadding hoyden, Gerd had craved
To govern more sight than given to a woman
By wits alone: to foresee her lover's faith
And their future lot, she braved
Church curse to ken that crooked oath
Whereby one hires a demon.

A flash like doomcrack rent night's black:
God's work stood anchored in that glare
Focusing all time's day-suns in one
So beggar Gerd might aim her look
At gorgon-prospects with power to strike to stone
Hearts of those who pierced time's core.

What Gerd saw then engraved her mind
Plague-pitted as the moon: each bud
Shriveling to cinders at its source,
Each love blazing blind to its gutted end—
And, fixed in the crystal center, grinning fierce:
Earth's ever-green death's head.

43   November Graveyard

The scene stands stubborn: skinflint trees
Hoard last year's leaves, won't mourn, wear sackcloth, or turn
To elegiac dryads, and dour grass
Guards the hard-hearted emerald of its grassiness
However the grandiloquent mind may scorn
Such poverty. No dead men's cries

Flower forget-me-nots between the stones
Paving this grave ground. Here's honest rot
To unpick the heart, pare bone
Free of the fictive vein. When one stark skeleton
Bulks real, all saints' tongues fall quiet:
Flies watch no resurrections in the sun.

At the essential landscape stare, stare
Till your eyes foist a vision dazzling on the wind:
Whatever lost ghosts flare,
Damned, howling in their shrouds across the moor
Rave on the leash of the starving mind
Which peoples the bare room, the blank, untenanted air.

44   Black Rook in Rainy Weather

On the stiff twig up there
Hunches a wet black rook
Arranging and rearranging its feathers in the rain.
I do not expect a miracle
Or an accident

1956

To set the sight on fire
In my eye, nor seek
Any more in the desultory weather some design,
But let spotted leaves fall as they fall,
Without ceremony, or portent.

Although, I admit, I desire,
Occasionally, some backtalk
From the mute sky, I can't honestly complain:
A certain minor light may still
Lean incandescent

Out of kitchen table or chair
As if a celestial burning took
Possession of the most obtuse objects now and then—
Thus hallowing an interval
Otherwise inconsequent

By bestowing largesse, honor,
One might say love. At any rate, I now walk
Wary (for it could happen
Even in this dull, ruinous landscape); skeptical,
Yet politic; ignorant

Of whatever angel may choose to flare
Suddenly at my elbow. I only know that a rook
Ordering its black feathers can so shine
As to seize my senses, haul
My eyelids up, and grant

A brief respite from fear
Of total neutrality. With luck,
Trekking stubborn through this season
Of fatigue, I shall
Patch together a content

Of sorts. Miracles occur,
If you care to call those spasmodic
Tricks of radiance miracles. The wait's begun again,
The long wait for the angel,
For that rare, random descent.

1957

The Snowman on the Moor

Stalemated their armies stood, with tottering banners:
She flung from a room
Still ringing with bruit of insults and dishonors

And in fury left him
Glowering at the coal-fire: 'Come find me'—her last taunt.
He did not come

But sat on, guarding his grim battlement.
By the doorstep
Her winter-beheaded daisies, marrowless, gaunt,

Warned her to keep
Indoors with politic goodwill, not haste
Into a landscape

Of stark wind-harrowed hills and weltering mist;
But from the house
She stalked intractable as a driven ghost

Across moor snows
Pocked by rook-claw and rabbit-track: she must yet win
Him to his knees—

Let him send police and hounds to bring her in.
Nursing her rage
Through bare whistling heather, over stiles of black stone,

1957

To the world's white edge
She came, and called hell to subdue an unruly man
And join her siege.

It was no fire-blurting fork-tailed demon
Volcanoed hot
From marble snow-heap of moor to ride that woman

With spur and knout
Down from pride's size: instead, a grisly-thewed,
Austere, corpse-white

Giant heaved into the distance, stone-hatcheted,
Sky-high, and snow
Floured his whirling beard, and at his tread

Ambushed birds by
Dozens dropped dead in the hedges: o she felt
No love in his eye,

Worse—saw dangling from that spike-studded belt
Ladies' sheaved skulls:
Mournfully the dry tongues clacked their guilt:

'Our wit made fools
Of kings, unmanned kings' sons: our masteries
Amused court halls:

For that brag, we barnacle these iron thighs.'
Throned in the thick
Of a blizzard, the giant roared up with his chittering trophies.

From brunt of axe-crack
She shied sideways: a white fizz! and the giant, pursuing,
Crumbled to smoke.

Humbled then, and crying,
The girl bent homeward, brimful of gentle talk
And mild obeying.

46   Mayflower

Throughout black winter the red haws withstood
Assault of snow-flawed winds from the dour skies
And, bright as blood-drops, proved no brave branch dies
If root's firm-fixed and resolution good.
Now, as green sap ascends the steepled wood,
Each hedge with such white bloom astounds our eyes
As sprang from Joseph's rod, and testifies
How best beauty's born of hardihood.

So when staunch island stock chose forfeiture
Of the homeland hearth to plough their pilgrim way
Across Atlantic furrows, dark, unsure—
Remembering the white, triumphant spray
On hawthorn boughs, with goodwill to endure
They named their ship after the flower of May.

47   Sow

God knows how our neighbor managed to breed
His great sow:
Whatever his shrewd secret, he kept it hid

In the same way
He kept the sow—impounded from public stare,
Prize ribbon and pig show.

But one dusk our questions commended us to a tour
Through his lantern-lit
Maze of barns to the lintel of the sunk sty door

To gape at it:
This was no rose-and-larkspurred china suckling
With a penny slot

For thrifty children, nor dolt pig ripe for heckling,
About to be
Glorified for prime flesh and golden crackling

In a parsley halo;
Nor even one of the common barnyard sows,
Mire-smirched, blowzy,

Maunching thistle and knotweed on her snout-cruise—
Bloat tun of milk
On the move, hedged by a litter of feat-foot ninnies

Shrilling her hulk
To halt for a swig at the pink teats. No. This vast
Brobdingnag bulk

Of a sow lounged belly-bedded on that black compost,
Fat-rutted eyes
Dream-filmed. What a vision of ancient hoghood must

Thus wholly engross
The great grandam!—our marvel blazoned a knight,
Helmed, in cuirass,

Unhorsed and shredded in the grove of combat
By a grisly-bristled
Boar, fabulous enough to straddle that sow's heat.

But our farmer whistled,
Then, with a jocular fist thwacked the barrel nape,
And the green-copse-castled

Pig hove, letting legend like dried mud drop,
Slowly, grunt
On grunt, up in the flickering light to shape

A monument
Prodigious in gluttonies as that hog whose want
Made lean Lent

Of kitchen slops and, stomaching no constraint,
Proceeded to swill
The seven troughed seas and every earthquaking continent.

48

The Everlasting Monday

Thou shalt have an everlasting
Monday and stand in the moon.

The moon's man stands in his shell,
Bent under a bundle
Of sticks. The light falls chalk and cold
Upon our bedspread.
His teeth are chattering among the leprous
Peaks and craters of those extinct volcanoes.

He also against black frost
Would pick sticks, would not rest
Until his own lit room outshone
Sunday's ghost of sun;
Now works his hell of Mondays in the moon's ball,
Fireless, seven chill seas chained to his ankle.

49

Hardcastle Crags

Flintlike, her feet struck
Such a racket of echoes from the steely street,
Tacking in moon-blued crooks from the black
Stone-built town, that she heard the quick air ignite
Its tinder and shake

A firework of echoes from wall
To wall of the dark, dwarfed cottages.
But the echoes died at her back as the walls
Gave way to fields and the incessant seethe of grasses
Riding in the full

Of the moon, manes to the wind,
Tireless, tied, as a moon-bound sea
Moves on its root. Though a mist-wraith wound
Up from the fissured valley and hung shoulder-high
Ahead, it fattened

To no family-featured ghost,
Nor did any word body with a name
The blank mood she walked in. Once past
The dream-peopled village, her eyes entertained no dream,
And the sandman's dust

Lost lustre under her footsoles.
The long wind, paring her person down
To a pinch of flame, blew its burdened whistle
In the whorl of her ear, and like a scooped-out pumpkin crown
Her head cupped the babel.

All the night gave her, in return
For the paltry gift of her bulk and the beat
Of her heart, was the humped indifferent iron
Of its hills, and its pastures bordered by black stone set
On black stone. Barns

Guarded broods and litters
Behind shut doors; the dairy herds
Knelt in the meadow mute as boulders;
Sheep drowsed stoneward in their tussocks of wool, and birds,
Twig-sleeping, wore

Granite ruffs, their shadows
The guise of leaves. The whole landscape
Loomed absolute as the antique world was
Once, in its earliest sway of lymph and sap,
Unaltered by eyes,

Enough to snuff the quick
Of her small heat out, but before the weight
Of stones and hills of stones could break
Her down to mere quartz grit in that stony light
She turned back.

The Thin People

They are always with us, the thin people
Meager of dimension as the gray people

On a movie-screen. They
Are unreal, we say:

It was only in a movie, it was only
In a war making evil headlines when we

Were small that they famished and
Grew so lean and would not round

Out their stalky limbs again though peace
Plumped the bellies of the mice

Under the meanest table.
It was during the long hunger-battle

They found their talent to persevere
In thinness, to come, later,

Into our bad dreams, their menace
Not guns, not abuses,

But a thin silence.
Wrapped in flea-ridden donkey skins,

Empty of complaint, forever
Drinking vinegar from tin cups: they wore

The insufferable nimbus of the lot-drawn
Scapegoat. But so thin,

So weedy a race could not remain in dreams,
Could not remain outlandish victims

In the contracted country of the head
Any more than the old woman in her mud hut could

Keep from cutting fat meat
Out of the side of the generous moon when it

Set foot nightly in her yard
Until her knife had pared

The moon to a rind of little light.
Now the thin people do not obliterate

Themselves as the dawn
Grayness blues, reddens, and the outline

Of the world comes clear and fills with color.
They persist in the sunlit room: the wallpaper

Frieze of cabbage-roses and cornflowers pales
Under their thin-lipped smiles,

Their withering kingship.
How they prop each other up!

We own no wildernesses rich and deep enough
For stronghold against their stiff

Battalions. See, how the tree boles flatten
And lose their good browns

If the thin people simply stand in the forest,
Making the world go thin as a wasp's nest

And grayer; not even moving their bones.

On the Difficulty of Conjuring Up a Dryad

51

Ravening through the persistent bric-à-brac
Of blunt pencils, rose-sprigged coffee cup,
Postage stamps, stacked books' clamor and yawp,

Neighborhood cockcrow—all nature's prodigal backtalk,
  The vaunting mind
  Snubs impromptu spiels of wind
  And wrestles to impose
  Its own order on what is.

'With my fantasy alone,' brags the importunate head,
Arrogant among rook-tongued spaces,
Sheep greens, finned falls, 'I shall compose a crisis
To stun sky black out, drive gibbering mad
  Trout, cock, ram,
  That bulk so calm
  On my jealous stare,
  Self-sufficient as they are.'

But no hocus-pocus of green angels
Damasks with dazzle the threadbare eye;
'My trouble, doctor, is: I see a tree,
And that damn scrupulous tree won't practice wiles
  To beguile sight:
  E.g., by cant of light
  Concoct a Daphne;
  My tree stays tree.

'However I wrench obstinate bark and trunk
To my sweet will, no luminous shape
Steps out radiant in limb, eye, lip,
To hoodwink the honest earth which pointblank
  Spurns such fiction
  As nymphs; cold vision
  Will have no counterfeit
  Palmed off on it.

'No doubt now in dream-propertied fall some moon-eyed,
Star-lucky sleight-of-hand man watches
My jilting lady squander coin, gold leaf stock ditches,
And the opulent air go studded with seed,
  While this beggared brain
  Hatches no fortune,
  But from leaf, from grass,
  Thieves what it has.'

On the Plethora of Dryads

Hearing a white saint rave
About a quintessential beauty
Visible only to the paragon heart,
I tried my sight on an apple-tree
That for eccentric knob and wart
Had all my love.

Without meat or drink I sat
Starving my fantasy down
To discover that metaphysical Tree which hid
From my worldling look its brilliant vein
Far deeper in gross wood
Than axe could cut.

But before I might blind sense
To see with the spotless soul,
Each particular quirk so ravished me
Every pock and stain bulked more beautiful
Than flesh of any body
Flawed by love's prints.

Battle however I would
To break through that patchwork
Of leaves' bicker and whisk in babel tongues,
Streak and mottle of tawn bark,
No visionary lightnings
Pierced my dense lid.

Instead, a wanton fit
Dragged each dazzled sense apart
Surfeiting eye, ear, taste, touch, smell;
Now, snared by this miraculous art,
I ride earth's burning carrousel
Day in, day out,

And such grit corrupts my eyes
I must watch sluttish dryads twitch

Their multifarious silks in the holy grove
Until no chaste tree but suffers blotch
Under flux of those seductive
Reds, greens, blues.

The Other Two

All summer we moved in a villa brimful of echoes,
Cool as the pearled interior of a conch.
Bells, hooves, of the high-stepping black goats woke us.
Around our bed the baronial furniture
Foundered through levels of light seagreen and strange.
Not one leaf wrinkled in the clearing air.
We dreamed how we were perfect, and we were.

Against bare, whitewashed walls, the furniture
Anchored itself, griffin-legged and darkly grained.
Two of us in a place meant for ten more—
Our footsteps multiplied in the shadowy chambers,
Our voices fathomed a profounder sound:
The walnut banquet table, the twelve chairs
Mirrored the intricate gestures of two others.

Heavy as statuary, shapes not ours
Performed a dumbshow in the polished wood,
That cabinet without windows or doors:
He lifts an arm to bring her close, but she
Shies from his touch: his is an iron mood.
Seeing her freeze, he turns his face away.
They poise and grieve as in some old tragedy.

Moon-blanched and implacable, he and she
Would not be eased, released. Our each example
Of tenderness dove through their purgatory
Like a planet, a stone, swallowed in a great darkness,
Leaving no sparky track, setting up no ripple.
Nightly we left them in their desert place.
Lights out, they dogged us, sleepless and envious:

We dreamed their arguments, their stricken voices.
We might embrace, but those two never did,
Come, so unlike us, to a stiff impasse,
Burdened in such a way we seemed the lighter—
Ourselves the haunters, and they, flesh and blood;
As if, above love's ruinage, we were
The heaven those two dreamed of, in despair.

54   The Lady and the Earthenware Head

Fired in sanguine clay, the model head
Fit nowhere: brickdust-complected, eye under a dense lid,
On the long bookshelf it stood
Stolidly propping thick volumes of prose: spite-set
Ape of her look. Best rid
Hearthstone at once of the outrageous head;
Still, she felt loath to junk it.

No place, it seemed, for the effigy to fare
Free from all molesting. Rough boys,
Spying a pate to spare
Glowering sullen and pompous from an ash-heap,
Might well seize this prize,
Maltreat the hostage head in shocking wise,
And waken the sly nerve up

That knits to each original its coarse copy. A dark tarn
She thought of then, thick-silted, with weeds obscured,
To serve her exacting turn:
But out of the watery aspic, laureled by fins,
The simulacrum leered,
Lewdly beckoning, and her courage wavered:
She blenched, as one who drowns,

And resolved more ceremoniously to lodge
The mimic head—in a crotched willow, green-
Vaulted by foliage:
Let bell-tongued birds descant in blackest feather
On the rendering, grain by grain,

Of that uncouth shape to simple sod again
Through drear and dulcet weather.

Yet, shrined on her shelf, the grisly visage endured,
Despite her wrung hands, her tears, her praying: Vanish!
Steadfast and evil-starred,
It ogled through rock-fault, wind-flaw and fisted wave—
An antique hag-head, too tough for knife to finish,
Refusing to diminish
By one jot its basilisk-look of love.

55

All the Dead Dears

In the Archaeological Museum in Cambridge is a stone coffin of the fourth century A.D. containing the skeletons of a woman, a mouse and a shrew. The ankle-bone of the woman has been slightly gnawn.

Rigged poker-stiff on her back
With a granite grin
This antique museum-cased lady
Lies, companioned by the gimcrack
Relics of a mouse and a shrew
That battened for a day on her ankle-bone.

These three, unmasked now, bear
Dry witness
To the gross eating game
We'd wink at if we didn't hear
Stars grinding, crumb by crumb,
Our own grist down to its bony face.

How they grip us through thin and thick,
These barnacle dead!
This lady here's no kin
Of mine, yet kin she is: she'll suck
Blood and whistle my marrow clean
To prove it. As I think now of her head,

From the mercury-backed glass
Mother, grandmother, greatgrandmother
Reach hag hands to haul me in,

And an image looms under the fishpond surface
Where the daft father went down
With orange duck-feet winnowing his hair —

All the long gone darlings: they
Get back, though, soon,
Soon: be it by wakes, weddings,
Childbirths or a family barbecue:
Any touch, taste, tang's
Fit for those outlaws to ride home on,

And to sanctuary: usurping the armchair
Between tick
And tack of the clock, until we go,
Each skulled-and-crossboned Gulliver
Riddled with ghosts, to lie
Deadlocked with them, taking root as cradles rock.

56   Natural History

That lofty monarch, Monarch Mind,
Blue-blooded in coarse country reigned;
Though he bedded in ermine, gorged on roast,
Pure Philosophy his love engrossed:
While subjects hungered, empty-pursed,
With stars, with angels, he conversed

Till, sick of their ruler's godling airs,
In one body those earthborn commoners
Rose up and put royal nerves to the rack:
King Egg-Head saw his domain crack,
His crown usurped by the low brow
Of the base, barbarous Prince Ow.

57   Two Views of Withens

Above whorled, spindling gorse,
Sheepfoot-flattened grasses,
Stone wall and ridgepole rise

Prow-like through blurs
Of fog in that hinterland few
Hikers get to:

Home of uncatchable
Sage hen and spry rabbit,
Where second wind, hip boot
Help over hill
And hill, and through peaty water.
I found bare moor,

A colorless weather,
And the House of Eros
Low-lintelled, no palace;
You, luckier,
Report white pillars, a blue sky,
The ghosts, kindly.

58   The Great Carbuncle

We came over the moor-top
Through air streaming and green-lit,
Stone farms foundering in it,
Valleys of grass altering
In a light neither of dawn

Nor nightfall, our hands, faces
Lucent as porcelain, the earth's
Claim and weight gone out of them.
Some such transfiguring moved
The eight pilgrims towards its source—

Toward that great jewel: shown often,
Never given; hidden, yet
Simultaneously seen
On moor-top, at sea-bottom,
Knowable only by light

Other than noon, than moon, stars—
The once-known way becoming

Wholly other, and ourselves
Estranged, changed, suspended where
Angels are rumored, clearly

Floating, among the floating
Tables and chairs. Gravity's
Lost in the lift and drift of
An easier element
Than earth, and there is nothing

So fine we cannot do it.
But nearing means distancing:
At the common homecoming
Light withdraws. Chairs, tables drop
Down: the body weighs like stone.

Words for a Nursery

59

Rosebud, knot of worms,
Heir of the first five
Shapers, I open:
Five moony crescents
For eyes to light me
Toward what I can grab,
Milk-spout, big finger
So many ladders
Giving a leg up
To these limber hooks.

I learn, good circus
Dog that I am, how
To move, serve, steer food,
Index the arrow,
Thumbhead, blunt helper,
My master's fetcher,
Whipper of itches,
No pocket dozer,
I shut on the key
Of this blue-green toy.

Five-antlered, branching
Touchy antenna,
I nose out the lay
Of thistle and silk,
Cold pole and hot plate.
Old historian,
My page this desert
Crossed by three causeways,
Leathery, treeless,
With five whorled landspits.

Brown-backed, white-bellied
As a flatfish, I
Swim the Sea of Do,
The left my lackey,
My backward image.
Penbearer, scrubnurse,
The captain's batman,
By heart here I hold
Coin, button, trigger
And his love's body.

Ill-served he'll be when
Age manhandles me
(A crab to nap on
Chairarms and tables,
Five wickless candles
To wag at the dark)
And worse-served when death
Makes off with this rose,
Five worms in a box
To feed the thin crows.

60   ## The Disquieting Muses

Mother, mother, what illbred aunt
Or what disfigured and unsightly
Cousin did you so unwisely keep
Unasked to my christening, that she
Sent these ladies in her stead

With heads like darning-eggs to nod
And nod and nod at foot and head
And at the left side of my crib?

Mother, who made to order stories
Of Mixie Blackshort the heroic bear,
Mother, whose witches always, always
Got baked into gingerbread, I wonder
Whether you saw them, whether you said
Words to rid me of those three ladies
Nodding by night around my bed,
Mouthless, eyeless, with stitched bald head.

In the hurricane, when father's twelve
Study windows bellied in
Like bubbles about to break, you fed
My brother and me cookies and Ovaltine
And helped the two of us to choir:
"Thor is angry: boom boom boom!
Thor is angry: we don't care!"
But those ladies broke the panes.

When on tiptoe the schoolgirls danced,
Blinking flashlights like fireflies
And singing the glowworm song, I could
Not lift a foot in the twinkle-dress
But, heavy-footed, stood aside
In the shadow cast by my dismal-headed
Godmothers, and you cried and cried:
And the shadow stretched, the lights went out.

Mother, you sent me to piano lessons
And praised my arabesques and trills
Although each teacher found my touch
Oddly wooden in spite of scales
And the hours of practicing, my ear
Tone-deaf and yes, unteachable.
I learned, I learned, I learned elsewhere,
From muses unhired by you, dear mother.

I woke one day to see you, mother,
Floating above me in bluest air

75

On a green balloon bright with a million
Flowers and bluebirds that never were
Never, never, found anywhere.
But the little planet bobbed away
Like a soap-bubble as you called: Come here!
And I faced my traveling companions.

Day now, night now, at head, side, feet,
They stand their vigil in gowns of stone,
Faces blank as the day I was born,
Their shadows long in the setting sun
That never brightens or goes down.
And this is the kingdom you bore me to,
Mother, mother. But no frown of mine
Will betray the company I keep.

61

Night Shift

It was not a heart, beating,
That muted boom, that clangor
Far off, not blood in the ears
Drumming up any fever

To impose on the evening.
The noise came from outside:
A metal detonating
Native, evidently, to

These stilled suburbs: nobody
Startled at it, though the sound
Shook the ground with its pounding.
It took root at my coming

Till the thudding source, exposed,
Confounded inept guesswork:
Framed in windows of Main Street's
Silver factory, immense

Hammers hoisted, wheels turning,
Stalled, let fall their vertical

Tonnage of metal and wood;
Stunned the marrow. Men in white

Undershirts circled, tending
Without stop those greased machines,
Tending, without stop, the blunt
Indefatigable fact.

Ouija

62

It is a chilly god, a god of shades,
Rises to the glass from his black fathoms.
At the window, those unborn, those undone
Assemble with the frail paleness of moths,
An envious phosphorescence in their wings.
Vermilions, bronzes, colors of the sun
In the coal fire will not wholly console them.
Imagine their deep hunger, deep as the dark
For the blood-heat that would ruddle or reclaim.
The glass mouth sucks blood-heat from my forefinger.
The old god dribbles, in return, his words.

The old god, too, writes aureate poetry
In tarnished modes, maundering among the wastes,
Fair chronicler of every foul declension.
Age, and ages of prose, have uncoiled
His talking whirlwind, abated his excessive temper
When words, like locusts, drummed the darkening air
And left the cobs to rattle, bitten clean.
Skies once wearing a blue, divine hauteur
Ravel above us, mistily descend,
Thickening with motes, to a marriage with the mire.

He hymns the rotten queen with saffron hair
Who has saltier aphrodisiacs
Than virgins' tears. That bawdy queen of death,
Her wormy couriers are at his bones.
Still he hymns juice of her, hot nectarine.
I see him, horny-skinned and tough, construe
What flinty pebbles the ploughblade upturns
As ponderable tokens of her love.

He, godly, doddering, spells
No succinct Gabriel from the letters here
But floridly, his amorous nostalgias.

63   On the Decline of Oracles

My father kept a vaulted conch
By two bronze bookends of ships in sail,
And as I listened its cold teeth seethed
With voices of that ambiguous sea
Old Böcklin missed, who held a shell
To hear the sea he could not hear.
What the seashell spoke to his inner ear
He knew, but no peasants know.

My father died, and when he died
He willed his books and shell away.
The books burned up, sea took the shell,
But I, I keep the voices he
Set in my ear, and in my eye
The sight of those blue, unseen waves
For which the ghost of Böcklin grieves.
The peasants feast and multiply.

Eclipsing the spitted ox I see
Neither brazen swan nor burning star,
Heraldry of a starker age,
But three men entering the yard,
And those men coming up the stair.
Profitless, their gossiping images
Invade the cloistral eye like pages
From a gross comic strip, and toward

The happening of this happening
The earth turns now. In half an hour
I shall go down the shabby stair and meet,
Coming up, those three. Worth
Less than present, past—this future.
Worthless such vision to eyes gone dull
That once descried Troy's towers fall,
Saw evil break out of the north.

64   Snakecharmer

As the gods began one world, and man another,
So the snakecharmer begins a snaky sphere
With moon-eye, mouth-pipe. He pipes. Pipes green. Pipes water.

Pipes water green until green waters waver
With reedy lengths and necks and undulatings.
And as his notes twine green, the green river

Shapes its images around his songs.
He pipes a place to stand on, but no rocks,
No floor: a wave of flickering grass tongues

Supports his foot. He pipes a world of snakes,
Of sways and coilings, from the snake-rooted bottom
Of his mind. And now nothing but snakes

Is visible. The snake-scales have become
Leaf, become eyelid; snake-bodies, bough, breast
Of tree and human. And he within this snakedom

Rules the writhings which make manifest
His snakehood and his might with pliant tunes
From his thin pipe. Out of this green nest

As out of Eden's navel twist the lines
Of snaky generations: let there be snakes!
And snakes there were, are, will be—till yawns

Consume this piper and he tires of music
And pipes the world back to the simple fabric
Of snake-warp, snake-weft. Pipes the cloth of snakes

To a melting of green waters, till no snake
Shows its head, and those green waters back to
Water, to green, to nothing like a snake.
Puts up his pipe, and lids his moony eye.

1957

A Lesson in Vengeance

65

In the dour ages
Of drafty cells and draftier castles,
Of dragons breathing without the frame of fables,
Saint and king unfisted obstruction's knuckles
By no miracle or majestic means,

But by such abuses
As smack of spite and the overscrupulous
Twisting of thumbscrews: one soul tied in sinews,
One white horse drowned, and all the unconquered pinnacles
Of God's city and Babylon's

Must wait, while here Suso's
Hand hones his tacks and needles,
Scourging to sores his own red sluices
For the relish of heaven, relentless, dousing with prickles
Of horsehair and lice his horny loins;

While there irate Cyrus
Squanders a summer and the brawn of his heroes
To rebuke the horse-swallowing River Gyndes:
He split it into three hundred and sixty trickles
A girl could wade without wetting her shins.

Still, latter-day sages,
Smiling at this behavior, subjugating their enemies
Neatly, nicely, by disbelief or bridges,
Never grip, as their grandsires did, that devil who chuckles
From grain of the marrow and the river-bed grains.

1958

Virgin in a Tree

How this tart fable instructs
And mocks! Here's the parody of that moral mousetrap
Set in the proverbs stitched on samplers
Approving chased girls who get them to a tree
And put on bark's nun-black

Habit which deflects
All amorous arrows. For to sheathe the virgin shape
In a scabbard of wood baffles pursuers,
Whether goat-thighed or god-haloed. Ever since that first Daphne
Switched her incomparable back

For a bay-tree hide, respect's
Twined to her hard limbs like ivy: the puritan lip
Cries: 'Celebrate Syrinx whose demurs
Won her the frog-colored skin, pale pith and watery
Bed of a reed. Look:

Pine-needle armor protects
Pitys from Pan's assault! And though age drop
Their leafy crowns, their fame soars,
Eclipsing Eva, Cleo and Helen of Troy:
For which of those would speak

For a fashion that constricts
White bodies in a wooden girdle, root to top
Unfaced, unformed, the nipple-flowers
Shrouded to suckle darkness? Only they
Who keep cool and holy make

A sanctum to attract
Green virgins, consecrating limb and lip
To chastity's service: like prophets, like preachers,
They descant on the serene and seraphic beauty
Of virgins for virginity's sake.'

Be certain some such pact's
Been struck to keep all glory in the grip
Of ugly spinsters and barren sirs
As you etch on the inner window of your eye
This virgin on her rack:

She, ripe and unplucked, 's
Lain splayed too long in the tortuous boughs: overripe
Now, dour-faced, her fingers
Stiff as twigs, her body woodenly
Askew, she'll ache and wake

Though doomsday bud. Neglect's
Given her lips that lemon-tasting droop:
Untongued, all beauty's bright juice sours.
Tree-twist will ape this gross anatomy
Till irony's bough break.

Perseus

67

The Triumph of Wit Over Suffering

Head alone shows you in the prodigious act
Of digesting what centuries alone digest:
The mammoth, lumbering statuary of sorrow,
Indissoluble enough to riddle the guts
Of a whale with holes and holes, and bleed him white
Into salt seas. Hercules had a simple time,
Rinsing those stables: a baby's tears would do it.
But who'd volunteer to gulp the Laocoön,
The Dying Gaul and those innumerable pietàs
Festering on the dim walls of Europe's chapels,
Museums and sepulchers? You.

                    You
Who borrowed feathers for your feet, not lead,
Not nails, and a mirror to keep the snaky head
In safe perspective, could outface the gorgon-grimace
Of human agony: a look to numb
Limbs: not a basilisk-blink, nor a double whammy,
But all the accumulated last grunts, groans,
Cries and heroic couplets concluding the million
Enacted tragedies on these blood-soaked boards,
And every private twinge a hissing asp
To petrify your eyes, and every village
Catastrophe a writhing length of cobra,
And the decline of empires the thick coil of a vast
Anaconda.
            Imagine: the world
Fisted to a foetus head, ravined, seamed
With suffering from conception upwards, and there
You have it in hand. Grit in the eye or a sore
Thumb can make anyone wince, but the whole globe
Expressive of grief turns gods, like kings, to rocks.
Those rocks, cleft and worn, themselves then grow
Ponderous and extend despair on earth's
Dark face.
            So might rigor mortis come to stiffen
All creation, were it not for a bigger belly
Still than swallows joy.
                    You enter now,
Armed with feathers to tickle as well as fly,
And a fun-house mirror that turns the tragic muse
To the beheaded head of a sullen doll, one braid,
A bedraggled snake, hanging limp as the absurd mouth
Hangs in its lugubrious pout. Where are
The classic limbs of stubborn Antigone?
The red, royal robes of Phèdre? The tear-dazzled
Sorrows of Malfi's gentle duchess?
                    Gone
In the deep convulsion gripping your face, muscles
And sinews bunched, victorious, as the cosmic
Laugh does away with the unstitching, plaguey wounds
Of an eternal sufferer.

1958

To you
Perseus, the palm, and may you poise
And repoise until time stop, the celestial balance
Which weighs our madness with our sanity.

68

Battle-Scene

From the Comic Operatic Fantasy *The Seafarer*

It beguiles—
This little Odyssey
In pink and lavender
Over a surface of gently-
Graded turquoise tiles
That represent a sea
With chequered waves and gaily
Bear up the seafarer,
Gaily, gaily,
In his pink plume and armor.

A lantern-frail
Gondola of paper
Ferries the fishpond Sindbad
Who poises his pastel spear
Toward three pinky-purple
Monsters which uprear
Off the ocean-floor
With fanged and dreadful head.
Beware, beware
The whale, the shark, the squid.

But fins and scales
Of each scrolled sea-beast
Troll no slime, no weed.
They are polished for the joust,
They gleam like easter eggshells,
Rose and amethyst.
Ahab, fulfill your boast:
Bring home each storied head.
One thrust, one thrust,
One thrust: and they are sped.

84

So fables go.
And so all children sing
Their bathtub battles deep,
Hazardous and long,
But oh, sage grownups know
Sea-dragon for sofa, fang
For pasteboard, and siren-song
For fever in a sleep.
Laughing, laughing
Of graybeards wakes us up.

69

Yadwigha, on a Red Couch, Among Lilies

A Sestina for the Douanier

Yadwigha, the literalists once wondered how you
Came to be lying on this baroque couch
Upholstered in red velvet, under the eye
Of uncaged tigers and a tropical moon,
Set in an intricate wilderness of green
Heart-shaped leaves, like catalpa leaves, and lilies

Of monstrous size, like no well-bred lilies.
It seems the consistent critics wanted you
To choose between your world of jungle green
And the fashionable monde of the red couch
With its prim bric-à-brac, without a moon
To turn you luminous, without the eye

Of tigers to be stilled by your dark eye
And body whiter than its frill of lilies:
They'd have had yellow silk screening the moon,
Leaves and lilies flattened to paper behind you
Or, at most, to a mille-fleurs tapestry. But the couch
Stood stubborn in its jungle: red against green,

Red against fifty variants of green,
The couch glared out at the prosaic eye.

So Rousseau, to explain why the red couch
Persisted in the picture with the lilies,
Tigers, snakes, and the snakecharmer and you,
And birds of paradise, and the round moon,

Described how you fell dreaming at full of moon
On a red velvet couch within your green-
Tessellated boudoir. Hearing flutes, you
Dreamed yourself away in the moon's eye
To a beryl jungle, and dreamed that bright moon-lilies
Nodded their petaled heads around your couch.

And that, Rousseau told the critics, was why the couch
Accompanied you. So they nodded at the couch with the moon
And the snakecharmer's song and the gigantic lilies,
Marvelingly numbered the many shades of green.
But to a friend, in private, Rousseau confessed his eye
So possessed by the glowing red of the couch which you,

Yadwigha, pose on, that he put you on the couch
To feed his eye with red: such red! under the moon,
In the midst of all that green and those great lilies!

27 March 1958

70

A Winter's Tale

On Boston Common a red star
Gleams, wired to a tall Ulmus
Americana. Magi near
The domed State House.

Old Joseph holds an alpenstock.
Two waxen oxen flank the Child.
A black sheep leads the shepherds' flock.
Mary looks mild.

Angels—more feminine and douce
Than models from Bonwit's or Jay's,

1958

Haloes lustrous as Sirius—
Gilt trumpets raise.

By S. S. Pierce, by S. S. Pierce,
The red-nosed, blue-caped women ring
For money. Lord, the crowds are fierce!
There's caroling

On Winter Street, on Temple Place.
Poodles are baking cookies in
Filene's show windows. Grant us grace,
Donner, Blitzen,

And all you Santa's deer who browse
By leave of the Park Commission
On grass that once fed Boston cows.
In unison

On Pinckney, Mount Vernon, Chestnut,
The wreathed doors open to the crowd.
Noel! Noel! No mouth is shut.
Off key and loud

The populace sings toward the sill
Of windows with odd violet panes.
O Little City on a Hill!
The cordial strains

Of bellringers and singers rouse
Frost-bitten pigeons, eddy forth
From Charles Street to the Custom House,
From South Station to North.

Above the Oxbow

Here in this valley of discreet academies
We have not mountains, but mounts, truncated hillocks
To the Adirondacks, to northern Monadnock,
Themselves mere rocky hillocks to an Everest.

Still, they're our best mustering of height: by
Comparison with the sunken silver-grizzled
Back of the Connecticut, the river-level
Flats of Hadley farms, they're lofty enough
Elevations to be called something more than hills.
Green, wholly green, they stand their knobby spine
Against our sky: they are what we look southward to
Up Pleasant Street at Main. Poising their shapes
Between the snuff and red tar-paper apartments,
They mound a summer coolness in our view.

To people who live in the bottom of valleys
A rise in the landscape, hummock or hogback, looks
To be meant for climbing. A peculiar logic
In going up for the coming down if the post
We start at's the same post we finish by,
But it's the clear conversion at the top can hold
Us to the oblique road, in spite of a fitful
Wish for even ground, and it's the last cliff
Ledge will dislodge our cramped concept of space, unwall
Horizons beyond vision, spill vision
After the horizons, stretching the narrowed eye
To full capacity. We climb in hopes
Of such seeing up the leaf-shuttered escarpments,
Blindered by green, under a green-grained sky

Into the blue. Tops define themselves as places
Where nothing higher's to be looked to. Downward looks
Follow the black arrow-backs of swifts on their track
Of the air eddies' loop and arc though air's at rest
To us, since we see no leaf edge stir high
Here on a mount overlaid with leaves. The paint-peeled
Hundred-year-old hotel sustains its ramshackle
Four-way veranda, view-keeping above
The fallen timbers of its once remarkable
Funicular railway, witness to gone
Time, and to graces gone with the time. A state view-
Keeper collects half-dollars for the slopes
Of state scenery, sells soda, shows off viewpoints.
A ruddy skylight paints the gray oxbow

And paints the river's pale circumfluent stillness
As roses broach their carmine in a mirror. Flux
Of the desultory currents—all that unique
Stipple of shifting wave-tips is ironed out, lost
In the simplified orderings of sky-
Lorded perspectives. Maplike, the far fields are ruled
By correct green lines and no seedy free-for-all
Of asparagus heads. Cars run their suave
Colored beads on the strung roads, and the people stroll
Straightforwardly across the springing green.
All's peace and discipline down there. Till lately we
Lived under the shadow of hot rooftops
And never saw how coolly we might move. For once
A high hush quietens the crickets' cry.

Memoirs of a Spinach-Picker

72

They called the place Lookout Farm.

                         Back then, the sun
Didn't go down in such a hurry. How it
Lit things, that lamp of the Possible!

                               Wet yet
Lay over the leaves like a clear cellophane,
A pane of dragonfly wing, when they left me
With a hundred bushel baskets on the edge
Of the spinach patch.

                       Bunch after bunch of green
Upstanding spinach-tips wedged in a circle—
Layer on layer, and you had a basket
Irreproachable as any lettuce head,
Pure leafage. A hundred baskets by day's end.

Sun and sky mirrored the green of the spinach.
In the tin pail shaded by yellow paper
Well-water kept cool at the start of the rows.
The water had an iron taste, and the air,
Even, a tang of metal.

                     Day in, day out,
I bent over the plants in my leather-kneed

Dungarees, proud as a lady in a sea
Of prize roses, culling the fullest florets;
My world pyramided with laden baskets.

I'd only to set one foot in wilderness—
A whole sea of spinach-heads leaned to my hand.

The Ghost's Leavetaking

73

Enter the chilly no-man's land of about
Five o'clock in the morning, the no-color void
Where the waking head rubbishes out the draggled lot
Of sulfurous dreamscapes and obscure lunar conundrums
Which seemed, when dreamed, to mean so profoundly much,

Gets ready to face the ready-made creation
Of chairs and bureaus and sleep-twisted sheets.
This is the kingdom of the fading apparition,
The oracular ghost who dwindles on pin-legs
To a knot of laundry, with a classic bunch of sheets

Upraised, as a hand, emblematic of farewell.
At this joint between two worlds and two entirely
Incompatible modes of time, the raw material
Of our meat-and-potato thoughts assumes the nimbus
Of ambrosial revelation. And so departs.

Chair and bureau are the hieroglyphs
Of some godly utterance wakened heads ignore:
So these posed sheets, before they thin to nothing,
Speak in sign language of a lost otherworld,
A world we lose by merely waking up.

Trailing its telltale tatters only at the outermost
Fringe of mundane vision, this ghost goes
Hand aloft, goodbye, goodbye, not down
Into the rocky gizzard of the earth,
But toward a region where our thick atmosphere

Diminishes, and God knows what is there.
A point of exclamation marks that sky
In ringing orange like a stellar carrot.
Its round period, displaced and green,
Suspends beside it the first point, the starting

Point of Eden, next the new moon's curve.
Go, ghost of our mother and father, ghost of us,
And ghost of our dreams' children, in those sheets
Which signify our origin and end,
To the cloud-cuckoo land of color wheels

And pristine alphabets and cows that moo
And moo as they jump over moons as new
As that crisp cusp towards which you voyage now.
Hail and farewell. Hello, goodbye. O keeper
Of the profane grail, the dreaming skull.

74

Sculptor

For Leonard Baskin

To his house the bodiless
Come to barter endlessly
Vision, wisdom, for bodies
Palpable as his, and weighty.

Hands moving move priestlier
Than priest's hands, invoke no vain
Images of light and air
But sure stations in bronze, wood, stone.

Obdurate, in dense-grained wood,
A bald angel blocks and shapes
The flimsy light; arms folded
Watches his cumbrous world eclipse

Inane worlds of wind and cloud.
Bronze dead dominate the floor,

Resistive, ruddy-bodied,
Dwarfing us. Our bodies flicker

Toward extinction in those eyes
Which, without him, were beggared
Of place, time, and their bodies.
Emulous spirits make discord,

Try entry, enter nightmares
Until his chisel bequeaths
Them life livelier than ours,
A solider repose than death's.

75

Full Fathom Five

Old man, you surface seldom.
Then you come in with the tide's coming
When seas wash cold, foam-

Capped: white hair, white beard, far-flung,
A dragnet, rising, falling, as waves
Crest and trough. Miles long

Extend the radial sheaves
Of your spread hair, in which wrinkling skeins
Knotted, caught, survives

The old myth of origins
Unimaginable. You float near
As keeled ice-mountains

Of the north, to be steered clear
Of, not fathomed. All obscurity
Starts with a danger:

Your dangers are many. I
Cannot look much but your form suffers
Some strange injury

And seems to die: so vapors
Ravel to clearness on the dawn sea.
The muddy rumors

Of your burial move me
To half-believe: your reappearance
Proves rumors shallow,

For the archaic trenched lines
Of your grained face shed time in runnels:
Ages beat like rains

On the unbeaten channels
Of the ocean. Such sage humor and
Durance are whirlpools

To make away with the ground-
Work of the earth and the sky's ridgepole.
Waist down, you may wind

One labyrinthine tangle
To root deep among knuckles, shinbones,
Skulls. Inscrutable,

Below shoulders not once
Seen by any man who kept his head,
You defy questions;

You defy other godhood.
I walk dry on your kingdom's border
Exiled to no good.

Your shelled bed I remember.
Father, this thick air is murderous.
I would breathe water.

Lorelei

It is no night to drown in:
A full moon, river lapsing
Black beneath bland mirror-sheen,

The blue water-mists dropping
Scrim after scrim like fishnets
Though fishermen are sleeping,

The massive castle turrets
Doubling themselves in a glass
All stillness. Yet these shapes float

Up toward me, troubling the face
Of quiet. From the nadir
They rise, their limbs ponderous

With richness, hair heavier
Than sculpted marble. They sing
Of a world more full and clear

Than can be. Sisters, your song
Bears a burden too weighty
For the whorled ear's listening

Here, in a well-steered country,
Under a balanced ruler.
Deranging by harmony

Beyond the mundane order,
Your voices lay siege. You lodge
On the pitched reefs of nightmare,

Promising sure harborage;
By day, descant from borders
Of hebetude, from the ledge

Also of high windows. Worse
Even than your maddening
Song, your silence. At the source

Of your ice-hearted calling—
Drunkenness of the great depths.
O river, I see drifting

Deep in your flux of silver
Those great goddesses of peace.
Stone, stone, ferry me down there.

Mussel Hunter at Rock Harbor

77

I came before the water-
Colorists came to get the
Good of the Cape light that scours
Sand grit to sided crystal
And buffs and sleeks the blunt hulls
Of the three fishing smacks beached
On the bank of the river's

Backtracking tail. I'd come for
Free fish-bait: the blue mussels
Clumped like bulbs at the grass-root
Margin of the tidal pools.
Dawn tide stood dead low. I smelt
Mud stench, shell guts, gulls' leavings;
Heard a queer crusty scrabble

Cease, and I neared the silenced
Edge of a cratered pool-bed
The mussels hung dull blue and
Conspicuous, yet it seemed
A sly world's hinges had swung
Shut against me. All held still.
Though I counted scant seconds,

Enough ages lapsed to win
Confidence of safe-conduct

1958

In the wary otherworld
Eyeing me. Grass put forth claws;
Small mud knobs, nudged from under,
Displaced their domes as tiny
Knights might doff their casques. The crabs

Inched from their pigmy burrows
And from the trench-dug mud, all
Camouflaged in mottled mail
Of browns and greens. Each wore one
Claw swollen to a shield large
As itself—no fiddler's arm
Grown Gargantuan by trade,

But grown grimly, and grimly
Borne, for a use beyond my
Guessing of it. Sibilant
Mass-motived hordes, they sidled
Out in a converging stream
Toward the pool-mouth, perhaps to
Meet the thin and sluggish thread

Of sea retracing its tide-
Way up the river-basin.
Or to avoid me. They moved
Obliquely with a dry-wet
Sound, with a glittery wisp
And trickle. Could they feel mud
Pleasurable under claws

As I could between bare toes?
That question ended it—I
Stood shut out, for once, for all,
Puzzling the passage of their
Absolutely alien
Order as I might puzzle
At the clear tail of Halley's

Comet coolly giving my
Orbit the go-by, made known
By a family name it

Knew nothing of. So the crabs
Went about their business, which
Wasn't fiddling, and I filled
A big handkerchief with blue

Mussels. From what the crabs saw,
If they could see, I was one
Two-legged mussel-picker.
High on the airy thatching
Of the dense grasses I found
The husk of a fiddler-crab,
Intact, strangely strayed above

His world of mud—green color
And innards bleached and blown off
Somewhere by much sun and wind;
There was no telling if he'd
Died recluse or suicide
Or headstrong Columbus crab.
The crab-face, etched and set there,

Grimaced as skulls grimace: it
Had an Oriental look,
A samurai death mask done
On a tiger tooth, less for
Art's sake than God's. Far from sea—
Where red-freckled crab-backs, claws
And whole crabs, dead, their soggy

Bellies pallid and upturned,
Perform their shambling waltzes
On the waves' dissolving turn
And return, losing themselves
Bit by bit to their friendly
Element—this relic saved
Face, to face the bald-faced sun.

Moonrise

Grub-white mulberries redden among leaves.
I'll go out and sit in white like they do,
Doing nothing. July's juice rounds their nubs.

This park is fleshed with idiot petals.
White catalpa flowers tower, topple,
Cast a round white shadow in their dying.

A pigeon rudders down. Its fan-tail's white.
Vocation enough: opening, shutting
White petals, white fan-tails, ten white fingers.

Enough for fingernails to make half-moons
Redden in white palms no labor reddens.
White bruises toward color, else collapses.

Berries redden. A body of whiteness
Rots, and smells of rot under its headstone
Though the body walk out in clean linen.

I smell that whiteness here, beneath the stones
Where small ants roll their eggs, where grubs fatten.
Death may whiten in sun or out of it.

Death whitens in the egg and out of it.
I can see no color for this whiteness.
White: it is a complexion of the mind.

I tire, imagining white Niagaras
Build up from a rock root, as fountains build
Against the weighty image of their fall.

Lucina, bony mother, laboring
Among the socketed white stars, your face
Of candor pares white flesh to the white bone,

Who drag our ancient father at the heel,
White-bearded, weary. The berries purple
And bleed. The white stomach may ripen yet.

Frog Autumn

Summer grows old, cold-blooded mother.
The insects are scant, skinny.
In these palustral homes we only
Croak and wither.

Mornings dissipate in somnolence.
The sun brightens tardily
Among the pithless reeds. Flies fail us.
The fen sickens.

Frost drops even the spider. Clearly
The genius of plenitude
Houses himself elsewhere. Our folk thin
Lamentably.

In Midas' Country

Meadows of gold dust. The silver
Currents of the Connecticut fan
And meander in bland pleatings under
River-verge farms where rye-heads whiten.
All's polished to a dull luster

In the sulfurous noon. We move
With the languor of idols below
The sky's great bell glass and briefly engrave
Our limbs' image on a field of straw
And goldenrod as on gold leaf.

It might be heaven, this static
Plenitude: apples gold on the bough,
Goldfinch, goldfish, golden tiger cat stock-
Still in one gigantic tapestry—
And lovers affable, dovelike.

But now the water-skiers race,
Bracing their knees. On unseen towlines

They cleave the river's greening patinas;
The mirror quivers to smithereens.
They stunt like clowns in the circus.

So we are hauled, though we would stop
On this amber bank where grasses bleach.
Already the farmer's after his crop,
August gives over its Midas touch,
Wind bares a flintier landscape.

81   # Incommunicado

The groundhog on the mountain did not run
But fatly scuttled into the splayed fern
And faced me, back to a ledge of dirt, to rattle
Her sallow rodent teeth like castanets
Against my leaning down, would not exchange
For that wary clatter sound or gesture
Of love: claws braced, at bay, my currency not hers.

Such meetings never occur in märchen
Where love-met groundhogs love one in return,
Where straight talk is the rule, whether warm or hostile,
Which no gruff animal misinterprets.
From what grace am I fallen. Tongues are strange,
Signs say nothing. The falcon who spoke clear
To Canacee cries gibberish to coarsened ears.

82   # Child's Park Stones

In sunless air, under pines
  Green to the point of blackness, some
    Founding father set these lobed, warped stones
  To loom in the leaf-filtered gloom
Black as the charred knuckle-bones

Of a giant or extinct
  Animal, come from another
    Age, another planet surely. Flanked
  By the orange and fuchsia bonfire
Of azaleas, sacrosanct

These stones guard a dark repose
  And keep their shapes intact while sun
    Alters shadows of rose and iris—
  Long, short, long—in the lit garden
And kindles a day's-end blaze

Colored to dull the pigment
  Of the azaleas, yet burnt out
    Quick as they. To follow the light's tint
  And intensity by midnight
By noon and throughout the brunt

Of various weathers is
  To know the still heart of the stones:
    Stones that take the whole summer to lose
  Their dream of the winter's cold; stones
Warming at core only as

Frost forms. No man's crowbar could
  Uproot them: their beards are ever-
    Green. Nor do they, once in a hundred
  Years, go down to drink the river:
No thirst disturbs a stone's bed.

Owl

83

Clocks belled twelve. Main Street showed otherwise
Than its suburb of woods: nimbus-
Lit, but unpeopled, held its windows
Of wedding pastries,

Diamond rings, potted roses, fox-skins
Ruddy on the wax mannequins

In a glassed tableau of affluence.
From deep-sunk basements

What moved the pale, raptorial owl
Then, to squall above the level
Of streetlights and wires, its wall to wall
Wingspread in control

Of the ferrying currents, belly
Dense-feathered, fearfully soft to
Look upon? Rats' teeth gut the city
Shaken by owl cry.

26 June 1958

84

Whiteness I Remember

Whiteness being what I remember
About Sam: whiteness and the great run
He gave me. I've gone nowhere since but
Going's been tame deviation. White,
Not of heraldic stallions: off-white
Of the stable horse whose history's
Humdrum, unexceptionable, his
Tried sobriety hiring him out
To novices and to the timid.
Yet the dapple toning his white down
To safe gray never grayed his temper.

I see him one-tracked, stubborn, white horse,
First horse under me, high as the roofs,
His neat trot pitching my tense poise up,
Unsettling the steady-rooted green
Of country hedgerows and cow pastures
To a giddy jog. Then for ill will
Or to try me he suddenly set
Green grass streaming, houses a river
Of pale fronts, straw thatchings, the hard road
An anvil, hooves four hammers to jolt
Me off into their space of beating,

Stirrups undone, and decorum. And
Wouldn't slow for the hauled reins, his name,
Or shouts of walkers: crossroad traffic
Stalling curbside at his oncoming,
The world subdued to his run of it.
I hung on his neck. Resoluteness
Simplified me: a rider, riding
Hung out over hazard, over hooves
Loud on earth's bedrock. Almost thrown, not
Thrown: fear, wisdom, at one: all colors
Spinning to still in his one whiteness.

9 July 1958

Fable of the Rhododendron Stealers

I walked the unwalked garden of rose-beds
In the public park; at home felt the want
Of a single rose present to imagine
The garden's remainder in full paint.

The stone lion-head set in the wall
Let drop its spittle of sluggish green
Into the stone basin. I snipped
An orange bud, pocketed it. When

It had opened its orange in my vase,
Retrogressed to blowze, I next chose red;
Argued my conscience clear which robbed
The park of less red than withering did.

Musk satisfied my nose, red my eye,
The petals' nap my fingertips:
I considered the poetry I rescued
From blind air, from complete eclipse.

Yet today, a yellow bud in my hand,
I stalled at sudden noisy crashes
From the laurel thicket. No one approached.
A spasm took the rhododendron bushes:

Three girls, engrossed, were wrenching full clusters
Of cerise and pink from the rhododendron,
Mountaining them on spread newspaper.
They brassily picked, slowed by no chagrin,

And wouldn't pause for my straight look.
But gave me pause, my rose a charge,
Whether nicety stood confounded by love,
Or petty thievery by large.

86 ## The Death of Myth-Making

Two virtues ride, by stallion, by nag,
    To grind our knives and scissors:
Lantern-jawed Reason, squat Common Sense,
One courting doctors of all sorts,
    One, housewives and shopkeepers.

The trees are lopped, the poodles trim,
    The laborer's nails pared level
Since those two civil servants set
Their whetstone to the blunted edge
    And minced the muddling devil

Whose owl-eyes in the scraggly wood
    Scared mothers to miscarry,
Drove the dogs to cringe and whine,
And turned the farmboy's temper wolfish,
    The housewife's, desultory.

87 ## Green Rock, Winthrop Bay

No lame excuses can gloss over
Barge-tar clotted at the tide-line, the wrecked pier
I should have known better.

1958

Fifteen years between me and the bay
Profited memory, but did away with the old scenery
And patched this shoddy

Makeshift of a view to quit
My promise of an idyll. the blue's worn out:
It's a niggard estate,

Inimical now. The great green rock
We gave good use as ship and house is black
With tarry muck

And periwinkles, shrunk to common
Size. The cries of scavenging gulls sound thin
In the traffic of planes

From Logan Airport opposite.
Gulls circle gray under shadow of a steelier flight.
Loss cancels profit.

Unless you do this tawdry harbor
A service and ignore it, I go a liar
Gilding what's eyesore,

Or must take loophole and blame time
For the rock's dwarfed lump, for the drabbled scum,
For a churlish welcome.

88

The Companionable Ills

The nose-end that twitches, the old imperfections —
Tolerable now as moles on the face
Put up with until chagrin gives place
To a wry complaisance —

Dug in first as God's spurs
To start the spirit out of the mud
It stabled in; long-used, became well-loved
Bedfellows of the spirit's debauch, fond masters.

I Want, I Want

Open-mouthed, the baby god
Immense, bald, though baby-headed,
Cried out for the mother's dug.
The dry volcanoes cracked and spit,

Sand abraded the milkless lip.
Cried then for the father's blood
Who set wasp, wolf and shark to work,
Engineered the gannet's beak.

Dry-eyed, the inveterate patriarch
Raised his men of skin and bone,
Barbs on the crown of gilded wire,
Thorns on the bloody rose-stem.

Poems, Potatoes

The word, defining, muzzles; the drawn line
Ousts mistier peers and thrives, murderous,
In establishments which imagined lines

Can only haunt. Sturdy as potatoes,
Stones, without conscience, word and line endure,
Given an inch. Not that they're gross (although

Afterthought often would have them alter
To delicacy, to poise) but that they
Shortchange me continuously: whether

More or other, they still dissatisfy.
Unpoemed, unpictured, the potato
Bunches its knobby browns on a vastly
Superior page; the blunt stone also.

1958

The Times Are Tidy

Unlucky the hero born
In this province of the stuck record
Where the most watchful cooks go jobless
And the mayor's rôtisserie turns
Round of its own accord.

There's no career in the venture
Of riding against the lizard,
Himself withered these latter-days
To leaf-size from lack of action:
History's beaten the hazard.

The last crone got burnt up
More than eight decades back
With the love-hot herb, the talking cat,
But the children are better for it,
The cow milks cream an inch thick.

1959

The Bull of Bendylaw

The black bull bellowed before the sea.
The sea, till that day orderly,
Hove up against Bendylaw.

The queen in the mulberry arbor stared
Stiff as a queen on a playing card.
The king fingered his beard.

A blue sea, four horny bull-feet,
A bull-snouted sea that wouldn't stay put,
Bucked at the garden gate.

Along box-lined walks in the florid sun
Toward the rowdy bellow and back again
The lords and ladies ran.

The great bronze gate began to crack,
The sea broke in at every crack,
Pellmell, blueblack.

The bull surged up, the bull surged down,
Not to be stayed by a daisy chain
Nor by any learned man.

O the king's tidy acre is under the sea,
And the royal rose in the bull's belly,
And the bull on the king's highway.

The Eye-mote

Blameless as daylight I stood looking
At a field of horses, necks bent, manes blown,
Tails streaming against the green
Backdrop of sycamores. Sun was striking
While chapel pinnacles over the roofs,
Holding the horses, the clouds, the leaves

Steadily rooted though they were all flowing
Away to the left like reeds in a sea
When the splinter flew in and stuck my eye,
Needling it dark. Then I was seeing
A melding of shapes in a hot rain:
Horses warped on the altering green,

Outlandish as double-humped camels or unicorns,
Grazing at the margins of a bad monochrome,
Beasts of oasis, a better time.
Abrading my lid, the small grain burns:
Red cinder around which I myself,
Horses, planets and spires revolve.

Neither tears nor the easing flush
Of eyebaths can unseat the speck:
It sticks, and it has stuck a week.
I wear the present itch for flesh,
Blind to what will be and what was.
I dream that I am Oedipus.

What I want back is what I was
Before the bed, before the knife,
Before the brooch-pin and the salve
Fixed me in this parenthesis;
Horses fluent in the wind,
A place, a time gone out of mind.

Point Shirley

From Water-Tower Hill to the brick prison
The shingle booms, bickering under
The sea's collapse.
Snowcakes break and welter. This year
The gritted wave leaps
The seawall and drops onto a bier
Of quahog chips,
Leaving a salty mash of ice to whiten

In my grandmother's sand yard. She is dead,
Whose laundry snapped and froze here, who
Kept house against
What the sluttish, rutted sea could do.
Squall waves once danced
Ship timbers in through the cellar window;
A thresh-tailed, lanced
Shark littered in the geranium bed—

Such collusion of mulish elements
She wore her broom straws to the nub.
Twenty years out
Of her hand, the house still hugs in each drab
Stucco socket
The purple egg-stones: from Great Head's knob
To the filled-in Gut
The sea in its cold gizzard ground those rounds.

Nobody wintering now behind
The planked-up windows where she set
Her wheat loaves
And apple cakes to cool. What is it
Survives, grieves
So, over this battered, obstinate spit
Of gravel? The waves'
Spewed relics clicker masses in the wind,

Grey waves the stub-necked eiders ride.
A labor of love, and that labor lost.
Steadily the sea

Eats at Point Shirley. She died blessed,
And I come by
Bones, bones only, pawed and tossed,
A dog-faced sea.
The sun sinks under Boston, bloody red.

I would get from these dry-papped stones
The milk your love instilled in them.
The black ducks dive.
And though your graciousness might stream,
And I contrive,
Grandmother, stones are nothing of home
To that spumiest dove.
Against both bar and tower the black sea runs.

Goatsucker

95

Old goatherds swear how all night long they hear
The warning whirr and burring of the bird
Who wakes with darkness and till dawn works hard
Vampiring dry of milk each great goat udder.
Moon full, moon dark, the chary dairy farmer
Dreams that his fattest cattle dwindle, fevered
By claw-cuts of the Goatsucker, alias Devil-bird,
Its eye, flashlit, a chip of ruby fire.

So fables say the Goatsucker moves, masked from men's sight
In an ebony air, on wings of witch cloth,
Well-named, ill-famed a knavish fly-by-night,
Yet it never milked any goat, nor dealt cow death
And shadows only—cave-mouth bristle beset—
Cockchafers and the wan, green luna moth.

Watercolor of Grantchester Meadows

96

There, spring lambs jam the sheepfold. In air
Stilled, silvered as water in a glass
Nothing is big or far.

1959

The small shrew chitters from its wilderness
Of grassheads and is heard.
Each thumb-size bird
Flits nimble-winged in thickets, and of good color.

Cloudwrack and owl-hollowed willows slanting over
The bland Granta double their white and green
World under the sheer water
And ride that flux at anchor, upside down.
The punter sinks his pole.
In Byron's pool
Cat-tails part where the tame cygnets steer.

It is a country on a nursery plate.
Spotted cows revolve their jaws and crop
Red clover or gnaw beetroot
Bellied on a nimbus of sun-glazed buttercup.
Hedging meadows of benign
Arcadian green
The blood-berried hawthorn hides its spines with white.

Droll, vegetarian, the water rat
Saws down a reed and swims from his limber grove,
While the students stroll or sit,
Hands laced, in a moony indolence of love—
Black-gowned, but unaware
How in such mild air
The owl shall stoop from his turret, the rat cry out.

19 February 1959

A Winter Ship

97

At this wharf there are no grand landings to speak of.
Red and orange barges list and blister
Shackled to the dock, outmoded, gaudy,
And apparently indestructible.
The sea pulses under a skin of oil.

1959

A gull holds his pose on a shanty ridgepole,
Riding the tide of the wind, steady
As wood and formal, in a jacket of ashes,
The whole flat harbor anchored in
The round of his yellow eye-button.

A blimp swims up like a day-moon or tin
Cigar over his rink of fishes.
The prospect is dull as an old etching.
They are unloading three barrels of little crabs.
The pier pilings seem about to collapse

And with them that rickety edifice
Of warehouses, derricks, smokestacks and bridges
In the distance. All around us the water slips
And gossips in its loose vernacular,
Ferrying the smells of dead cod and tar.

Farther out, the waves will be mouthing icecakes—
A poor month for park-sleepers and lovers.
Even our shadows are blue with cold.
We wanted to see the sun come up
And are met, instead, by this iceribbed ship,

Bearded and blown, an albatross of frost,
Relic of tough weather, every winch and stay
Encased in a glassy pellicle.
The sun will diminish it soon enough:
Each wave-tip glitters like a knife.

Aftermath

Compelled by calamity's magnet
They loiter and stare as if the house
Burnt-out were theirs, or as if they thought
Some scandal might any minute ooze
From a smoke-choked closet into light;
No deaths, no prodigious injuries
Glut these hunters after an old meat,
Blood-spoor of the austere tragedies.

98

113

Mother Medea in a green smock
Moves humbly as any housewife through
Her ruined apartments, taking stock
Of charred shoes, the sodden upholstery:
Cheated of the pyre and the rack,
The crowd sucks her last tear and turns away.

Two Views of a Cadaver Room

99

(1)

The day she visited the dissecting room
They had four men laid out, black as burnt turkey,
Already half unstrung. A vinegary fume
Of the death vats clung to them;
The white-smocked boys started working.
The head of his cadaver had caved in,
And she could scarcely make out anything
In that rubble of skull plates and old leather.
A sallow piece of string held it together.

In their jars the snail-nosed babies moon and glow.
He hands her the cut-out heart like a cracked heirloom.

(2)

In Brueghel's panorama of smoke and slaughter
Two people only are blind to the carrion army:
He, afloat in the sea of her blue satin
Skirts, sings in the direction
Of her bare shoulder, while she bends,
Fingering a leaflet of music, over him,
Both of them deaf to the fiddle in the hands
Of the death's-head shadowing their song.
These Flemish lovers flourish; not for long.

Yet desolation, stalled in paint, spares the little country
Foolish, delicate, in the lower right hand corner.

Suicide off Egg Rock

Behind him the hotdogs split and drizzled
On the public grills, and the ochreous salt flats,
Gas tanks, factory stacks—that landscape
Of imperfections his bowels were part of—
Rippled and pulsed in the glassy updraught.
Sun struck the water like a damnation.
No pit of shadow to crawl into,
And his blood beating the old tattoo
I am, I am, I am. Children
Were squealing where combers broke and the spindrift
Raveled wind-ripped from the crest of the wave.
A mongrel working his legs to a gallop
Hustled a gull flock to flap off the sandspit.

He smoldered, as if stone-deaf, blindfold,
His body beached with the sea's garbage,
A machine to breathe and beat forever.
Flies filing in through a dead skate's eyehole
Buzzed and assailed the vaulted brainchamber.
The words in his book wormed off the pages.
Everything glittered like blank paper.

Everything shrank in the sun's corrosive
Ray but Egg Rock on the blue wastage.
He heard when he walked into the water

The forgetful surf creaming on those ledges.

The Ravaged Face

Outlandish as a circus, the ravaged face
Parades the marketplace, lurid and stricken
By some unutterable chagrin,
Maudlin from leaky eye to swollen nose.
Two pinlegs stagger underneath the mass.
Grievously purpled, mouth skewered on a groan,
Past keeping to the house, past all discretion—
Myself, myself!—obscene, lugubrious.

1959

Better the flat leer of the idiot,
The stone face of the man who doesn't feel,
The velvet dodges of the hypocrite:
Better, better, and more acceptable
To timorous children, to the lady on the street.
O Oedipus. O Christ. You use me ill.

19 March 1959

Metaphors

I'm a riddle in nine syllables,
An elephant, a ponderous house,
A melon strolling on two tendrils.
O red fruit, ivory, fine timbers!
This loaf's big with its yeasty rising.
Money's new-minted in this fat purse.
I'm a means, a stage, a cow in calf.
I've eaten a bag of green apples,
Boarded the train there's no getting off.

20 March 1959

Electra on Azalea Path

The day you died I went into the dirt,
Into the lightless hibernaculum
Where bees, striped black and gold, sleep out the blizzard
Like hieratic stones, and the ground is hard.
It was good for twenty years, that wintering—
As if you had never existed, as if I came
God-fathered into the world from my mother's belly:
Her wide bed wore the stain of divinity.
I had nothing to do with guilt or anything
When I wormed back under my mother's heart.

Small as a doll in my dress of innocence
I lay dreaming your epic, image by image.
Nobody died or withered on that stage.

1959

Everything took place in a durable whiteness.
The day I woke, I woke on Churchyard Hill.
I found your name, I found your bones and all
Enlisted in a cramped necropolis,
Your speckled stone askew by an iron fence.

In this charity ward, this poorhouse, where the dead
Crowd foot to foot, head to head, no flower
Breaks the soil. This is Azalea Path.
A field of burdock opens to the south.
Six feet of yellow gravel cover you.
The artificial red sage does not stir
In the basket of plastic evergreens they put
At the headstone next to yours, nor does it rot,
Although the rains dissolve a bloody dye:
The ersatz petals drip, and they drip red.

Another kind of redness bothers me:
The day your slack sail drank my sister's breath
The flat sea purpled like that evil cloth
My mother unrolled at your last homecoming.
I borrow the stilts of an old tragedy.
The truth is, one late October, at my birth-cry
A scorpion stung its head, an ill-starred thing;
My mother dreamed you face down in the sea.

The stony actors poise and pause for breath.
I brought my love to bear, and then you died.
It was the gangrene ate you to the bone
My mother said; you died like any man.
How shall I age into that state of mind?
I am the ghost of an infamous suicide,
My own blue razor rusting in my throat.
O pardon the one who knocks for pardon at
Your gate, father—your hound-bitch, daughter, friend.
It was my love that did us both to death.

The Beekeeper's Daughter

A garden of mouthings. Purple, scarlet-speckled, black
The great corollas dilate, peeling back their silks.
Their musk encroaches, circle after circle,
A well of scents almost too dense to breathe in.
Hieratical in your frock coat, maestro of the bees,
You move among the many-breasted hives,

My heart under your foot, sister of a stone.

Trumpet-throats open to the beaks of birds.
The Golden Rain Tree drips its powders down.
In these little boudoirs streaked with orange and red
The anthers nod their heads, potent as kings
To father dynasties. The air is rich.
Here is a queenship no mother can contest—

A fruit that's death to taste: dark flesh, dark parings.

In burrows narrow as a finger, solitary bees
Keep house among the grasses. Kneeling down
I set my eye to a hole-mouth and meet an eye
Round, green, disconsolate as a tear.
Father, bridegroom, in this Easter egg
Under the coronal of sugar roses

The queen bee marries the winter of your year.

The Hermit at Outermost House

Sky and sea, horizon-hinged
Tablets of blank blue, couldn't,
Clapped shut, flatten this man out.

The great gods, Stone-Head, Claw-Foot,
Winded by much rock-bumping
And claw-threat, realized that.

For what, then, had they endured
Dourly the long hots and colds,
Those old despots, if he sat

Laugh-shaken on his doorsill,
Backbone unbendable as
Timbers of his upright hut?

Hard gods were there, nothing else.
Still he thumbed out something else.
Thumbed no stony, horny pot,

But a certain meaning green.
He withstood them, that hermit.
Rock-face, crab-claw verged on green.

Gulls mulled in the greenest light.

Man in Black

Where the three magenta
Breakwaters take the shove
And suck of the gray sea

To the left, and the wave
Unfists against the dun
Barb-wired headland of

The Deer Island prison
With its trim piggeries,
Hen huts and cattle green

To the right, and March ice
Glazes the rock pools yet,
Snuff-colored sand cliffs rise

Over a great stone spit
Bared by each falling tide,
And you, across those white

Stones, strode out in your dead
Black coat, black shoes, and your
Black hair till there you stood,

Fixed vortex on the far
Tip, riveting stones, air,
All of it, together.

Old Ladies' Home

107

Sharded in black, like beetles,
Frail as antique earthenware
One breath might shiver to bits,
The old women creep out here
To sun on the rocks or prop
Themselves up against the wall
Whose stones keep a little heat.

Needles knit in a bird-beaked
Counterpoint to their voices:
Sons, daughters, daughters and sons,
Distant and cold as photos,
Grandchildren nobody knows.
Age wears the best black fabric
Rust-red or green as lichens.

At owl-call the old ghosts flock
To hustle them off the lawn.
From beds boxed-in like coffins
The bonneted ladies grin.
And Death, that bald-head buzzard,
Stalls in halls where the lamp wick
Shortens with each breath drawn.

The Net-Menders

Halfway up from the little harbor of sardine boats,
Halfway down from groves where the thin, bitter almond pips
Fatten in green-pocked pods, the three net-menders sit out,
Dressed in black, everybody in mourning for someone.
They set their stout chairs back to the road and face the dark
Dominoes of their doorways.

                      Sun grains their crow-colors,
Purples the fig in the leaf's shadow, turns the dust pink.
On the road named for Tomas Ortunio, mica
Winks like money under the ringed toes of the chickens.
The houses are white as sea-salt goats lick from the rocks.

While their fingers work with the coarse mesh and the fine
Their eyes revolve the whole town like a blue and green ball.
Nobody dies or is born without their knowing it.
They talk of bride-lace, of lovers spunky as gamecocks.

The moon leans, a stone madonna, over the lead sea
And the iron hills that enclose them. Earthen fingers
Twist old words into the web-threads:

                    Tonight may the fish
Be a harvest of silver in the nets, and the lamps
Of our husbands and sons move sure among the low stars.

Magnolia Shoals

Up here among the gull cries
    we stroll through a maze of pale
red-mottled relics, shells, claws

as if it were summer still.
    That season has turned its back.
Though the green sea gardens stall,

bow, and recover their look
    of the imperishable
gardens in an antique book

or tapestries on a wall,
    leaves behind us warp and lapse.
The late month withers, as well.

Below us a white gull keeps
    the weed-slicked shelf for his own,
hustles other gulls off. Crabs

rove over his field of stone;
    mussels cluster blue as grapes:
his beak brings the harvest in.

The watercolorist grips
    his brush in the stringent air.
The horizon's bare of ships,

the beach and the rocks are bare.
    He paints a blizzard of gulls,
wings drumming in the winter.

October 1959

The Sleepers

110

No map traces the street
Where those two sleepers are.
We have lost track of it.
They lie as if under water
In a blue, unchanging light,
The French window ajar

Curtained with yellow lace.
Through the narrow crack
Odors of wet earth rise.
The snail leaves a silver track;

1959

Dark thickets hedge the house.
We take a backward look.

Among petals pale as death
And leaves steadfast in shape
They sleep on, mouth to mouth.
A white mist is going up.
The small green nostrils breathe,
And they turn in their sleep.

Ousted from that warm bed
We are a dream they dream.
Their eyelids keep the shade.
No harm can come to them.
We cast our skins and slide
Into another time.

III Yaddo: The Grand Manor

Woodsmoke and a distant loudspeaker
Filter into this clear
Air, and blur.

The red tomato's in, the green bean;
The cook lugs a pumpkin
From the vine

For pies. The fir tree's thick with grackles.
Gold carp loom in the pools.
A wasp crawls

Over windfalls to sip cider-juice.
Guests in the studios
Muse, compose.

Indoors, Tiffany's phoenix rises
Above the fireplace;
Two carved sleighs

Rest on orange plush near the newel post.
Wood stoves burn warm as toast.
The late guest

Wakens, mornings, to a cobalt sky,
A diamond-paned window,
Zinc-white snow.

Medallion

By the gate with star and moon
Worked into the peeled orange wood
The bronze snake lay in the sun

Inert as a shoelace; dead
But pliable still, his jaw
Unhinged and his grin crooked,

Tongue a rose-colored arrow.
Over my hand I hung him.
His little vermilion eye

Ignited with a glassed flame
As I turned him in the light;
When I split a rock one time

The garnet bits burned like that.
Dust dulled his back to ochre
The way sun ruins a trout.

Yet his belly kept its fire
Going under the chainmail,
The old jewels smoldering there

In each opaque belly-scale:
Sunset looked at through milk glass.
And I saw white maggots coil

1959

Thin as pins in the dark bruise
Where his innards bulged as if
He were digesting a mouse.

Knifelike, he was chaste enough,
Pure death's-metal. The yardman's
Flung brick perfected his laugh.

The Manor Garden

113

The fountains are dry and the roses over.
Incense of death. Your day approaches.
The pears fatten like little buddhas.
A blue mist is dragging the lake.

You move through the era of fishes,
The smug centuries of the pig—
Head, toe and finger
Come clear of the shadow. History

Nourishes these broken flutings,
These crowns of acanthus,
And the crow settles her garments.
You inherit white heather, a bee's wing,

Two suicides, the family wolves,
Hours of blankness. Some hard stars
Already yellow the heavens.
The spider on its own string

Crosses the lake. The worms
Quit their usual habitations.
The small birds converge, converge
With their gifts to a difficult borning.

Blue Moles

(1)

They're out of the dark's ragbag, these two
Moles dead in the pebbled rut,
Shapeless as flung gloves, a few feet apart—
Blue suede a dog or fox has chewed.
One, by himself, seemed pitiable enough,
Little victim unearthed by some large creature
From his orbit under the elm root.
The second carcass makes a duel of the affair:
Blind twins bitten by bad nature.

The sky's far dome is sane and clear.
Leaves, undoing their yellow caves
Between the road and the lake water,
Bare no sinister spaces. Already
The moles look neutral as the stones.
Their corkscrew noses, their white hands
Uplifted, stiffen in a family pose.
Difficult to imagine how fury struck—
Dissolved now, smoke of an old war.

(2)

Nightly the battle-shouts start up
In the ear of the veteran, and again
I enter the soft pelt of the mole.
Light's death to them: they shrivel in it.
They move through their mute rooms while I sleep,
Palming the earth aside, grubbers
After the fat children of root and rock.
By day, only the topsoil heaves.
Down there one is alone.

Outsize hands prepare a path,
They go before: opening the veins,
Delving for the appendages
Of beetles, sweetbreads, shards—to be eaten

Over and over. And still the heaven
Of final surfeit is just as far
From the door as ever. What happens between us
Happens in darkness, vanishes
Easy and often as each breath.

Dark Wood, Dark Water

This wood burns a dark
Incense. Pale moss drips
In elbow-scarves, beards

From the archaic
Bones of the great trees.
Blue mists move over

A lake thick with fish.
Snails scroll the border
Of the glazed water

With coils of ram's-horn.
Out in the open
Down there the late year

Hammers her rare and
Various metals.
Old pewter roots twist

Up from the jet-backed
Mirror of water
And while the air's clear

Hourglass sifts a
Drift of goldpieces
Bright waterlights are

Sliding their quoits one
After the other
Down boles of the fir.

Polly's Tree

A dream tree, Polly's tree:
  a thicket of sticks,
    each speckled twig

ending in a thin-paned
  leaf unlike any
    other on it

or in a ghost flower
  flat as paper and
    of a color

vaporish as frost-breath,
  more finical than
    any silk fan

the Chinese ladies use
  to stir robin's egg
    air. The silver-

haired seed of the milkweed
  comes to roost there, frail
    as the halo

rayed round a candle flame,
  a will-o'-the-wisp
    nimbus, or puff

of cloud-stuff, tipping her
  queer candelabrum.
    Palely lit by

snuff-ruffed dandelions,
  white daisy wheels and
    a tiger-faced

pansy, it glows. O it's
  no family tree,
    Polly's tree, nor

a tree of heaven, though
   it marry quartz-flake,
      feather and rose.

It sprang from her pillow
   whole as a cobweb,
      ribbed like a hand,

a dream tree. Polly's tree
   wears a valentine
      arc of tear-pearled

bleeding hearts on its sleeve
   and, crowning it, one
      blue larkspur star.

The Colossus

I shall never get you put together entirely,
Pieced, glued, and properly jointed.
Mule-bray, pig-grunt and bawdy cackles
Proceed from your great lips.
It's worse than a barnyard.

Perhaps you consider yourself an oracle,
Mouthpiece of the dead, or of some god or other.
Thirty years now I have labored
To dredge the silt from your throat.
I am none the wiser.

Scaling little ladders with gluepots and pails of Lysol
I crawl like an ant in mourning
Over the weedy acres of your brow
To mend the immense skull-plates and clear
The bald, white tumuli of your eyes.

A blue sky out of the Oresteia
Arches above us. O father, all by yourself
You are pithy and historical as the Roman Forum.

1959

I open my lunch on a hill of black cypress.
Your fluted bones and acanthine hair are littered

In their old anarchy to the horizon-line.
It would take more than a lightning-stroke
To create such a ruin.
Nights, I squat in the cornucopia
Of your left ear, out of the wind,

Counting the red stars and those of plum-color.
The sun rises under the pillar of your tongue.
My hours are married to shadow.
No longer do I listen for the scrape of a keel
On the blank stones of the landing.

Private Ground

First frost, and I walk among the rose-fruit, the marble toes
Of the Greek beauties you brought
Off Europe's relic heap
To sweeten your neck of the New York woods.
Soon each white lady will be boarded up
Against the cracking climate.

All morning, with smoking breath, the handyman
Has been draining the goldfish ponds.
They collapse like lungs, the escaped water
Threading back, filament by filament, to the pure
Platonic table where it lives. The baby carp
Litter the mud like orangepeel.

Eleven weeks, and I know your estate so well
I need hardly go out at all.
A superhighway seals me off.
Trading their poisons, the north and south bound cars
Flatten the doped snakes to ribbon. In here, the grasses
Unload their griefs on my shoes,

The woods creak and ache, and the day forgets itself.
I bend over this drained basin where the small fish
Flex as the mud freezes.
They glitter like eyes, and I collect them all.
Morgue of old logs and old images, the lake
Opens and shuts, accepting them among its reflections.

Poem for a Birthday

1. Who

The month of flowering's finished. The fruit's in,
Eaten or rotten. I am all mouth.
October's the month for storage.

This shed's fusty as a mummy's stomach:
Old tools, handles and rusty tusks.
I am at home here among the dead heads.

Let me sit in a flowerpot,
The spiders won't notice.
My heart is a stopped geranium.

If only the wind would leave my lungs alone.
Dogbody noses the petals. They bloom upside down.
They rattle like hydrangea bushes.

Moldering heads console me,
Nailed to the rafters yesterday:
Inmates who don't hibernate.

Cabbageheads: wormy purple, silver-glaze,
A dressing of mule ears, mothy pelts, but green-hearted,
Their veins white as porkfat.

O the beauty of usage!
The orange pumpkins have no eyes.
These halls are full of women who think they are birds.

This is a dull school.
I am a root, a stone, an owl pellet,
Without dreams of any sort.

Mother, you are the one mouth
I would be a tongue to. Mother of otherness
Eat me. Wastebasket gaper, shadow of doorway.

I said: I must remember this, being small.
There were such enormous flowers,
Purple and red mouths, utterly lovely.

The hoops of blackberry stems made me cry.
Now they light me up like an electric bulb.
For weeks I can remember nothing at all.

2. Dark House

This is a dark house, very big.
I made it myself,
Cell by cell from a quiet corner,
Chewing at the gray paper,
Oozing the glue drops,
Whistling, wiggling my ears,
Thinking of something else.

It has so many cellars,
Such eelish delvings!
I am round as an owl,
I see by my own light.
Any day I may litter puppies
Or mother a horse. My belly moves.
I must make more maps.

These marrowy tunnels!
Moley-handed, I eat my way.
All-mouth licks up the bushes
And the pots of meat.
He lives in an old well,
A stony hole. He's to blame.
He's a fat sort.

1959

Pebble smells, turnipy chambers.
Small nostrils are breathing.
Little humble loves!
Footlings, boneless as noses,
It is warm and tolerable
In the bowel of the root.
Here's a cuddly mother.

3. Maenad

Once I was ordinary:
Sat by my father's bean tree
Eating the fingers of wisdom.
The birds made milk.
When it thundered I hid under a flat stone.

The mother of mouths didn't love me.
The old man shrank to a doll.
O I am too big to go backward:
Birdmilk is feathers,
The bean leaves are dumb as hands.

This month is fit for little.
The dead ripen in the grapeleaves.
A red tongue is among us.
Mother, keep out of my barnyard,
I am becoming another.

Dog-head, devourer:
Feed me the berries of dark.
The lids won't shut. Time
Unwinds from the great umbilicus of the sun
Its endless glitter.

I must swallow it all.

Lady, who are these others in the moon's vat—
Sleepdrunk, their limbs at odds?
In this light the blood is black.
Tell me my name.

4. The Beast

He was bullman earlier,
King of the dish, my lucky animal.
Breathing was easy in his airy holding.
The sun sat in his armpit.
Nothing went moldy. The little invisibles
Waited on him hand and foot.
The blue sisters sent me to another school.
Monkey lived under the dunce cap.
He kept blowing me kisses.
I hardly knew him.

He won't be got rid of:
Mumblepaws, teary and sorry,
Fido Littlesoul, the bowel's familiar.
A dustbin's enough for him.
The dark's his bone.
Call him any name, he'll come to it.

Mud-sump, happy sty-face.
I've married a cupboard of rubbish.
I bed in a fish puddle.
Down here the sky is always falling.
Hogwallow's at the window.
The star bugs won't save me this month.
I housekeep in Time's gut-end
Among emmets and mollusks,
Duchess of Nothing,
Hairtusk's bride.

5. Flute Notes from a Reedy Pond

Now coldness comes sifting down, layer after layer,
To our bower at the lily root.
Overhead the old umbrellas of summer
Wither like pithless hands. There is little shelter.

Hourly the eye of the sky enlarges its blank
Dominion. The stars are no nearer.
Already frog-mouth and fish-mouth drink
The liquor of indolence, and all things sink

Into a soft caul of forgetfulness.
The fugitive colors die.
Caddis worms drowse in their silk cases,
The lamp-headed nymphs are nodding to sleep like statues.

Puppets, loosed from the strings of the puppet-master,
Wear masks of horn to bed.
This is not death, it is something safer.
The wingy myths won't tug at us any more:

The molts are tongueless that sang from above the water
Of golgotha at the tip of a reed,
And how a god flimsy as a baby's finger
Shall unhusk himself and steer into the air.

6. Witch Burning

In the marketplace they are piling the dry sticks.
A thicket of shadows is a poor coat. I inhabit
The wax image of myself, a doll's body.
Sickness begins here: I am a dartboard for witches.
Only the devil can eat the devil out.
In the month of red leaves I climb to a bed of fire.

It is easy to blame the dark: the mouth of a door,
The cellar's belly. They've blown my sparkler out.
A black-sharded lady keeps me in a parrot cage.
What large eyes the dead have!
I am intimate with a hairy spirit.
Smoke wheels from the beak of this empty jar.

If I am a little one, I can do no harm.
If I don't move about, I'll knock nothing over. So I said,
Sitting under a potlid, tiny and inert as a rice grain.
They are turning the burners up, ring after ring.
We are full of starch, my small white fellows. We grow.
It hurts at first. The red tongues will teach the truth.

Mother of beetles, only unclench your hand:
I'll fly through the candle's mouth like a singeless moth.

Give me back my shape. I am ready to construe the days
I coupled with dust in the shadow of a stone.
My ankles brighten. Brightness ascends my thighs.
I am lost, I am lost, in the robes of all this light.

7. The Stones

This is the city where men are mended.
I lie on a great anvil.
The flat blue sky-circle

Flew off like the hat of a doll
When I fell out of the light. I entered
The stomach of indifference, the wordless cupboard.

The mother of pestles diminished me.
I became a still pebble.
The stones of the belly were peaceable,

The head-stone quiet, jostled by nothing.
Only the mouth-hole piped out,
Importunate cricket

In a quarry of silences.
The people of the city heard it.
They hunted the stones, taciturn and separate,

The mouth-hole crying their locations.
Drunk as a foetus
I suck at the paps of darkness.

The food tubes embrace me. Sponges kiss my lichens away.
The jewelmaster drives his chisel to pry
Open one stone eye.

This is the after-hell: I see the light.
A wind unstoppers the chamber
Of the ear, old worrier.

1959

Water mollifies the flint lip,
And daylight lays its sameness on the wall.
The grafters are cheerful,

Heating the pincers, hoisting the delicate hammers.
A current agitates the wires
Volt upon volt. Catgut stitches my fissures.

A workman walks by carrying a pink torso.
The storerooms are full of hearts.
This is the city of spare parts.

My swaddled legs and arms smell sweet as rubber.
Here they can doctor heads, or any limb.
On Fridays the little children come

To trade their hooks for hands.
Dead men leave eyes for others.
Love is the uniform of my bald nurse.

Love is the bone and sinew of my curse.
The vase, reconstructed, houses
The elusive rose.

Ten fingers shape a bowl for shadows.
My mendings itch. There is nothing to do.
I shall be good as new.

4 November 1959

The Burnt-out Spa

An old beast ended in this place:

A monster of wood and rusty teeth.
Fire smelted his eyes to lumps
Of pale blue vitreous stuff, opaque
As resin drops oozed from pine bark.

1959

The rafters and struts of his body wear
Their char of karakul still. I can't tell
How long his carcass has foundered under
The rubbish of summers, the black-leaved falls.

Now little weeds insinuate
Soft suede tongues between his bones.
His armorplate, his toppled stones
Are an esplanade for crickets.

I pick and pry like a doctor or
Archaeologist among
Iron entrails, enamel bowls,
The coils and pipes that made him run.

The small dell eats what ate it once.
And yet the ichor of the spring
Proceeds clear as it ever did
From the broken throat, the marshy lip.

It flows off below the green and white
Balustrade of a sag-backed bridge.
Leaning over, I encounter one
Blue and improbable person

Framed in a basketwork of cat-tails.
O she is gracious and austere,
Seated beneath the toneless water!
It is not I, it is not I.

No animal spoils on her green doorstep.
And we shall never enter there
Where the durable ones keep house.
The stream that hustles us

Neither nourishes nor heals.

11 November 1959

Mushrooms

Overnight, very
Whitely, discreetly,
Very quietly

Our toes, our noses
Take hold on the loam,
Acquire the air.

Nobody sees us,
Stops us, betrays us;
The small grains make room.

Soft fists insist on
Heaving the needles,
The leafy bedding,

Even the paving.
Our hammers, our rams,
Earless and eyeless,

Perfectly voiceless,
Widen the crannies,
Shoulder through holes. We

Diet on water,
On crumbs of shadow,
Bland-mannered, asking

Little or nothing.
So many of us!
So many of us!

We are shelves, we are
Tables, we are meek,
We are edible,

Nudgers and shovers
In spite of ourselves.
Our kind multiplies:

1959

We shall by morning
Inherit the earth.
Our foot's in the door.

13 November 1959

1960

You're

Clownlike, happiest on your hands,
Feet to the stars, and moon-skulled,
Gilled like a fish. A common-sense
Thumbs-down on the dodo's mode.
Wrapped up in yourself like a spool,
Trawling your dark as owls do.
Mute as a turnip from the Fourth
Of July to All Fools' Day,
O high-riser, my little loaf.

Vague as fog and looked for like mail.
Farther off than Australia.
Bent-backed Atlas, our traveled prawn.
Snug as a bud and at home
Like a sprat in a pickle jug.
A creel of eels, all ripples.
Jumpy as a Mexican bean.
Right, like a well-done sum.
A clean slate, with your own face on.

January/February 1960

The Hanging Man

By the roots of my hair some god got hold of me.
I sizzled in his blue volts like a desert prophet.

The nights snapped out of sight like a lizard's eyelid:
A world of bald white days in a shadeless socket.

A vulturous boredom pinned me in this tree.
If he were I, he would do what I did.

Stillborn

124

These poems do not live: it's a sad diagnosis.
They grew their toes and fingers well enough,
Their little foreheads bulged with concentration.
If they missed out on walking about like people
It wasn't for any lack of mother-love.

O I cannot understand what happened to them!
They are proper in shape and number and every part.
They sit so nicely in the pickling fluid!
They smile and smile and smile and smile at me.
And still the lungs won't fill and the heart won't start.

They are not pigs, they are not even fish,
Though they have a piggy and a fishy air—
It would be better if they were alive, and that's what they were.
But they are dead, and their mother near dead with distraction,
And they stupidly stare, and do not speak of her.

On Deck

125

Midnight in the mid-Atlantic. On deck.
Wrapped up in themselves as in thick veiling
And mute as mannequins in a dress shop,
Some few passengers keep track
Of the old star-map on the ceiling.
Tiny and far, a single ship

Lit like a two-tiered wedding cake
Carries its candles slowly off.
Now there is nothing much to look at.
Still nobody will move or speak—
The bingo players, the players at love
On a square no bigger than a carpet

Are hustled over the crests and troughs,
Each stalled in his particular minute
And castled in it like a king.
Small drops spot their coats, their gloves:
They fly too fast to feel the wet.
Anything can happen where they are going.

The untidy lady revivalist
For whom the good Lord provides (He gave
Her a pocketbook, a pearl hatpin
And seven winter coats last August)
Prays under her breath that she may save
The art students in West Berlin.

The astrologer at her elbow (a Leo)
Picked his trip-date by the stars.
He is gratified by the absence of icecakes.
He'll be rich in a year (and he should know)
Selling the Welsh and English mothers
Nativities at two-and-six.

And the white-haired jeweler from Denmark is
       carving
A perfectly faceted wife to wait
On him hand and foot, quiet as a diamond.
Moony balloons tied by a string
To their owners' wrists, the light dreams float
To be let loose at news of land.

July 1960

Sleep in the Mojave Desert

Out here there are no hearthstones,
Hot grains, simply. It is dry, dry.
And the air dangerous. Noonday acts queerly
On the mind's eye, erecting a line
Of poplars in the middle distance, the only
Object beside the mad, straight road
One can remember men and houses by.

A cool wind should inhabit those leaves
And a dew collect on them, dearer than money,
In the blue hour before sunup.
Yet they recede, untouchable as tomorrow,
Or those glittery fictions of spilt water
That glide ahead of the very thirsty.

I think of the lizards airing their tongues
In the crevice of an extremely small shadow
And the toad guarding his heart's droplet.
The desert is white as a blind man's eye,
Comfortless as salt. Snake and bird
Doze behind the old masks of fury.
We swelter like firedogs in the wind.
The sun puts its cinder out. Where we lie
The heat-cracked crickets congregate
In their black armorplate and cry.
The day-moon lights up like a sorry mother,
And the crickets come creeping into our hair
To fiddle the short night away.

5 July 1960

127   Two Campers in Cloud Country

(Rock Lake, Canada)

In this country there is neither measure nor balance
To redress the dominance of rocks and woods,
The passage, say, of these man-shaming clouds.

No gesture of yours or mine could catch their attention,
No word make them carry water or fire the kindling
Like local trolls in the spell of a superior being.

Well, one wearies of the Public Gardens: one wants a vacation
Where trees and clouds and animals pay no notice;
Away from the labeled elms, the tame tea-roses.

1960

It took three days driving north to find a cloud
The polite skies over Boston couldn't possibly accommodate.
Here on the last frontier of the big, brash spirit

The horizons are too far off to be chummy as uncles;
The colors assert themselves with a sort of vengeance.
Each day concludes in a huge splurge of vermilions

And night arrives in one gigantic step.
It is comfortable, for a change, to mean so little.
These rocks offer no purchase to herbage or people:

They are conceiving a dynasty of perfect cold.
In a month we'll wonder what plates and forks are for.
I lean to you, numb as a fossil. Tell me I'm here.

The Pilgrims and Indians might never have happened.
Planets pulse in the lake like bright amoebas;
The pines blot our voices up in their lightest sighs.

Around our tent the old simplicities sough
Sleepily as Lethe, trying to get in.
We'll wake blank-brained as water in the dawn.

July 1960

128   Leaving Early

Lady, your room is lousy with flowers.
When you kick me out, that's what I'll remember,
Me, sitting here bored as a leopard
In your jungle of wine-bottle lamps,
Velvet pillows the colour of blood pudding
And the white china flying fish from Italy.
I forget you, hearing the cut flowers
Sipping their liquids from assorted pots,
Pitchers and Coronation goblets
Like Monday drunkards. The milky berries
Bow down, a local constellation,

145

1960

Toward their admirers in the tabletop:
Mobs of eyeballs looking up.
Are those petals or leaves you've paired them with—
Those green-striped ovals of silver tissue?
The red geraniums I know.
Friends, friends. They stink of armpits
And the involved maladies of autumn,
Musky as a lovebed the morning after.
My nostrils prickle with nostalgia.
Henna hags: cloth of your cloth.
They toe old water thick as fog.

The roses in the toby jug
Gave up the ghost last night. High time.
Their yellow corsets were ready to split.
You snored, and I heard the petals unlatch,
Tapping and ticking like nervous fingers.
You should have junked them before they died.
Daybreak discovered the bureau lid
Littered with Chinese hands. Now I'm stared at
By chrysanthemums the size
Of Holofernes' head, dipped in the same
Magenta as this fubsy sofa.
In the mirror their doubles back them up.
Listen: your tenant mice
Are rattling the cracker packets. Fine flour
Muffles their bird-feet: they whistle for joy.
And you doze on, nose to the wall.
This mizzle fits me like a sad jacket.
How did we make it up to your attic?
You handed me gin in a glass bud vase.
We slept like stones. Lady, what am I doing
With a lung full of dust and a tongue of wood,
Knee-deep in the cold and swamped by flowers?

25 September 1960

1960

Love Letter

Not easy to state the change you made.
If I'm alive now, then I was dead,
Though, like a stone, unbothered by it,
Staying put according to habit.
You didn't just toe me an inch, no—
Nor leave me to set my small bald eye
Skyward again, without hope, of course,
Of apprehending blueness, or stars.

That wasn't it. I slept, say: a snake
Masked among black rocks as a black rock
In the white hiatus of winter—
Like my neighbors, taking no pleasure
In the million perfectly-chiseled
Cheeks alighting each moment to melt
My cheek of basalt. They turned to tears,
Angels weeping over dull natures,
But didn't convince me. Those tears froze.
Each dead head had a visor of ice.

And I slept on like a bent finger.
The first thing I saw was sheer air
And the locked drops rising in a dew
Limpid as spirits. Many stones lay
Dense and expressionless round about.
I didn't know what to make of it.
I shone, mica-scaled, and unfolded
To pour myself out like a fluid
Among bird feet and the stems of plants.
I wasn't fooled. I knew you at once.

Tree and stone glittered, without shadows.
My finger-length grew lucent as glass.
I started to bud like a March twig:
An arm and a leg, an arm, a leg.
From stone to cloud, so I ascended.
Now I resemble a sort of god
Floating through the air in my soul-shift
Pure as a pane of ice. It's a gift.

16 October 1960

Magi

The abstracts hover like dull angels:
Nothing so vulgar as a nose or an eye
Bossing the ethereal blanks of their face-ovals.

Their whiteness bears no relation to laundry,
Snow, chalk or suchlike. They're
The real thing, all right: the Good, the True—

Salutary and pure as boiled water,
Loveless as the multiplication table.
While the child smiles into thin air.

Six months in the world, and she is able
To rock on all fours like a padded hammock.
For her, the heavy notion of Evil

Attending her cot is less than a belly ache,
And Love the mother of milk, no theory.
They mistake their star, these papery godfolk.

They want the crib of some lamp-headed Plato.
Let them astound his heart with their merit.
What girl ever flourished in such company?

Candles

They are the last romantics, these candles:
Upside down hearts of light tipping wax fingers,
And the fingers, taken in by their own haloes,
Grown milky, almost clear, like the bodies of saints.
It is touching, the way they'll ignore

A whole family of prominent objects
Simply to plumb the deeps of an eye
In its hollow of shadows, its fringe of reeds,
And the owner past thirty, no beauty at all.
Daylight would be more judicious,

Giving everybody a fair hearing.
They should have gone out with balloon flights and the stereopticon.
This is no time for the private point of view.
When I light them, my nostrils prickle.
Their pale, tentative yellows

Drag up false, Edwardian sentiments,
And I remember my maternal grandmother from Vienna.
As a schoolgirl she gave roses to Franz Josef.
The burghers sweated and wept. The children wore white.
And my grandfather moped in the Tyrol,

Imagining himself a headwaiter in America,
Floating in a high-church hush
Among ice buckets, frosty napkins.
These little globes of light are sweet as pears.
Kindly with invalids and mawkish women,

They mollify the bald moon.
Nun-souled, they burn heavenward and never marry.
The eyes of the child I nurse are scarcely open.
In twenty years I shall be retrograde
As these draughty ephemerids.

I watch their spilt tears cloud and dull to pearls.
How shall I tell anything at all
To this infant still in a birth-drowse?
Tonight, like a shawl, the mild light enfolds her,
The shadows stoop over like guests at a christening.

17 October 1960

132 ## A Life

Touch it: it won't shrink like an eyeball,
This egg-shaped bailiwick, clear as a tear.
Here's yesterday, last year—
Palm-spear and lily distinct as flora in the vast
Windless threadwork of a tapestry.

1960

Flick the glass with your fingernail:
It will ping like a Chinese chime in the slightest air stir
Though nobody in there looks up or bothers to answer.
The inhabitants are light as cork,
Every one of them permanently busy.

At their feet, the sea waves bow in single file,
Never trespassing in bad temper:
Stalling in midair,
Short-reined, pawing like paradeground horses.
Overhead, the clouds sit tasseled and fancy

As Victorian cushions. This family
Of valentine-faces might please a collector:
They ring true, like good china.

Elsewhere the landscape is more frank.
The light falls without letup, blindingly.

A woman is dragging her shadow in a circle
About a bald, hospital saucer.
It resembles the moon, or a sheet of blank paper
And appears to have suffered a sort of private blitzkrieg.
She lives quietly

With no attachments, like a foetus in a bottle,
The obsolete house, the sea, flattened to a picture
She has one too many dimensions to enter.
Grief and anger, exorcized,
Leave her alone now.

The future is a gray seagull
Tattling in its cat-voice of departure, departure.
Age and terror, like nurses, attend her,
And a drowned man, complaining of the great cold,
Crawls up out of the sea.

18 November 1960

Waking in Winter

I can taste the tin of the sky—the real tin thing.
Winter dawn is the color of metal,
The trees stiffen into place like burnt nerves.
All night I have dreamed of destruction, annihilations—
An assembly-line of cut throats, and you and I
Inching off in the gray Chevrolet, drinking the green
Poison of stilled lawns, the little clapboard gravestones,
Noiseless, on rubber wheels, on the way to the sea resort.

How the balconies echoed! How the sun lit up
The skulls, the unbuckled bones facing the view!
Space! Space! The bed linen was giving out entirely.
Cot legs melted in terrible attitudes, and the nurses—
Each nurse patched her soul to a wound and disappeared.
The deathly guests had not been satisfied
With the rooms, or the smiles, or the beautiful rubber plants,
Or the sea, hushing their peeled sense like Old Mother Morphia.

1961

Parliament Hill Fields

On this bald hill the new year hones its edge.
Faceless and pale as china
The round sky goes on minding its business.
Your absence is inconspicuous;
Nobody can tell what I lack.

Gulls have threaded the river's mud bed back
To this crest of grass. Inland, they argue,
Settling and stirring like blown paper
Or the hands of an invalid. The wan
Sun manages to strike such tin glints

From the linked ponds that my eyes wince
And brim; the city melts like sugar.
A crocodile of small girls
Knotting and stopping, ill-assorted, in blue uniforms,
Opens to swallow me. I'm a stone, a stick,

One child drops a barrette of pink plastic;
None of them seem to notice.
Their shrill, gravelly gossip's funneled off.
Now silence after silence offers itself.
The wind stops my breath like a bandage.

Southward, over Kentish Town, an ashen smudge
Swaddles roof and tree.
It could be a snowfield or a cloudbank.
I suppose it's pointless to think of you at all.
Already your doll grip lets go.

1961

The tumulus, even at noon, guards its black shadow:
You know me less constant,
Ghost of a leaf, ghost of a bird.
I circle the writhen trees. I am too happy.
These faithful dark-boughed cypresses

Brood, rooted in their heaped losses.
Your cry fades like the cry of a gnat.
I lose sight of you on your blind journey,
While the heath grass glitters and the spindling rivulets
Unspool and spend themselves. My mind runs with them,

Pooling in heel-prints, fumbling pebble and stem.
The day empties its images
Like a cup or a room. The moon's crook whitens,
Thin as the skin seaming a scar.
Now, on the nursery wall,

The blue night plants, the little pale blue hill
In your sister's birthday picture start to glow.
The orange pompons, the Egyptian papyrus
Light up. Each rabbit-eared
Blue shrub behind the glass

Exhales an indigo nimbus,
A sort of cellophane balloon.
The old dregs, the old difficulties take me to wife.
Gulls stiffen to their chill vigil in the drafty half-light;
I enter the lit house.

11 February 1961

Whitsun

This is not what I meant:
Stucco arches, the banked rocks sunning in rows,
Bald eyes or petrified eggs,
Grownups coffined in stockings and jackets,
Lard-pale, sipping the thin
Air like a medicine.

The stopped horse on his chromium pole
Stares through us; his hooves chew the breeze.
Your shirt of crisp linen
Bloats like a spinnaker. Hat-brims
Deflect the watery dazzle; the people idle
As if in hospital.

I can smell the salt, all right.
At our feet, the weed-mustachioed sea
Exhibits its glaucous silks,
Bowing and truckling like an old-school Oriental.
You're no happier than I about it.
A policeman points out a vacant cliff

Green as a pool table, where cabbage butterflies
Peel off to sea as gulls do,
And we picnic in the death-stench of a hawthorn.
The waves pulse and pulse like hearts.
Beached under the spumy blooms, we lie
Seasick and fever-dry.

14 February 1961

136

Zoo Keeper's Wife

I can stay awake all night, if need be —
Cold as an eel, without eyelids.
Like a dead lake the dark envelops me,
Blueblack, a spectacular plum fruit.
No airbubbles start from my heart, I am lungless
And ugly, my belly a silk stocking
Where the heads and tails of my sisters decompose.
Look, they are melting like coins in the powerful juices —

The spidery jaws, the spine bones bared for a moment
Like the white lines on a blueprint.
Should I stir, I think this pink and purple plastic
Guts bag would clack like a child's rattle,
Old grievances jostling each other, so many loose teeth.

But what do you know about that
My fat pork, my marrowy sweetheart, face-to-the-wall?
Some things of this world are indigestible.

You wooed me with the wolf-headed fruit bats
Hanging from their scorched hooks in the moist
Fug of the Small Mammal House.
The armadillo dozed in his sandbin
Obscene and bald as a pig, the white mice
Multiplied to infinity like angels on a pinhead
Out of sheer boredom. Tangled in the sweat-wet sheets
I remember the bloodied chicks and the quartered rabbits.

You checked the diet charts and took me to play
With the boa constrictor in the Fellows' Garden.
I pretended I was the Tree of Knowledge.
I entered your bible, I boarded your ark
With the sacred baboon in his wig and wax ears
And the bear-furred, bird-eating spider
Clambering round its glass box like an eight-fingered hand.
I can't get it out of my mind

How our courtship lit the tindery cages—
Your two-horned rhinoceros opened a mouth
Dirty as a bootsole and big as a hospital sink
For my cube of sugar: its bog breath
Gloved my arm to the elbow.
The snails blew kisses like black apples.
Nightly now I flog apes owls bears sheep
Over their iron stile. And still don't sleep.

14 February 1961

137   Face Lift

You bring me good news from the clinic,
Whipping off your silk scarf, exhibiting the tight white
Mummy-cloths, smiling: I'm all right.
When I was nine, a lime-green anesthetist

Fed me banana gas through a frog-mask. The nauseous vault
Boomed with bad dreams and the Jovian voices of surgeons.
Then mother swam up, holding a tin basin.
O I was sick.

They've changed all that. Traveling
Nude as Cleopatra in my well-boiled hospital shift,
Fizzy with sedatives and unusually humorous,
I roll to an anteroom where a kind man
Fists my fingers for me. He makes me feel something precious
Is leaking from the finger-vents. At the count of two
Darkness wipes me out like chalk on a blackboard. . .
I don't know a thing.

For five days I lie in secret,
Tapped like a cask, the years draining into my pillow.
Even my best friend thinks I'm in the country.
Skin doesn't have roots, it peels away easy as paper.
When I grin, the stitches tauten. I grow backward. I'm twenty,
Broody and in long skirts on my first husband's sofa, my fingers
Buried in the lambswool of the dead poodle;
I hadn't a cat yet.

Now she's done for, the dewlapped lady
I watched settle, line by line, in my mirror —
Old sock-face, sagged on a darning egg.
They've trapped her in some laboratory jar.
Let her die there, or wither incessantly for the next fifty years,
Nodding and rocking and fingering her thin hair.
Mother to myself, I wake swaddled in gauze,
Pink and smooth as a baby.

15 February 1961

Morning Song

Love set you going like a fat gold watch.
The midwife slapped your footsoles, and your bald cry
Took its place among the elements.

1961

Our voices echo, magnifying your arrival. New statue.
In a drafty museum, your nakedness
Shadows our safety. We stand round blankly as walls.

I'm no more your mother
Than the cloud that distills a mirror to reflect its own slow
Effacement at the wind's hand.

All night your moth-breath
Flickers among the flat pink roses. I wake to listen:
A far sea moves in my ear.

One cry, and I stumble from bed, cow-heavy and floral
In my Victorian nightgown.
Your mouth opens clean as a cat's. The window square

Whitens and swallows its dull stars. And now you try
Your handful of notes;
The clear vowels rise like balloons.

19 February 1961

139

Barren Woman

Empty, I echo to the least footfall,
Museum without statues, grand with pillars, porticoes, rotundas.
In my courtyard a fountain leaps and sinks back into itself,
Nun-hearted and blind to the world. Marble lilies
Exhale their pallor like scent.

I imagine myself with a great public,
Mother of a white Nike and several bald-eyed Apollos.
Instead, the dead injure me with attentions, and nothing can happen.
The moon lays a hand on my forehead,
Blank-faced and mum as a nurse.

21 February 1961

Heavy Women

Irrefutable, beautifully smug
As Venus, pedestaled on a half-shell
Shawled in blond hair and the salt
Scrim of a sea breeze, the women
Settle in their belling dresses.
Over each weighty stomach a face
Floats calm as a moon or a cloud.

Smiling to themselves, they meditate
Devoutly as the Dutch bulb
Forming its twenty petals.
The dark still nurses its secret.
On the green hill, under the thorn trees,
They listen for the millennium,
The knock of the small, new heart.

Pink-buttocked infants attend them.
Looping wool, doing nothing in particular,
They step among the archetypes.
Dusk hoods them in Mary-blue
While far off, the axle of winter
Grinds round, bearing down with the straw,
The star, the wise gray men.

26 February 1961

In Plaster

I shall never get out of this! There are two of me now:
This new absolutely white person and the old yellow one,
And the white person is certainly the superior one.
She doesn't need food, she is one of the real saints.
At the beginning I hated her, she had no personality—
She lay in bed with me like a dead body
And I was scared, because she was shaped just the way I was

Only much whiter and unbreakable and with no complaints.
I couldn't sleep for a week, she was so cold.

I blamed her for everything, but she didn't answer.
I couldn't understand her stupid behavior!
When I hit her she held still, like a true pacifist.
Then I realized what she wanted was for me to love her:
She began to warm up, and I saw her advantages.

Without me, she wouldn't exist, so of course she was grateful.
I gave her a soul, I bloomed out of her as a rose
Blooms out of a vase of not very valuable porcelain,
And it was I who attracted everybody's attention,
Not her whiteness and beauty, as I had at first supposed.
I patronized her a little, and she lapped it up—
You could tell almost at once she had a slave mentality.

I didn't mind her waiting on me, and she adored it.
In the morning she woke me early, reflecting the sun
From her amazingly white torso, and I couldn't help but notice
Her tidiness and her calmness and her patience:
She humored my weakness like the best of nurses,
Holding my bones in place so they would mend properly.
In time our relationship grew more intense.

She stopped fitting me so closely and seemed offish.
I felt her criticizing me in spite of herself,
As if my habits offended her in some way.
She let in the drafts and became more and more absent-minded.
And my skin itched and flaked away in soft pieces
Simply because she looked after me so badly.
Then I saw what the trouble was: she thought she was immortal.

She wanted to leave me, she thought she was superior,
And I'd been keeping her in the dark, and she was resentful—
Wasting her days waiting on a half-corpse!
And secretly she began to hope I'd die.
Then she could cover my mouth and eyes, cover me entirely,
And wear my painted face the way a mummy-case
Wears the face of a pharaoh, though it's made of mud and water.

I wasn't in any position to get rid of her.
She'd supported me for so long I was quite limp—
I had even forgotten how to walk or sit,

So I was careful not to upset her in any way
Or brag ahead of time how I'd avenge myself.
Living with her was like living with my own coffin:
Yet I still depended on her, though I did it regretfully.

I used to think we might make a go of it together—
After all, it was a kind of marriage, being so close.
Now I see it must be one or the other of us.
She may be a saint, and I may be ugly and hairy,
But she'll soon find out that that doesn't matter a bit.
I'm collecting my strength; one day I shall manage without her,
And she'll perish with emptiness then, and begin to miss me.

18 March 1961

142

Tulips

The tulips are too excitable, it is winter here.
Look how white everything is, how quiet, how snowed-in.
I am learning peacefulness, lying by myself quietly
As the light lies on these white walls, this bed, these hands.
I am nobody; I have nothing to do with explosions.
I have given my name and my day-clothes up to the nurses
And my history to the anesthetist and my body to surgeons.

They have propped my head between the pillow and the sheet–cuff
Like an eye between two white lids that will not shut.
Stupid pupil, it has to take everything in.
The nurses pass and pass, they are no trouble,
They pass the way gulls pass inland in their white caps,
Doing things with their hands, one just the same as another,
So it is impossible to tell how many there are.

My body is a pebble to them, they tend it as water
Tends to the pebbles it must run over, smoothing them gently.
They bring me numbness in their bright needles, they bring me sleep.
Now I have lost myself I am sick of baggage——
My patent leather overnight case like a black pillbox,
My husband and child smiling out of the family photo;
Their smiles catch onto my skin, little smiling hooks.

1961

I have let things slip, a thirty-year-old cargo boat
Stubbornly hanging on to my name and address.
They have swabbed me clear of my loving associations.
Scared and bare on the green plastic-pillowed trolley
I watched my teaset, my bureaus of linen, my books
Sink out of sight, and the water went over my head.
I am a nun now, I have never been so pure.

I didn't want any flowers, I only wanted
To lie with my hands turned up and be utterly empty.
How free it is, you have no idea how free——
The peacefulness is so big it dazes you,
And it asks nothing, a name tag, a few trinkets.
It is what the dead close on, finally; I imagine them
Shutting their mouths on it, like a Communion tablet.

The tulips are too red in the first place, they hurt me.
Even through the gift paper I could hear them breathe
Lightly, through their white swaddlings, like an awful baby.
Their redness talks to my wound, it corresponds.
They are subtle: they seem to float, though they weigh me down,
Upsetting me with their sudden tongues and their color,
A dozen red lead sinkers round my neck.

Nobody watched me before, now I am watched.
The tulips turn to me, and the window behind me
Where once a day the light slowly widens and slowly thins,
And I see myself, flat, ridiculous, a cut-paper shadow
Between the eye of the sun and the eyes of the tulips,
And I have no face, I have wanted to efface myself.
The vivid tulips eat my oxygen.

Before they came the air was calm enough,
Coming and going, breath by breath, without any fuss.
Then the tulips filled it up like a loud noise.
Now the air snags and eddies round them the way a river
Snags and eddies round a sunken rust-red engine.
They concentrate my attention, that was happy
Playing and resting without committing itself.

The walls, also, seem to be warming themselves.
The tulips should be behind bars like dangerous animals;
They are opening like the mouth of some great African cat,
And I am aware of my heart: it opens and closes
Its bowl of red blooms out of sheer love of me.
The water I taste is warm and salt, like the sea,
And comes from a country far away as health.

18 March 1961

I Am Vertical

143

But I would rather be horizontal.
I am not a tree with my root in the soil
Sucking up minerals and motherly love
So that each March I may gleam into leaf,
Nor am I the beauty of a garden bed
Attracting my share of Ahs and spectacularly painted,
Unknowing I must soon unpetal.
Compared with me, a tree is immortal
And a flower-head not tall, but more startling,
And I want the one's longevity and the other's daring.

Tonight, in the infinitesimal light of the stars,
The trees and flowers have been strewing their cool odors.
I walk among them, but none of them are noticing.
Sometimes I think that when I am sleeping
I must most perfectly resemble them —
Thoughts gone dim.
It is more natural to me, lying down.
Then the sky and I are in open conversation,
And I shall be useful when I lie down finally:
Then the trees may touch me for once, and the flowers have time for me.

28 March 1961

Insomniac

The night sky is only a sort of carbon paper,
Blueblack, with the much-poked periods of stars
Letting in the light, peephole after peephole—
A bonewhite light, like death, behind all things.
Under the eyes of the stars and the moon's rictus
He suffers his desert pillow, sleeplessness
Stretching its fine, irritating sand in all directions.

Over and over the old, granular movie
Exposes embarrassments—the mizzling days
Of childhood and adolescence, sticky with dreams,
Parental faces on tall stalks, alternately stern and tearful,
A garden of buggy roses that made him cry.
His forehead is bumpy as a sack of rocks.
Memories jostle each other for face-room like obsolete film stars.

He is immune to pills: red, purple, blue—
How they lit the tedium of the protracted evening!
Those sugary planets whose influence won for him
A life baptized in no-life for a while,
And the sweet, drugged waking of a forgetful baby.
Now the pills are worn-out and silly, like classical gods.
Their poppy-sleepy colors do him no good.

His head is a little interior of gray mirrors.
Each gesture flees immediately down an alley
Of diminishing perspectives, and its significance
Drains like water out the hole at the far end.
He lives without privacy in a lidless room,
The bald slots of his eyes stiffened wide-open
On the incessant heat-lightning flicker of situations.

Nightlong, in the granite yard, invisible cats
Have been howling like women, or damaged instruments.
Already he can feel daylight, his white disease,
Creeping up with her hatful of trivial repetitions.
The city is a map of cheerful twitters now,
And everywhere people, eyes mica-silver and blank,
Are riding to work in rows, as if recently brainwashed.

May 1961

Widow

Widow. The word consumes itself—
Body, a sheet of newsprint on the fire
Levitating a numb minute in the updraft
Over the scalding, red topography
That will put her heart out like an only eye.

Widow. The dead syllable, with its shadow
Of an echo, exposes the panel in the wall
Behind which the secret passage lies—stale air,
Fusty remembrances, the coiled-spring stair
That opens at the top onto nothing at all. . . .

Widow. The bitter spider sits
And sits in the center of her loveless spokes.
Death is the dress she wears, her hat and collar.
The moth-face of her husband, moonwhite and ill,
Circles her like a prey she'd love to kill

A second time, to have him near again—
A paper image to lay against her heart
The way she laid his letters, till they grew warm
And seemed to give her warmth, like a live skin.
But it is she who is paper now, warmed by no one.

Widow: that great, vacant estate!
The voice of God is full of draftiness,
Promising simply the hard stars, the space
Of immortal blankness between stars
And no bodies, singing like arrows up to heaven.

Widow, the compassionate trees bend in,
The trees of loneliness, the trees of mourning.
They stand like shadows about the green landscape—
Or even like black holes cut out of it.
A widow resembles them, a shadow-thing,

Hand folding hand, and nothing in between.
A bodiless soul could pass another soul
In this clear air and never notice it—

One soul pass through the other, frail as smoke
And utterly ignorant of the way it took.

That is the fear she has—the fear
His soul may beat and be beating at her dull sense
Like blue Mary's angel, dovelike against a pane
Blinded to all but the gray, spiritless room
It looks in on, and must go on looking in on.

16 May 1961

Stars Over the Dordogne

146

Stars are dropping thick as stones into the twiggy
Picket of trees whose silhouette is darker
Than the dark of the sky because it is quite starless.
The woods are a well. The stars drop silently.
They seem large, yet they drop, and no gap is visible.
Nor do they send up fires where they fall
Or any signal of distress or anxiousness.
They are eaten immediately by the pines.

Where I am at home, only the sparsest stars
Arrive at twilight, and then after some effort.
And they are wan, dulled by much travelling.
The smaller and more timid never arrive at all
But stay, sitting far out, in their own dust.
They are orphans. I cannot see them. They are lost.
But tonight they have discovered this river with no trouble,
They are scrubbed and self-assured as the great planets.

The Big Dipper is my only familiar.
I miss Orion and Cassiopeia's Chair. Maybe they are
Hanging shyly under the studded horizon
Like a child's too-simple mathematical problem.
Infinite number seems to be the issue up there.
Or else they are present, and their disguise so bright
I am overlooking them by looking too hard.
Perhaps it is the season that is not right.

And what if the sky here is no different,
And it is my eyes that have been sharpening themselves?
Such a luxury of stars would embarrass me.
The few I am used to are plain and durable;
I think they would not wish for this dressy backcloth
Or much company, or the mildness of the south.
They are too puritan and solitary for that—
When one of them falls it leaves a space,

A sense of absence in its old shining place.
And where I lie now, back to my own dark star,
I see those constellations in my head,
Unwarmed by the sweet air of this peach orchard.
There is too much ease here; these stars treat me too well.
On this hill, with its view of lit castles, each swung bell
Is accounting for its cow. I shut my eyes
And drink the small night chill like news of home.

147

The Rival

If the moon smiled, she would resemble you.
You leave the same impression
Of something beautiful, but annihilating.
Both of you are great light borrowers.
Her O-mouth grieves at the world; yours is unaffected,

And your first gift is making stone out of everything.
I wake to a mausoleum; you are here,
Ticking your fingers on the marble table, looking for cigarettes,
Spiteful as a woman, but not so nervous,
And dying to say something unanswerable.

The moon, too, abases her subjects,
But in the daytime she is ridiculous.
Your dissatisfactions, on the other hand,
Arrive through the mailslot with loving regularity,
White and blank, expansive as carbon monoxide.

No day is safe from news of you,
Walking about in Africa maybe, but thinking of me.

July 1961

148   # Wuthering Heights

The horizons ring me like faggots,
Tilted and disparate, and always unstable.
Touched by a match, they might warm me,
And their fine lines singe
The air to orange
Before the distances they pin evaporate,
Weighting the pale sky with a solider color.
But they only dissolve and dissolve
Like a series of promises, as I step forward.

There is no life higher than the grasstops
Or the hearts of sheep, and the wind
Pours by like destiny, bending
Everything in one direction.
I can feel it trying
To funnel my heat away.
If I pay the roots of the heather
Too close attention, they will invite me
To whiten my bones among them.

The sheep know where they are,
Browsing in their dirty wool-clouds,
Gray as the weather.
The black slots of their pupils take me in.
It is like being mailed into space,
A thin, silly message.
They stand about in grandmotherly disguise,
All wig curls and yellow teeth
And hard, marbly baas.

I come to wheel ruts, and water
Limpid as the solitudes

That flee through my fingers.
Hollow doorsteps go from grass to grass;
Lintel and sill have unhinged themselves.
Of people the air only
Remembers a few odd syllables.
It rehearses them moaningly:
Black stone, black stone.

The sky leans on me, me, the one upright
Among all horizontals.
The grass is beating its head distractedly.
It is too delicate
For a life in such company;
Darkness terrifies it.
Now, in valleys narrow
And black as purses, the house lights
Gleam like small change.

September 1961

149   Blackberrying

Nobody in the lane, and nothing, nothing but blackberries,
Blackberries on either side, though on the right mainly,
A blackberry alley, going down in hooks, and a sea
Somewhere at the end of it, heaving. Blackberries
Big as the ball of my thumb, and dumb as eyes
Ebon in the hedges, fat
With blue-red juices. These they squander on my fingers.
I had not asked for such a blood sisterhood; they must love me.
They accommodate themselves to my milkbottle, flattening their sides.

Overhead go the choughs in black, cacophonous flocks—
Bits of burnt paper wheeling in a blown sky.
Theirs is the only voice, protesting, protesting.
I do not think the sea will appear at all.
The high, green meadows are glowing, as if lit from within.
I come to one bush of berries so ripe it is a bush of flies,
Hanging their bluegreen bellies and their wing panes in a Chinese screen.

The honey-feast of the berries has stunned them; they believe in heaven.
One more hook, and the berries and bushes end.

The only thing to come now is the sea.
From between two hills a sudden wind funnels at me,
Slapping its phantom laundry in my face.
These hills are too green and sweet to have tasted salt.
I follow the sheep path between them. A last hook brings me
To the hills' northern face, and the face is orange rock
That looks out on nothing, nothing but a great space
Of white and pewter lights, and a din like silversmiths
Beating and beating at an intractable metal.

23 September 1961

Finisterre

This was the land's end: the last fingers, knuckled and rheumatic,
Cramped on nothing. Black
Admonitory cliffs, and the sea exploding
With no bottom, or anything on the other side of it,
Whitened by the faces of the drowned.
Now it is only gloomy, a dump of rocks —
Leftover soldiers from old, messy wars.
The sea cannons into their ear, but they don't budge.
Other rocks hide their grudges under the water.

The cliffs are edged with trefoils, stars and bells
Such as fingers might embroider, close to death,
Almost too small for the mists to bother with.
The mists are part of the ancient paraphernalia —
Souls, rolled in the doom-noise of the sea.
They bruise the rocks out of existence, then resurrect them.
They go up without hope, like sighs.
I walk among them, and they stuff my mouth with cotton.
When they free me, I am beaded with tears.

Our Lady of the Shipwrecked is striding toward the horizon,
Her marble skirts blown back in two pink wings.

A marble sailor kneels at her foot distractedly, and at his foot
A peasant woman in black
Is praying to the monument of the sailor praying.
Our Lady of the Shipwrecked is three times life size,
Her lips sweet with divinity.
She does not hear what the sailor or the peasant is saying—
She is in love with the beautiful formlessness of the sea.

Gull-colored laces flap in the sea drafts
Beside the postcard stalls.
The peasants anchor them with conches. One is told:
'These are the pretty trinkets the sea hides,
Little shells made up into necklaces and toy ladies.
They do not come from the Bay of the Dead down there,
But from another place, tropical and blue,
We have never been to.
These are our crêpes. Eat them before they blow cold.'

29 September 1961

The Surgeon at 2 a.m.

151

The white light is artificial, and hygienic as heaven.
The microbes cannot survive it.
They are departing in their transparent garments, turned aside
From the scalpels and the rubber hands.
The scalded sheet is a snowfield, frozen and peaceful.
The body under it is in my hands.
As usual there is no face. A lump of Chinese white
With seven holes thumbed in. The soul is another light.
I have not seen it; it does not fly up.
Tonight it has receded like a ship's light.

It is a garden I have to do with—tubers and fruits
Oozing their jammy substances,
A mat of roots. My assistants hook them back.
Stenches and colors assail me.
This is the lung-tree.
These orchids are splendid. They spot and coil like snakes.

1961

The heart is a red-bell-bloom, in distress.
I am so small
In comparison to these organs!
I worm and hack in a purple wilderness.

The blood is a sunset. I admire it.
I am up to my elbows in it, red and squeaking.
Still it seeps up, it is not exhausted.
So magical! A hot spring
I must seal off and let fill
The intricate, blue piping under this pale marble.
How I admire the Romans —
Aqueducts, the Baths of Caracalla, the eagle nose!
The body is a Roman thing.
It has shut its mouth on the stone pill of repose.

It is a statue the orderlies are wheeling off.
I have perfected it.
I am left with an arm or a leg,
A set of teeth, or stones
To rattle in a bottle and take home,
And tissue in slices — a pathological salami.
Tonight the parts are entombed in an icebox.
Tomorrow they will swim
In vinegar like saints' relics.
Tomorrow the patient will have a clean, pink plastic limb.

Over one bed in the ward, a small blue light
Announces a new soul. The bed is blue.
Tonight, for this person, blue is a beautiful color.
The angels of morphia have borne him up.
He floats an inch from the ceiling,
Smelling the dawn drafts.
I walk among sleepers in gauze sarcophagi.
The red night lights are flat moons. They are dull with blood.
I am the sun, in my white coat,
Gray faces, shuttered by drugs, follow me like flowers.

29 September 1961

Last Words

I do not want a plain box, I want a sarcophagus
With tigery stripes, and a face on it
Round as the moon, to stare up.
I want to be looking at them when they come
Picking among the dumb minerals, the roots.
I see them already—the pale, star-distance faces.
Now they are nothing, they are not even babies.
I imagine them without fathers or mothers, like the first gods.
They will wonder if I was important.
I should sugar and preserve my days like fruit!
My mirror is clouding over—
A few more breaths, and it will reflect nothing at all.
The flowers and the faces whiten to a sheet.

I do not trust the spirit. It escapes like steam
In dreams, through mouth-hole or eye-hole. I can't stop it.
One day it won't come back. Things aren't like that.
They stay, their little particular lusters
Warmed by much handling. They almost purr.
When the soles of my feet grow cold,
The blue eye of my turquoise will comfort me.
Let me have my copper cooking pots, let my rouge pots
Bloom about me like night flowers, with a good smell.
They will roll me up in bandages, they will store my heart
Under my feet in a neat parcel.
I shall hardly know myself. It will be dark,
And the shine of these small things sweeter than the face of Ishtar.

21 October 1961

The Moon and the Yew Tree

This is the light of the mind, cold and planetary.
The trees of the mind are black. The light is blue.
The grasses unload their griefs on my feet as if I were God,
Prickling my ankles and murmuring of their humility.
Fumy, spiritous mists inhabit this place

1961

Separated from my house by a row of headstones.
I simply cannot see where there is to get to.

The moon is no door. It is a face in its own right,
White as a knuckle and terribly upset.
It drags the sea after it like a dark crime; it is quiet
With the O-gape of complete despair. I live here.
Twice on Sunday, the bells startle the sky——
Eight great tongues affirming the Resurrection.
At the end, they soberly bong out their names.

The yew tree points up. It has a Gothic shape.
The eyes lift after it and find the moon.
The moon is my mother. She is not sweet like Mary.
Her blue garments unloose small bats and owls.
How I would like to believe in tenderness——
The face of the effigy, gentled by candles,
Bending, on me in particular, its mild eyes.

I have fallen a long way. Clouds are flowering
Blue and mystical over the face of the stars.
Inside the church, the saints will be all blue,
Floating on their delicate feet over the cold pews,
Their hands and faces stiff with holiness.
The moon sees nothing of this. She is bald and wild.
And the message of the yew tree is blackness—blackness and silence.

22 October 1961

Mirror

154

I am silver and exact. I have no preconceptions.
Whatever I see I swallow immediately
Just as it is, unmisted by love or dislike.
I am not cruel, only truthful—
The eye of a little god, four-cornered.
Most of the time I meditate on the opposite wall.
It is pink, with speckles. I have looked at it so long
I think it is a part of my heart. But it flickers.
Faces and darkness separate us over and over.

Now I am a lake. A woman bends over me,
Searching my reaches for what she really is.
Then she turns to those liars, the candles or the moon.
I see her back, and reflect it faithfully.
She rewards me with tears and an agitation of hands.
I am important to her. She comes and goes.
Each morning it is her face that replaces the darkness.
In me she has drowned a young girl, and in me an old woman
Rises toward her day after day, like a terrible fish.

23 October 1961

155   The Babysitters

It is ten years, now, since we rowed to Children's Island.
The sun flamed straight down that noon on the water off Marblehead.
That summer we wore black glasses to hide our eyes.
We were always crying, in our spare rooms, little put-upon sisters,
In the two huge, white, handsome houses in Swampscott.
When the sweetheart from England appeared, with her cream skin and
     Yardley cosmetics,
I had to sleep in the same room with the baby on a too-short cot,
And the seven-year-old wouldn't go out unless his jersey stripes
Matched the stripes of his socks.

O it was richness!—eleven rooms and a yacht
With a polished mahogany stair to let into the water
And a cabin boy who could decorate cakes in six-colored frosting.
But I didn't know how to cook, and babies depressed me.
Nights, I wrote in my diary spitefully, my fingers red
With triangular scorch marks from ironing tiny ruchings and puffed
     sleeves.
When the sporty wife and her doctor husband went on one of their
     cruises
They left me a borrowed maid named Ellen, 'for protection',
And a small Dalmatian.

In your house, the main house, you were better off.
You had a rose garden and a guest cottage and a model apothecary shop

And a cook and a maid, and knew about the key to the bourbon.
I remember you playing 'Ja Da' in a pink piqué dress
On the gameroom piano, when the 'big people' were out,
And the maid smoked and shot pool under a green-shaded lamp.
The cook had one wall eye and couldn't sleep, she was so nervous.
On trial, from Ireland, she burned batch after batch of cookies
Till she was fired.

O what has come over us, my sister!
On that day-off the two of us cried so hard to get
We lifted a sugared ham and a pineapple from the grownups' icebox
And rented an old green boat. I rowed. You read
Aloud, crosslegged on the stern seat, from the *Generation of Vipers*.
So we bobbed out to the island. It was deserted—
A gallery of creaking porches and still interiors,
Stopped and awful as a photograph of somebody laughing,
But ten years dead.

The bold gulls dove as if they owned it all.
We picked up sticks of driftwood and beat them off,
Then stepped down the steep beach shelf and into the water.
We kicked and talked. The thick salt kept us up.
I see us floating there yet, inseparable—two cork dolls.
What keyhole have we slipped through, what door has shut?
The shadows of the grasses inched round like hands of a clock,
And from our opposite continents we wave and call.
Everything has happened.

29 October 1961

175

1962

New Year on Dartmoor

This is newness: every little tawdry
Obstacle glass-wrapped and peculiar,
Glinting and clinking in a saint's falsetto. Only you
Don't know what to make of the sudden slippiness,
The blind, white, awful, inaccessible slant.
There's no getting up it by the words you know.
No getting up by elephant or wheel or shoe.
We have only come to look. You are too new
To want the world in a glass hat.

Three Women
A Poem for Three Voices

Setting: A Maternity Ward and round about

FIRST VOICE:
I am slow as the world. I am very patient,
Turning through my time, the suns and stars
Regarding me with attention.
The moon's concern is more personal:
She passes and repasses, luminous as a nurse.
Is she sorry for what will happen? I do not think so.
She is simply astonished at fertility.

When I walk out, I am a great event.
I do not have to think, or even rehearse.
What happens in me will happen without attention.
The pheasant stands on the hill;
He is arranging his brown feathers.

I cannot help smiling at what it is I know.
Leaves and petals attend me. I am ready.

SECOND VOICE:
When I first saw it, the small red seep, I did not believe it.
I watched the men walk about me in the office. They were so flat!
There was something about them like cardboard, and now I had caught it,
That flat, flat, flatness from which ideas, destructions,
Bulldozers, guillotines, white chambers of shrieks proceed,
Endlessly proceed—and the cold angels, the abstractions.
I sat at my desk in my stockings, my high heels,

And the man I work for laughed: 'Have you seen something awful?
You are so white, suddenly.' And I said nothing.
I saw death in the bare trees, a deprivation.
I could not believe it. Is it so difficult
For the spirit to conceive a face, a mouth?
The letters proceed from these black keys, and these black keys proceed
From my alphabetical fingers, ordering parts,

Parts, bits, cogs, the shining multiples.
I am dying as I sit. I lose a dimension.
Trains roar in my ears, departures, departures!
The silver track of time empties into the distance,
The white sky empties of its promise, like a cup.
These are my feet, these mechanical echoes.
Tap, tap, tap, steel pegs. I am found wanting.

This is a disease I carry home, this is a death.
Again, this is a death. Is it the air,
The particles of destruction I suck up? Am I a pulse
That wanes and wanes, facing the cold angel?
Is this my lover then? This death, this death?
As a child I loved a lichen-bitten name.
Is this the one sin then, this old dead love of death?

THIRD VOICE:
I remember the minute when I knew for sure.
The willows were chilling,
The face in the pool was beautiful, but not mine—
It had a consequential look, like everything else,

And all I could see was dangers: doves and words,
Stars and showers of gold—conceptions, conceptions!
I remember a white, cold wing

And the great swan, with its terrible look,
Coming at me, like a castle, from the top of the river.
There is a snake in swans.
He glided by; his eye had a black meaning.
I saw the world in it—small, mean and black,
Every little word hooked to every little word, and act to act.
A hot blue day had budded into something.

I wasn't ready. The white clouds rearing
Aside were dragging me in four directions.
I wasn't ready.
I had no reverence.
I thought I could deny the consequence—
But it was too late for that. It was too late, and the face
Went on shaping itself with love, as if I was ready.

SECOND VOICE:
It is a world of snow now. I am not at home.
How white these sheets are. The faces have no features.
They are bald and impossible, like the faces of my children,
Those little sick ones that elude my arms.
Other children do not touch me: they are terrible.
They have too many colors, too much life. They are not quiet,
Quiet, like the little emptinesses I carry.

I have had my chances. I have tried and tried.
I have stitched life into me like a rare organ,
And walked carefully, precariously, like something rare.
I have tried not to think too hard. I have tried to be natural.
I have tried to be blind in love, like other women,
Blind in my bed, with my dear blind sweet one,
Not looking, through the thick dark, for the face of another.

I did not look. But still the face was there,
The face of the unborn one that loved its perfections,
The face of the dead one that could only be perfect
In its easy peace, could only keep holy so.

And then there were other faces. The faces of nations,
Governments, parliaments, societies,
The faceless faces of important men.

It is these men I mind:
They are so jealous of anything that is not flat! They are jealous gods
That would have the whole world flat because they are.
I see the Father conversing with the Son.
Such flatness cannot but be holy.
'Let us make a heaven,' they say.
'Let us flatten and launder the grossness from these souls.'

FIRST VOICE:
I am calm. I am calm. It is the calm before something awful:
The yellow minute before the wind walks, when the leaves
Turn up their hands, their pallors. It is so quiet here.
The sheets, the faces, are white and stopped, like clocks.
Voices stand back and flatten. Their visible hieroglyphs
Flatten to parchment screens to keep the wind off.
They paint such secrets in Arabic, Chinese!

I am dumb and brown. I am a seed about to break.
The brownness is my dead self, and it is sullen:
It does not wish to be more, or different.
Dusk hoods me in blue now, like a Mary.
O color of distance and forgetfulness! —
When will it be, the second when Time breaks
And eternity engulfs it, and I drown utterly?

I talk to myself, myself only, set apart —
Swabbed and lurid with disinfectants, sacrificial.
Waiting lies heavy on my lids. It lies like sleep,
Like a big sea. Far off, far off, I feel the first wave tug
Its cargo of agony toward me, inescapable, tidal.
And I, a shell, echoing on this white beach
Face the voices that overwhelm, the terrible element.

THIRD VOICE:
I am a mountain now, among mountainy women.
The doctors move among us as if our bigness
Frightened the mind. They smile like fools.

They are to blame for what I am, and they know it.
They hug their flatness like a kind of health.
And what if they found themselves surprised, as I did?
They would go mad with it.

And what if two lives leaked between my thighs?
I have seen the white clean chamber with its instruments.
It is a place of shrieks. It is not happy.
'This is where you will come when you are ready.'
The night lights are flat red moons. They are dull with blood.
I am not ready for anything to happen.
I should have murdered this, that murders me.

FIRST VOICE:
There is no miracle more cruel than this.
I am dragged by the horses, the iron hooves.
I last. I last it out. I accomplish a work.
Dark tunnel, through which hurtle the visitations,
The visitations, the manifestations, the startled faces.
I am the center of an atrocity.
What pains, what sorrows must I be mothering?

Can such innocence kill and kill? It milks my life.
The trees wither in the street. The rain is corrosive.
I taste it on my tongue, and the workable horrors,
The horrors that stand and idle, the slighted godmothers
With their hearts that tick and tick, with their satchels of instruments.
I shall be a wall and a roof, protecting.
I shall be a sky and a hill of good: O let me be!

A power is growing on me, an old tenacity.
I am breaking apart like the world. There is this blackness,
This ram of blackness. I fold my hands on a mountain.
The air is thick. It is thick with this working.
I am used. I am drummed into use.
My eyes are squeezed by this blackness.
I see nothing.

SECOND VOICE:
I am accused. I dream of massacres.
I am a garden of black and red agonies. I drink them,

Hating myself, hating and fearing. And now the world conceives
Its end and runs toward it, arms held out in love.
It is a love of death that sickens everything.
A dead sun stains the newsprint. It is red.
I lose life after life. The dark earth drinks them.

She is the vampire of us all. So she supports us,
Fattens us, is kind. Her mouth is red.
I know her. I know her intimately —
Old winter-face, old barren one, old time bomb.
Men have used her meanly. She will eat them.
Eat them, eat them, eat them in the end.
The sun is down. I die. I make a death.

FIRST VOICE:
Who is he, this blue, furious boy,
Shiny and strange, as if he had hurtled from a star?
He is looking so angrily!
He flew into the room, a shriek at his heel.
The blue color pales. He is human after all.
A red lotus opens in its bowl of blood;
They are stitching me up with silk, as if I were a material.

What did my fingers do before they held him?
What did my heart do, with its love?
I have never seen a thing so clear.
His lids are like the lilac-flower
And soft as a moth, his breath.
I shall not let go.
There is no guile or warp in him. May he keep so.

SECOND VOICE:
There is the moon in the high window. It is over.
How winter fills my soul! And that chalk light
Laying its scales on the windows, the windows of empty offices,
Empty schoolrooms, empty churches. O so much emptiness!
There is this cessation. This terrible cessation of everything.
These bodies mounded around me now, these polar sleepers —
What blue, moony ray ices their dreams?

I feel it enter me, cold, alien, like an instrument.
And that mad, hard face at the end of it, that O-mouth
Open in its gape of perpetual grieving.
It is she that drags the blood-black sea around
Month after month, with its voices of failure.
I am helpless as the sea at the end of her string.
I am restless. Restless and useless. I, too, create corpses.

I shall move north. I shall move into a long blackness.
I see myself as a shadow, neither man nor woman,
Neither a woman, happy to be like a man, nor a man
Blunt and flat enough to feel no lack. I feel a lack.
I hold my fingers up, ten white pickets.
See, the darkness is leaking from the cracks.
I cannot contain it. I cannot contain my life.

I shall be a heroine of the peripheral.
I shall not be accused by isolate buttons,
Holes in the heels of socks, the white mute faces
Of unanswered letters, coffined in a letter case.
I shall not be accused, I shall not be accused.
The clock shall not find me wanting, nor these stars
That rivet in place abyss after abyss.

THIRD VOICE:
I see her in my sleep, my red, terrible girl.
She is crying through the glass that separates us.
She is crying, and she is furious.
Her cries are hooks that catch and grate like cats.
It is by these hooks she climbs to my notice.
She is crying at the dark, or at the stars
That at such a distance from us shine and whirl.

I think her little head is carved in wood,
A red, hard wood, eyes shut and mouth wide open.
And from the open mouth issue sharp cries
Scratching at my sleep like arrows,
Scratching at my sleep, and entering my side.
My daughter has no teeth. Her mouth is wide.
It utters such dark sounds it cannot be good.

1962

FIRST VOICE:
What is it that flings these innocent souls at us?
Look, they are so exhausted, they are all flat out
In their canvas-sided cots, names tied to their wrists,
The little silver trophies they've come so far for.
There are some with thick black hair, there are some bald.
Their skin tints are pink or sallow, brown or red;
They are beginning to remember their differences.

I think they are made of water; they have no expression.
Their features are sleeping, like light on quiet water.
They are the real monks and nuns in their identical garments.
I see them showering like stars on to the world—
On India, Africa, America, these miraculous ones,
These pure, small images. They smell of milk.
Their footsoles are untouched. They are walkers of air.

Can nothingness be so prodigal?
Here is my son.
His wide eye is that general, flat blue.
He is turning to me like a little, blind, bright plant.
One cry. It is the hook I hang on.
And I am a river of milk.
I am a warm hill.

SECOND VOICE:
I am not ugly. I am even beautiful.
The mirror gives back a woman without deformity.
The nurses give back my clothes, and an identity.
It is usual, they say, for such a thing to happen.
It is usual in my life, and the lives of others.
I am one in five, something like that. I am not hopeless.
I am beautiful as a statistic. Here is my lipstick.

I draw on the old mouth.
The red mouth I put by with my identity
A day ago, two days, three days ago. It was a Friday.
I do not even need a holiday; I can go to work today.
I can love my husband, who will understand.
Who will love me through the blur of my deformity
As if I had lost an eye, a leg, a tongue.

And so I stand, a little sightless. So I walk
Away on wheels, instead of legs, they serve as well.
And learn to speak with fingers, not a tongue.
The body is resourceful.
The body of a starfish can grow back its arms
And newts are prodigal in legs. And may I be
As prodigal in what lacks me.

THIRD VOICE:
She is a small island, asleep and peaceful,
And I am a white ship hooting: Goodbye, goodbye.
The day is blazing. It is very mournful.
The flowers in this room are red and tropical.
They have lived behind glass all their lives, they have been cared for
        tenderly.
Now they face a winter of white sheets, white faces.
There is very little to go into my suitcase.

There are the clothes of a fat woman I do not know.
There is my comb and brush. There is an emptiness.
I am so vulnerable suddenly.
I am a wound walking out of hospital.
I am a wound that they are letting go.
I leave my health behind. I leave someone
Who would adhere to me: I undo her fingers like bandages: I go.

SECOND VOICE:
I am myself again. There are no loose ends.
I am bled white as wax, I have no attachments.
I am flat and virginal, which means nothing has happened,
Nothing that cannot be erased, ripped up and scrapped, begun again.
These little black twigs do not think to bud,
Nor do these dry, dry gutters dream of rain.
This woman who meets me in windows—she is neat.

So neat she is transparent, like a spirit.
How shyly she superimposes her neat self
On the inferno of African oranges, the heel-hung pigs.
She is deferring to reality.
It is I. It is I—
Tasting the bitterness between my teeth.
The incalculable malice of the everyday.

FIRST VOICE:
How long can I be a wall, keeping the wind off?
How long can I be
Gentling the sun with the shade of my hand,
Intercepting the blue bolts of a cold moon?
The voices of loneliness, the voices of sorrow
Lap at my back ineluctably.
How shall it soften them, this little lullaby?

How long can I be a wall around my green property?
How long can my hands
Be a bandage to his hurt, and my words
Bright birds in the sky, consoling, consoling?
It is a terrible thing
To be so open: it is as if my heart
Put on a face and walked into the world.

THIRD VOICE:
Today the colleges are drunk with spring.
My black gown is a little funeral:
It shows I am serious.
The books I carry wedge into my side.
I had an old wound once, but it is healing.
I had a dream of an island, red with cries.
It was a dream, and did not mean a thing.

FIRST VOICE:
Dawn flowers in the great elm outside the house.
The swifts are back. They are shrieking like paper rockets.
I hear the sound of the hours
Widen and die in the hedgerows. I hear the moo of cows.
The colors replenish themselves, and the wet
Thatch smokes in the sun.
The narcissi open white faces in the orchard.

I am reassured. I am reassured.
These are the clear bright colors of the nursery,
The talking ducks, the happy lambs.
I am simple again. I believe in miracles.
I do not believe in those terrible children
Who injure my sleep with their white eyes, their fingerless hands.
They are not mine. They do not belong to me.

I shall meditate upon normality.
I shall meditate upon my little son.
He does not walk. He does not speak a word.
He is still swaddled in white bands.
But he is pink and perfect. He smiles so frequently.
I have papered his room with big roses,
I have painted little hearts on everything.

I do not will him to be exceptional.
It is the exception that interests the devil.
It is the exception that climbs the sorrowful hill
Or sits in the desert and hurts his mother's heart.
I will him to be common,
To love me as I love him,
And to marry what he wants and where he will.

THIRD VOICE:
Hot noon in the meadows. The buttercups
Swelter and melt, and the lovers
Pass by, pass by.
They are black and flat as shadows.
It is so beautiful to have no attachments!
I am solitary as grass. What is it I miss?
Shall I ever find it, whatever it is?

The swans are gone. Still the river
Remembers how white they were.
It strives after them with its lights.
It finds their shapes in a cloud.
What is that bird that cries
With such sorrow in its voice?
I am young as ever, it says. What is it I miss?

SECOND VOICE:
I am at home in the lamplight. The evenings are lengthening.
I am mending a silk slip: my husband is reading.
How beautifully the light includes these things.
There is a kind of smoke in the spring air,
A smoke that takes the parks, the little statues
With pinkness, as if a tenderness awoke,
A tenderness that did not tire, something healing.

I wait and ache. I think I have been healing.
There is a great deal else to do. My hands
Can stitch lace neatly on to this material. My husband
Can turn and turn the pages of a book.
And so we are at home together, after hours.
It is only time that weighs upon our hands.
It is only time, and that is not material.

The streets may turn to paper suddenly, but I recover
From the long fall, and find myself in bed,
Safe on the mattress, hands braced, as for a fall.
I find myself again. I am no shadow
Though there is a shadow starting from my feet. I am a wife.
The city waits and aches. The little grasses
Crack through stone, and they are green with life.

March 1962

Little Fugue

The yew's black fingers wag;
Cold clouds go over.
So the deaf and dumb
Signal the blind, and are ignored.

I like black statements.
The featurelessness of that cloud, now!
White as an eye all over!
The eye of the blind pianist

At my table on the ship.
He felt for his food.
His fingers had the noses of weasels.
I couldn't stop looking.

He could hear Beethoven:
Black yew, white cloud,
The horrific complications.
Finger-traps—a tumult of keys.

1962

Empty and silly as plates,
So the blind smile.
I envy the big noises,
The yew hedge of the Grosse Fuge.

Deafness is something else.
Such a dark funnel, my father!
I see your voice
Black and leafy, as in my childhood,

A yew hedge of orders,
Gothic and barbarous, pure German.
Dead men cry from it.
I am guilty of nothing.

The yew my Christ, then.
Is it not as tortured?
And you, during the Great War
In the California delicatessen

Lopping the sausages!
They color my sleep,
Red, mottled, like cut necks.
There was a silence!

Great silence of another order.
I was seven, I knew nothing.
The world occurred.
You had one leg, and a Prussian mind.

Now similar clouds
Are spreading their vacuous sheets.
Do you say nothing?
I am lame in the memory.

I remember a blue eye,
A briefcase of tangerines.
This was a man, then!
Death opened, like a black tree, blackly.

I survive the while,
Arranging my morning.
These are my fingers, this my baby.
The clouds are a marriage dress, of that pallor.

2 April 1962

An Appearance

159

The smile of iceboxes annihilates me.
Such blue currents in the veins of my loved one!
I hear her great heart purr.

From her lips ampersands and percent signs
Exit like kisses.
It is Monday in her mind: morals

Launder and present themselves.
What am I to make of these contradictions?
I wear white cuffs, I bow.

Is this love then, this red material
Issuing from the steel needle that flies so blindingly?
It will make little dresses and coats,

It will cover a dynasty.
How her body opens and shuts—
A Swiss watch, jeweled in the hinges!

O heart, such disorganization!
The stars are flashing like terrible numerals.
ABC, her eyelids say.

4 April 1962

Crossing the Water

Black lake, black boat, two black, cut-paper people.
Where do the black trees go that drink here?
Their shadows must cover Canada.

A little light is filtering from the water flowers.
Their leaves do not wish us to hurry:
They are round and flat and full of dark advice.

Cold worlds shake from the oar.
The spirit of blackness is in us, it is in the fishes.
A snag is lifting a valedictory, pale hand;

Stars open among the lilies.
Are you not blinded by such expressionless sirens?
This is the silence of astounded souls.

4 April 1962

Among the Narcissi

Spry, wry, and gray as these March sticks,
Percy bows, in his blue peajacket, among the narcissi.
He is recuperating from something on the lung.

The narcissi, too, are bowing to some big thing:
It rattles their stars on the green hill where Percy
Nurses the hardship of his stitches, and walks and walks.

There is a dignity to this; there is a formality—
The flowers vivid as bandages, and the man mending.
They bow and stand: they suffer such attacks!

And the octogenarian loves the little flocks.
He is quite blue; the terrible wind tries his breathing.
The narcissi look up like children, quickly and whitely.

5 April 1962

1962

Pheasant

You said you would kill it this morning.
Do not kill it. It startles me still,
The jut of that odd, dark head, pacing

Through the uncut grass on the elm's hill.
It is something to own a pheasant,
Or just to be visited at all.

I am not mystical: it isn't
As if I thought it had a spirit.
It is simply in its element.

That gives it a kingliness, a right.
The print of its big foot last winter,
The tail-track, on the snow in our court—

The wonder of it, in that pallor,
Through crosshatch of sparrow and starling.
Is it its rareness, then? It is rare.

But a dozen would be worth having,
A hundred, on that hill—green and red,
Crossing and recrossing: a fine thing!

It is such a good shape, so vivid.
It's a little cornucopia.
It unclaps, brown as a leaf, and loud,

Settles in the elm, and is easy.
It was sunning in the narcissi.
I trespass stupidly. Let be, let be.

7 April 1962

Elm

For Ruth Fainlight

I know the bottom, she says. I know it with my great tap root:
It is what you fear.
I do not fear it: I have been there.

Is it the sea you hear in me,
Its dissatisfactions?
Or the voice of nothing, that was your madness?

Love is a shadow.
How you lie and cry after it
Listen: these are its hooves: it has gone off, like a horse.

All night I shall gallop thus, impetuously,
Till your head is a stone, your pillow a little turf,
Echoing, echoing.

Or shall I bring you the sound of poisons?
This is rain now, this big hush.
And this is the fruit of it: tin-white, like arsenic.

I have suffered the atrocity of sunsets.
Scorched to the root
My red filaments burn and stand, a hand of wires.

Now I break up in pieces that fly about like clubs.
A wind of such violence
Will tolerate no bystanding: I must shriek.

The moon, also, is merciless: she would drag me
Cruelly, being barren.
Her radiance scathes me. Or perhaps I have caught her.

I let her go. I let her go
Diminished and flat, as after radical surgery.
How your bad dreams possess and endow me.

I am inhabited by a cry.
Nightly it flaps out
Looking, with its hooks, for something to love.

I am terrified by this dark thing
That sleeps in me;
All day I feel its soft, feathery turnings, its malignity.

Clouds pass and disperse.
Are those the faces of love, those pale irretrievables?
Is it for such I agitate my heart?

I am incapable of more knowledge.
What is this, this face
So murderous in its strangle of branches?——

Its snaky acids kiss.
It petrifies the will. These are the isolate, slow faults
That kill, that kill, that kill.

19 April 1962

164

The Rabbit Catcher

It was a place of force—
The wind gagging my mouth with my own blown hair,
Tearing off my voice, and the sea
Blinding me with its lights, the lives of the dead
Unreeling in it, spreading like oil.

I tasted the malignity of the gorse,
Its black spikes,
The extreme unction of its yellow candle-flowers.
They had an efficiency, a great beauty,
And were extravagant, like torture.

There was only one place to get to.
Simmering, perfumed,
The paths narrowed into the hollow.

And the snares almost effaced themselves —
Zeros, shutting on nothing,

Set close, like birth pangs.
The absence of shrieks
Made a hole in the hot day, a vacancy.
The glassy light was a clear wall,
The thickets quiet.

I felt a still busyness, an intent.
I felt hands round a tea mug, dull, blunt,
Ringing the white china.
How they awaited him, those little deaths!
They waited like sweethearts. They excited him.

And we, too, had a relationship —
Tight wires between us,
Pegs too deep to uproot, and a mind like a ring
Sliding shut on some quick thing,
The constriction killing me also.

21 May 1962

165
Event

How the elements solidify! —
The moonlight, that chalk cliff
In whose rift we lie

Back to back. I hear an owl cry
From its cold indigo.
Intolerable vowels enter my heart.

The child in the white crib revolves and sighs,
Opens its mouth now, demanding.
His little face is carved in pained, red wood.

Then there are the stars — ineradicable, hard.
One touch: it burns and sickens.
I cannot see your eyes.

1962

Where apple bloom ices the night
I walk in a ring,
A groove of old faults, deep and bitter.

Love cannot come here.
A black gap discloses itself.
On the opposite lip

A small white soul is waving, a small white maggot.
My limbs, also, have left me.
Who has dismembered us?

The dark is melting. We touch like cripples.

21 May 1962

Apprehensions

There is this white wall, above which the sky creates itself—
Infinite, green, utterly untouchable.
Angels swim in it, and the stars, in indifference also.
They are my medium.
The sun dissolves on this wall, bleeding its lights.

A gray wall now, clawed and bloody.
Is there no way out of the mind?
Steps at my back spiral into a well.
There are no trees or birds in this world,
There is only a sourness.

This red wall winces continually:
A red fist, opening and closing,
Two gray, papery bags—
This is what I am made of, this and a terror
Of being wheeled off under crosses and a rain of pietàs.

On a black wall, unidentifiable birds
Swivel their heads and cry.

There is no talk of immortality among these!
Cold blanks approach us:
They move in a hurry.

28 May 1962

167 ## Berck-Plage

(1)

This is the sea, then, this great abeyance.
How the sun's poultice draws on my inflammation.

Electrifyingly-colored sherbets, scooped from the freeze
By pale girls, travel the air in scorched hands.

Why is it so quiet, what are they hiding?
I have two legs, and I move smilingly.

A sandy damper kills the vibrations;
It stretches for miles, the shrunk voices

Waving and crutchless, half their old size.
The lines of the eye, scalded by these bald surfaces,

Boomerang like anchored elastics, hurting the owner.
Is it any wonder he puts on dark glasses?

Is it any wonder he affects a black cassock?
Here he comes now, among the mackerel gatherers

Who wall up their backs against him.
They are handling the black and green lozenges like the parts of a body.

The sea, that crystallized these,
Creeps away, many-snaked, with a long hiss of distress.

1962

(2)

This black boot has no mercy for anybody.
Why should it, it is the hearse of a dead foot,

The high, dead, toeless foot of this priest
Who plumbs the well of his book,

The bent print bulging before him like scenery.
Obscene bikinis hide in the dunes,

Breasts and hips a confectioner's sugar
Of little crystals, titillating the light,

While a green pool opens its eye,
Sick with what it has swallowed——

Limbs, images, shrieks. Behind the concrete bunkers
Two lovers unstick themselves.

O white sea-crockery,
What cupped sighs, what salt in the throat. . . .

And the onlooker, trembling,
Drawn like a long material

Through a still virulence,
And a weed, hairy as privates.

(3)

On the balconies of the hotel, things are glittering.
Things, things——

Tubular steel wheelchairs, aluminum crutches.
Such salt-sweetness. Why should I walk

Beyond the breakwater, spotty with barnacles?
I am not a nurse, white and attendant,

1962

I am not a smile.
These children are after something, with hooks and cries,

And my heart too small to bandage their terrible faults.
This is the side of a man: his red ribs,

The nerves bursting like trees, and this is the surgeon:
One mirrory eye——

A facet of knowledge.
On a striped mattress in one room

An old man is vanishing.
There is no help in his weeping wife.

Where are the eye-stones, yellow and valuable,
And the tongue, sapphire of ash.

(4)

A wedding-cake face in a paper frill.
How superior he is now.

It is like possessing a saint.
The nurses in their wing-caps are no longer so beautiful;

They are browning, like touched gardenias.
The bed is rolled from the wall.

This is what it is to be complete. It is horrible.
Is he wearing pajamas or an evening suit

Under the glued sheet from which his powdery beak
Rises so whitely unbuffeted?

They propped his jaw with a book until it stiffened
And folded his hands, that were shaking: goodbye, goodbye.

Now the washed sheets fly in the sun,
The pillow cases are sweetening.

1962

It is a blessing, it is a blessing:
The long coffin of soap-colored oak,

The curious bearers and the raw date
Engraving itself in silver with marvelous calm.

(5)

The gray sky lowers, the hills like a green sea
Run fold upon fold far off, concealing their hollows,

The hollows in which rock the thoughts of the wife——
Blunt, practical boats

Full of dresses and hats and china and married daughters.
In the parlor of the stone house

One curtain is flickering from the open window,
Flickering and pouring, a pitiful candle.

This is the tongue of the dead man: remember, remember.
How far he is now, his actions

Around him like livingroom furniture, like a décor.
As the pallors gather——

The pallors of hands and neighborly faces,
The elate pallors of flying iris.

They are flying off into nothing: remember us.
The empty benches of memory look over stones,

Marble façades with blue veins, and jelly-glassfuls of daffodils.
It is so beautiful up here: it is a stopping place.

(6)

The natural fatness of these lime leaves!——
Pollarded green balls, the trees march to church.

1962

The voice of the priest, in thin air,
Meets the corpse at the gate,

Addressing it, while the hills roll the notes of the dead bell;
A glitter of wheat and crude earth.

What is the name of that color?——
Old blood of caked walls the sun heals,

Old blood of limb stumps, burnt hearts.
The widow with her black pocketbook and three daughters,

Necessary among the flowers,
Enfolds her face like fine linen,

Not to be spread again.
While a sky, wormy with put-by smiles,

Passes cloud after cloud.
And the bride flowers expend a freshness,

And the soul is a bride
In a still place, and the groom is red and forgetful, he is featureless.

(7)

Behind the glass of this car
The world purrs, shut-off and gentle.

And I am dark-suited and still, a member of the party,
Gliding up in low gear behind the cart.

And the priest is a vessel,
A tarred fabric, sorry and dull,

Following the coffin on its flowery cart like a beautiful woman,
A crest of breasts, eyelids and lips

Storming the hilltop.
Then, from the barred yard, the children

Smell the melt of shoe-blacking,
Their faces turning, wordless and slow,

Their eyes opening
On a wonderful thing——

Six round black hats in the grass and a lozenge of wood,
And a naked mouth, red and awkward.

For a minute the sky pours into the hole like plasma.
There is no hope, it is given up.

30 June 1962

168 # The Other

You come in late, wiping your lips.
What did I leave untouched on the doorstep—

White Nike,
Streaming between my walls?

Smilingly, blue lightning
Assumes, like a meathook, the burden of his parts.

The police love you, you confess everything.
Bright hair, shoe-black, old plastic,

Is my life so intriguing?
Is it for this you widen your eye-rings?

Is it for this the air motes depart?
They are not air motes, they are corpuscles.

Open your handbag. What is that bad smell?
It is your knitting, busily

Hooking itself to itself,
It is your sticky candies.

I have your head on my wall.
Navel cords, blue-red and lucent,

Shriek from my belly like arrows, and these I ride.
O moon-glow, o sick one,

The stolen horses, the fornications
Circle a womb of marble.

Where are you going
That you suck breath like mileage?

Sulfurous adulteries grieve in a dream.
Cold glass, how you insert yourself

Between myself and myself.
I scratch like a cat.

The blood that runs is dark fruit—
An effect, a cosmetic.

You smile.
No, it is not fatal.

2 July 1962

169 ## Words heard, by accident, over the phone

O mud, mud, how fluid!—
Thick as foreign coffee, and with a sluggy pulse.
Speak, speak! Who is it?
It is the bowel-pulse, lover of digestibles.
It is he who has achieved these syllables.

What are these words, these words?
They are plopping like mud.
O god, how shall I ever clean the phone table?

They are pressing out of the many-holed earpiece, they are looking for a
  listener.
Is he here?

Now the room is ahiss. The instrument
Withdraws its tentacle.
But the spawn percolate in my heart. They are fertile.
Muck funnel, muck funnel—
You are too big. They must take you back!

11 July 1962

170   Poppies in July

Little poppies, little hell flames,
Do you do no harm?

You flicker. I cannot touch you.
I put my hands among the flames. Nothing burns.

And it exhausts me to watch you
Flickering like that, wrinkly and clear red, like the skin of a mouth.

A mouth just bloodied.
Little bloody skirts!

There are fumes that I cannot touch.
Where are your opiates, your nauseous capsules?

If I could bleed, or sleep!——
If my mouth could marry a hurt like that!

Or your liquors seep to me, in this glass capsule,
Dulling and stilling.

But colorless. Colorless.

20 July 1962

Burning the Letters

I made a fire; being tired
Of the white fists of old
Letters and their death rattle
When I came too close to the wastebasket.
What did they know that I didn't?
Grain by grain, they unrolled
Sands where a dream of clear water
Grinned like a getaway car.
I am not subtle
Love, love, and well, I was tired
Of cardboard cartons the color of cement or a dog pack
Holding in its hate
Dully, under a pack of men in red jackets,
And the eyes and times of the postmarks.

This fire may lick and fawn, but it is merciless:
A glass case
My fingers would enter although
They melt and sag, they are told
Do not touch.
And here is an end to the writing,
The spry hooks that bend and cringe, and the smiles, the smiles.
And at least it will be a good place now, the attic.
At least I won't be strung just under the surface,
Dumb fish
With one tin eye,
Watching for glints,
Riding my Arctic
Between this wish and that wish.

So I poke at the carbon birds in my housedress.
They are more beautiful than my bodiless owl,
They console me—
Rising and flying, but blinded.
They would flutter off, black and glittering, they would be coal angels
Only they have nothing to say to anybody.
I have seen to that.
With the butt of a rake
I flake up papers that breathe like people,

I fan them out
Between the yellow lettuces and the German cabbage
Involved in its weird blue dreams,
Involved as a foetus.
And a name with black edges

Wilts at my foot,
Sinuous orchis
In a nest of root-hairs and boredom —
Pale eyes, patent-leather gutturals!
Warm rain greases my hair, extinguishes nothing.
My veins glow like trees.
The dogs are tearing a fox. This is what it is like —
A red burst and a cry
That splits from its ripped bag and does not stop
With the dead eye
And the stuffed expression, but goes on
Dyeing the air,
Telling the particles of the clouds, the leaves, the water
What immortality is. That it is immortal.

13 August 1962

For a Fatherless Son

172

You will be aware of an absence, presently,
Growing beside you, like a tree,
A death tree, color gone, an Australian gum tree —
Balding, gelded by lightning — an illusion,
And a sky like a pig's backside, an utter lack of attention.

But right now you are dumb.
And I love your stupidity,
The blind mirror of it. I look in
And find no face but my own, and you think that's funny.
It is good for me

To have you grab my nose, a ladder rung.
One day you may touch what's wrong

The small skulls, the smashed blue hills, the godawful hush.
Till then your smiles are found money.

26 September 1962

A Birthday Present

What is this, behind this veil, is it ugly, is it beautiful?
It is shimmering, has it breasts, has it edges?

I am sure it is unique, I am sure it is just what I want.
When I am quiet at my cooking I feel it looking, I feel it thinking

'Is this the one I am to appear for,
Is this the elect one, the one with black eye-pits and a scar?

Measuring the flour, cutting off the surplus,
Adhering to rules, to rules, to rules.

Is this the one for the annunciation?
My god, what a laugh!'

But it shimmers, it does not stop, and I think it wants me.
I would not mind if it was bones, or a pearl button.

I do not want much of a present, anyway, this year.
After all I am alive only by accident.

I would have killed myself gladly that time any possible way.
Now there are these veils, shimmering like curtains,

The diaphanous satins of a January window
White as babies' bedding and glittering with dead breath. O ivory!

It must be a tusk there, a ghost-column.
Can you not see I do not mind what it is.

Can you not give it to me?
Do not be ashamed—I do not mind if it is small.

1962

Do not be mean, I am ready for enormity.
Let us sit down to it, one on either side, admiring the gleam,

The glaze, the mirrory variety of it.
Let us eat our last supper at it, like a hospital plate.

I know why you will not give it to me,
You are terrified

The world will go up in a shriek, and your head with it,
Bossed, brazen, an antique shield,

A marvel to your great-grandchildren.
Do not be afraid, it is not so.

I will only take it and go aside quietly.
You will not even hear me opening it, no paper crackle,

No falling ribbons, no scream at the end.
I do not think you credit me with this discretion.

If you only knew how the veils were killing my days.
To you they are only transparencies, clear air.

But my god, the clouds are like cotton.
Armies of them. They are carbon monoxide.

Sweetly, sweetly I breathe in,
Filling my veins with invisibles, with the million

Probable motes that tick the years off my life.
You are silver-suited for the occasion. O adding machine——

Is it impossible for you to let something go and have it go whole?
Must you stamp each piece in purple,

Must you kill what you can?
There is this one thing I want today, and only you can give it to me.

It stands at my window, big as the sky.
It breathes from my sheets, the cold dead center

Where spilt lives congeal and stiffen to history.
Let it not come by the mail, finger by finger.

Let it not come by word of mouth, I should be sixty
By the time the whole of it was delivered, and too numb to use it.

Only let down the veil, the veil, the veil.
If it were death

I would admire the deep gravity of it, its timeless eyes.
I would know you were serious.

There would be a nobility then, there would be a birthday.
And the knife not carve, but enter

Pure and clean as the cry of a baby,
And the universe slide from my side.

30 September 1962

174

The Detective

What was she doing when it blew in
Over the seven hills, the red furrow, the blue mountain?
Was she arranging cups? It is important.
Was she at the window, listening?
In that valley the train shrieks echo like souls on hooks.

That is the valley of death, though the cows thrive.
In her garden the lies were shaking out their moist silks
And the eyes of the killer moving sluglike and sidelong,
Unable to face the fingers, those egotists.
The fingers were tamping a woman into a wall,

A body into a pipe, and the smoke rising.
This is the smell of years burning, here in the kitchen,
These are the deceits, tacked up like family photographs,
And this is a man, look at his smile,
The death weapon? No one is dead.

There is no body in the house at all.
There is the smell of polish, there are plush carpets.
There is the sunlight, playing its blades,
Bored hoodlum in a red room
Where the wireless talks to itself like an elderly relative.

Did it come like an arrow, did it come like a knife?
Which of the poisons is it?
Which of the nerve-curlers, the convulsors? Did it electrify?
This is a case without a body.
The body does not come into it at all.

It is a case of vaporization.
The mouth first, its absence reported
In the second year. It had been insatiable
And in punishment was hung out like brown fruit
To wrinkle and dry.

The breasts next.
These were harder, two white stones.
The milk came yellow, then blue and sweet as water.
There was no absence of lips, there were two children,
But their bones showed, and the moon smiled.

Then the dry wood, the gates,
The brown motherly furrows, the whole estate.
We walk on air, Watson.
There is only the moon, embalmed in phosphorus.
There is only a crow in a tree. Make notes.

1 October 1962

175   The Courage of Shutting-Up

The courage of the shut mouth, in spite of artillery!
The line pink and quiet, a worm, basking.
There are black disks behind it, the disks of outrage,
And the outrage of a sky, the lined brain of it.
The disks revolve, they ask to be heard—

1962

Loaded, as they are, with accounts of bastardies.
Bastardies, usages, desertions and doubleness,
The needle journeying in its groove,
Silver beast between two dark canyons,
A great surgeon, now a tattooist,

Tattooing over and over the same blue grievances,
The snakes, the babies, the tits
On mermaids and two-legged dreamgirls.
The surgeon is quiet, he does not speak.
He has seen too much death, his hands are full of it.

So the disks of the brain revolve, like the muzzles of cannon.
Then there is that antique billhook, the tongue,
Indefatigable, purple. Must it be cut out?
It has nine tails, it is dangerous.
And the noise it flays from the air, once it gets going!

No, the tongue, too, has been put by,
Hung up in the library with the engravings of Rangoon
And the fox heads, the otter heads, the heads of dead rabbits.
It is a marvelous object—
The things it has pierced in its time.

But how about the eyes, the eyes, the eyes?
Mirrors can kill and talk, they are terrible rooms
In which a torture goes on one can only watch.
The face that lived in this mirror is the face of a dead man.
Do not worry about the eyes—

They may be white and shy, they are no stool pigeons,
Their death rays folded like flags
Of a country no longer heard of,
An obstinate independency
Insolvent among the mountains.

2 October 1962

The Bee Meeting

Who are these people at the bridge to meet me? They are the
      villagers——
The rector, the midwife, the sexton, the agent for bees.
In my sleeveless summery dress I have no protection,
And they are all gloved and covered, why did nobody tell me?
They are smiling and taking out veils tacked to ancient hats.

I am nude as a chicken neck, does nobody love me?
Yes, here is the secretary of bees with her white shop smock,
Buttoning the cuffs at my wrists and the slit from my neck to my knees.
Now I am milkweed silk, the bees will not notice.
They will not smell my fear, my fear, my fear.

Which is the rector now, is it that man in black?
Which is the midwife, is that her blue coat?
Everybody is nodding a square black head, they are knights in visors,
Breastplates of cheesecloth knotted under the armpits.
Their smiles and their voices are changing. I am led through a beanfield.

Strips of tinfoil winking like people,
Feather dusters fanning their hands in a sea of bean flowers,
Creamy bean flowers with black eyes and leaves like bored hearts.
Is it blood clots the tendrils are dragging up that string?
No, no, it is scarlet flowers that will one day be edible.

Now they are giving me a fashionable white straw Italian hat
And a black veil that molds to my face, they are making me one of them.
They are leading me to the shorn grove, the circle of hives.
Is it the hawthorn that smells so sick?
The barren body of hawthorn, etherizing its children.

Is it some operation that is taking place?
It is the surgeon my neighbors are waiting for,
This apparition in a green helmet,
Shining gloves and white suit.
Is it the butcher, the grocer, the postman, someone I know?

I cannot run, I am rooted, and the gorse hurts me
With its yellow purses, its spiky armory.

I could not run without having to run forever.
The white hive is snug as a virgin,
Sealing off her brood cells, her honey, and quietly humming.

Smoke rolls and scarves in the grove.
The mind of the hive thinks this is the end of everything.
Here they come, the outriders, on their hysterical elastics.
If I stand very still, they will think I am cow-parsley,
A gullible head untouched by their animosity,

Not even nodding, a personage in a hedgerow.
The villagers open the chambers, they are hunting the queen.
Is she hiding, is she eating honey? She is very clever.
She is old, old, old, she must live another year, and she knows it.
While in their fingerjoint cells the new virgins

Dream of a duel they will win inevitably,
A curtain of wax dividing them from the bride flight,
The upflight of the murderess into a heaven that loves her.
The villagers are moving the virgins, there will be no killing.
The old queen does not show herself, is she so ungrateful?

I am exhausted, I am exhausted——
Pillar of white in a blackout of knives.
I am the magician's girl who does not flinch.
The villagers are untying their disguises, they are shaking hands.
Whose is that long white box in the grove, what have they accomplished,
      why am I cold.

3 October 1962

177   # The Arrival of the Bee Box

    I ordered this, this clean wood box
    Square as a chair and almost too heavy to lift.
    I would say it was the coffin of a midget
    Or a square baby
    Were there not such a din in it.

1962

The box is locked, it is dangerous.
I have to live with it overnight
And I can't keep away from it.
There are no windows, so I can't see what is in there.
There is only a little grid, no exit.

I put my eye to the grid.
It is dark, dark,
With the swarmy feeling of African hands
Minute and shrunk for export,
Black on black, angrily clambering.

How can I let them out?
It is the noise that appalls me most of all,
The unintelligible syllables.
It is like a Roman mob,
Small, taken one by one, but my god, together!

I lay my ear to furious Latin.
I am not a Caesar.
I have simply ordered a box of maniacs.
They can be sent back.
They can die, I need feed them nothing, I am the owner.

I wonder how hungry they are.
I wonder if they would forget me
If I just undid the locks and stood back and turned into a tree.
There is the laburnum, its blond colonnades,
And the petticoats of the cherry.

They might ignore me immediately
In my moon suit and funeral veil.
I am no source of honey
So why should they turn on me?
Tomorrow I will be sweet God, I will set them free.

The box is only temporary.

4 October 1962

213

Stings

Bare-handed, I hand the combs.
The man in white smiles, bare-handed,
Our cheesecloth gauntlets neat and sweet,
The throats of our wrists brave lilies.
He and I

Have a thousand clean cells between us,
Eight combs of yellow cups,
And the hive itself a teacup,
White with pink flowers on it,
With excessive love I enameled it

Thinking 'Sweetness, sweetness'.
Brood cells gray as the fossils of shells
Terrify me, they seem so old.
What am I buying, wormy mahogany?
Is there any queen at all in it?

If there is, she is old,
Her wings torn shawls, her long body
Rubbed of its plush——
Poor and bare and unqueenly and even shameful.
I stand in a column

Of winged, unmiraculous women,
Honey-drudgers.
I am no drudge
Though for years I have eaten dust
And dried plates with my dense hair.

And seen my strangeness evaporate,
Blue dew from dangerous skin.
Will they hate me,
These women who only scurry,
Whose news is the open cherry, the open clover?

It is almost over.
I am in control.
Here is my honey-machine,

It will work without thinking,
Opening, in spring, like an industrious virgin

To scour the creaming crests
As the moon, for its ivory powders, scours the sea.
A third person is watching.
He has nothing to do with the bee-seller or with me.
Now he is gone

In eight great bounds, a great scapegoat.
Here is his slipper, here is another,
And here the square of white linen
He wore instead of a hat.
He was sweet,

The sweat of his efforts a rain
Tugging the world to fruit.
The bees found him out,
Molding onto his lips like lies,
Complicating his features.

They thought death was worth it, but I
Have a self to recover, a queen.
Is she dead, is she sleeping?
Where has she been,
With her lion-red body, her wings of glass?

Now she is flying
More terrible than she ever was, red
Scar in the sky, red comet
Over the engine that killed her——
The mausoleum, the wax house.

6 October 1962

179
The Swarm

Somebody is shooting at something in our town —
A dull pom, pom in the Sunday street.
Jealousy can open the blood,

It can make black roses.
Who are they shooting at?

It is you the knives are out for
At Waterloo, Waterloo, Napoleon,
The hump of Elba on your short back,
And the snow, marshaling its brilliant cutlery
Mass after mass, saying Shh!

Shh! These are chess people you play with,
Still figures of ivory.
The mud squirms with throats,
Stepping stones for French bootsoles.
The gilt and pink domes of Russia melt and float off

In the furnace of greed. Clouds, clouds.
So the swarm balls and deserts
Seventy feet up, in a black pine tree.
It must be shot down. Pom! Pom!
So dumb it thinks bullets are thunder.

It thinks they are the voice of God
Condoning the beak, the claw, the grin of the dog
Yellow-haunched, a pack-dog,
Grinning over its bone of ivory
Like the pack, the pack, like everybody.

The bees have got so far. Seventy feet high!
Russia, Poland and Germany!
The mild hills, the same old magenta
Fields shrunk to a penny
Spun into a river, the river crossed.

The bees argue, in their black ball,
A flying hedgehog, all prickles.
The man with gray hands stands under the honeycomb
Of their dream, the hived station
Where trains, faithful to their steel arcs,

Leave and arrive, and there is no end to the country.
Pom! Pom! They fall
Dismembered, to a tod of ivy.
So much for the charioteers, the outriders, the Grand Army!
A red tatter, Napoleon!

The last badge of victory.
The swarm is knocked into a cocked straw hat.
Elba, Elba, bleb on the sea!
The white busts of marshals, admirals, generals
Worming themselves into niches.

How instructive this is!
The dumb, banded bodies
Walking the plank draped with Mother France's upholstery
Into a new mausoleum,
An ivory palace, a crotch pine.

The man with gray hands smiles —
The smile of a man of business, intensely practical.
They are not hands at all
But asbestos receptacles.
Pom! Pom! 'They would have killed *me*.'

Stings big as drawing pins!
It seems bees have a notion of honor,
A black intractable mind.
Napoleon is pleased, he is pleased with everything.
O Europe! O ton of honey!

7 October 1962

180   # Wintering

This is the easy time, there is nothing doing.
I have whirled the midwife's extractor,
I have my honey,
Six jars of it,
Six cat's eyes in the wine cellar,

1962

Wintering in a dark without window
At the heart of the house
Next to the last tenant's rancid jam
And the bottles of empty glitters——
Sir So-and-so's gin.

This is the room I have never been in.
This is the room I could never breathe in.
The black bunched in there like a bat,
No light
But the torch and its faint

Chinese yellow on appalling objects——
Black asininity. Decay.
Possession.
It is they who own me.
Neither cruel nor indifferent,

Only ignorant.
This is the time of hanging on for the bees—the bees
So slow I hardly know them,
Filing like soldiers
To the syrup tin

To make up for the honey I've taken.
Tate and Lyle keeps them going,
The refined snow.
It is Tate and Lyle they live on, instead of flowers.
They take it. The cold sets in.

Now they ball in a mass,
Black
Mind against all that white.
The smile of the snow is white.
It spreads itself out, a mile-long body of Meissen,

Into which, on warm days,
They can only carry their dead.
The bees are all women,
Maids and the long royal lady.
They have got rid of the men,

The blunt, clumsy stumblers, the boors.
Winter is for women——
The woman, still at her knitting,
At the cradle of Spanish walnut,
Her body a bulb in the cold and too dumb to think.

Will the hive survive, will the gladiolas
Succeed in banking their fires
To enter another year?
What will they taste of, the Christmas roses?
The bees are flying. They taste the spring.

9 October 1962

A Secret

A secret! A secret!
How superior.
You are blue and huge, a traffic policeman,
Holding up one palm—

A difference between us?
I have one eye, you have two.
The secret is stamped on you,
Faint, undulant watermark.

Will it show in the black detector?
Will it come out
Wavery, indelible, true
Through the African giraffe in its Edeny greenery,

The Moroccan hippopotamus?
They stare from a square, stiff frill.
They are for export,
One a fool, the other a fool.

A secret . . . An extra amber
Brandy finger
Roosting and cooing 'You, you'
Behind two eyes in which nothing is reflected but monkeys.

1962

A knife that can be taken out
To pare nails,
To lever the dirt.
'It won't hurt.'

An illegitimate baby—
That big blue head—
How it breathes in the bureau drawer!
'Is that lingerie, pet?

'It smells of salt cod, you had better
Stab a few cloves in an apple,
Make a sachet or
Do away with the bastard.

'Do away with it altogether.'
'No, no, it is happy there.'
'But it wants to get out!
Look, look! It is wanting to crawl.'

My god, there goes the stopper!
The cars in the Place de la Concorde—
Watch out!
A stampede, a stampede!

Horns twirling and jungle gutturals!
An exploded bottle of stout,
Slack foam in the lap.
You stumble out,

Dwarf baby,
The knife in your back.
'I feel weak.'
The secret is out.

10 October 1962

The Applicant

First, are you our sort of a person?
Do you wear
A glass eye, false teeth or a crutch,
A brace or a hook,
Rubber breasts or a rubber crotch,

Stitches to show something's missing? No, no? Then
How can we give you a thing?
Stop crying.
Open your hand.
Empty? Empty. Here is a hand

To fill it and willing
To bring teacups and roll away headaches
And do whatever you tell it.
Will you marry it?
It is guaranteed

To thumb shut your eyes at the end
And dissolve of sorrow.
We make new stock from the salt.
I notice you are stark naked.
How about this suit——

Black and stiff, but not a bad fit.
Will you marry it?
It is waterproof, shatterproof, proof
Against fire and bombs through the roof.
Believe me, they'll bury you in it.

Now your head, excuse me, is empty.
I have the ticket for that.
Come here, sweetie, out of the closet.
Well, what do you think of *that*?
Naked as paper to start

But in twenty-five years she'll be silver,
In fifty, gold.
A living doll, everywhere you look.

It can sew, it can cook,
It can talk, talk, talk.

It works, there is nothing wrong with it.
You have a hole, it's a poultice.
You have an eye, it's an image.
My boy, it's your last resort.
Will you marry it, marry it, marry it.

11 October 1962

183

Daddy

You do not do, you do not do
Any more, black shoe
In which I have lived like a foot
For thirty years, poor and white,
Barely daring to breathe or Achoo.

Daddy, I have had to kill you.
You died before I had time——
Marble-heavy, a bag full of God,
Ghastly statue with one gray toe
Big as a Frisco seal

And a head in the freakish Atlantic
Where it pours bean green over blue
In the waters off beautiful Nauset.
I used to pray to recover you.
Ach, du.

In the German tongue, in the Polish town
Scraped flat by the roller
Of wars, wars, wars.
But the name of the town is common.
My Polack friend

Says there are a dozen or two.
So I never could tell where you
Put your foot, your root,
I never could talk to you.
The tongue stuck in my jaw.

It stuck in a barb wire snare.
Ich, ich, ich, ich,
I could hardly speak.
I thought every German was you.
And the language obscene

An engine, an engine
Chuffing me off like a Jew.
A Jew to Dachau, Auschwitz, Belsen.
I began to talk like a Jew.
I think I may well be a Jew.

The snows of the Tyrol, the clear beer of Vienna
Are not very pure or true.
With my gipsy ancestress and my weird luck
And my Taroc pack and my Taroc pack
I may be a bit of a Jew.

I have always been scared of *you*,
With your Luftwaffe, your gobbledygoo.
And your neat mustache
And your Aryan eye, bright blue.
Panzer-man, panzer-man, O You——

Not God but a swastika
So black no sky could squeak through.
Every woman adores a Fascist,
The boot in the face, the brute
Brute heart of a brute like you.

You stand at the blackboard, daddy,
In the picture I have of you,
A cleft in your chin instead of your foot
But no less a devil for that, no not
Any less the black man who

1962

Bit my pretty red heart in two.
I was ten when they buried you.
At twenty I tried to die
And get back, back, back to you.
I thought even the bones would do.

But they pulled me out of the sack,
And they stuck me together with glue.
And then I knew what to do.
I made a model of you,
A man in black with a Meinkampf look

And a love of the rack and the screw.
And I said I do, I do.
So daddy, I'm finally through.
The black telephone's off at the root,
The voices just can't worm through.

If I've killed one man, I've killed two——
The vampire who said he was you
And drank my blood for a year,
Seven years, if you want to know.
Daddy, you can lie back now.

There's a stake in your fat black heart
And the villagers never liked you.
They are dancing and stamping on you.
They always *knew* it was you.
Daddy, daddy, you bastard, I'm through.

12 October 1962

Medusa

Off that landspit of stony mouth-plugs,
Eyes rolled by white sticks,
Ears cupping the sea's incoherences,
You house your unnerving head—God-ball,
Lens of mercies,

1962

Your stooges
Plying their wild cells in my keel's shadow,
Pushing by like hearts,
Red stigmata at the very center,
Riding the rip tide to the nearest point of departure,

Dragging their Jesus hair.
Did I escape, I wonder?
My mind winds to you
Old barnacled umbilicus, Atlantic cable,
Keeping itself, it seems, in a state of miraculous repair.

In any case, you are always there,
Tremulous breath at the end of my line,
Curve of water upleaping
To my water rod, dazzling and grateful,
Touching and sucking.

I didn't call you.
I didn't call you at all.
Nevertheless, nevertheless
You steamed to me over the sea,
Fat and red, a placenta

Paralysing the kicking lovers.
Cobra light
Squeezing the breath from the blood bells
Of the fuchsia. I could draw no breath,
Dead and moneyless,

Overexposed, like an X-ray.
Who do you think you are?
A Communion wafer? Blubbery Mary?
I shall take no bite of your body,
Bottle in which I live,

Ghastly Vatican.
I am sick to death of hot salt.

Green as eunuchs, your wishes
Hiss at my sins.
Off, off, eely tentacle!

There is nothing between us.

16 October 1962

185   # The Jailer

My night sweats grease his breakfast plate.
The same placard of blue fog is wheeled into position
With the same trees and headstones.
Is that all he can come up with,
The rattler of keys?

I have been drugged and raped.
Seven hours knocked out of my right mind
Into a black sack
Where I relax, foetus or cat,
Lever of his wet dreams.

Something is gone.
My sleeping capsule, my red and blue zeppelin
Drops me from a terrible altitude.
Carapace smashed,
I spread to the beaks of birds.

O little gimlets—
What holes this papery day is already full of!
He has been burning me with cigarettes,
Pretending I am a negress with pink paws.
I am myself. That is not enough.

The fever trickles and stiffens in my hair.
My ribs show. What have I eaten?
Lies and smiles.
Surely the sky is not that color,
Surely the grass should be rippling.

1962

All day, gluing my church of burnt matchsticks,
I dream of someone else entirely.
And he, for this subversion,
Hurts me, he
With his armor of fakery,

His high cold masks of amnesia.
How did I get here?
Indeterminate criminal,
I die with variety—
Hung, starved, burned, hooked.

I imagine him
Impotent as distant thunder,
In whose shadow I have eaten my ghost ration.
I wish him dead or away.
That, it seems, is the impossibility.

That being free. What would the dark
Do without fevers to eat?
What would the light
Do without eyes to knife, what would he
Do, do, do without me?

17 October 1962

Lesbos

Viciousness in the kitchen!
The potatoes hiss.
It is all Hollywood, windowless,
The fluorescent light wincing on and off like a terrible migraine,
Coy paper strips for doors—
Stage curtains, a widow's frizz.
And I, love, am a pathological liar,
And my child—look at her, face down on the floor,
Little unstrung puppet, kicking to disappear—
Why she is schizophrenic,
Her face red and white, a panic,
You have stuck her kittens outside your window
In a sort of cement well

Where they crap and puke and cry and she can't hear.
You say you can't stand her,
The bastard's a girl.
You who have blown your tubes like a bad radio
Clear of voices and history, the staticky
Noise of the new.
You say I should drown the kittens. Their smell!
You say I should drown my girl.
She'll cut her throat at ten if she's mad at two.
The baby smiles, fat snail,
From the polished lozenges of orange linoleum.
You could eat him. He's a boy.
You say your husband is just no good to you.
His Jew-Mama guards his sweet sex like a pearl.
You have one baby, I have two.
I should sit on a rock off Cornwall and comb my hair.
I should wear tiger pants, I should have an affair.
We should meet in another life, we should meet in air,
Me and you.

Meanwhile there's a stink of fat and baby crap.
I'm doped and thick from my last sleeping pill.
The smog of cooking, the smog of hell
Floats our heads, two venomous opposites,
Our bones, our hair.
I call you Orphan, orphan. You are ill.
The sun gives you ulcers, the wind gives you T.B.
Once you were beautiful.
In New York, in Hollywood, the men said: 'Through?
Gee baby, you are rare.'
You acted, acted, acted for the thrill.
The impotent husband slumps out for a coffee.
I try to keep him in,
An old pole for the lightning,
The acid baths, the skyfuls off of you.
He lumps it down the plastic cobbled hill,
Flogged trolley. The sparks are blue.
The blue sparks spill,
Splitting like quartz into a million bits.

O jewel! O valuable!
That night the moon
Dragged its blood bag, sick
Animal
Up over the harbor lights.
And then grew normal,
Hard and apart and white.
The scale-sheen on the sand scared me to death.
We kept picking up handfuls, loving it,
Working it like dough, a mulatto body,
The silk grits.
A dog picked up your doggy husband. He went on.

Now I am silent, hate
Up to my neck,
Thick, thick.
I do not speak.
I am packing the hard potatoes like good clothes,
I am packing the babies,
I am packing the sick cats.
O vase of acid,
It is love you are full of. You know who you hate.
He is hugging his ball and chain down by the gate
That opens to the sea
Where it drives in, white and black,
Then spews it back.
Every day you fill him with soul-stuff, like a pitcher.
You are so exhausted.
Your voice my ear-ring,
Flapping and sucking, blood-loving bat.
That is that. That is that.
You peer from the door,
Sad hag. 'Every woman's a whore.
I can't communicate.'

I see your cute décor
Close on you like the fist of a baby
Or an anemone, that sea
Sweetheart, that kleptomaniac.
I am still raw.

I say I may be back.
You know what lies are for.

Even in your Zen heaven we shan't meet.

18 October 1962

187 ## Stopped Dead

A squeal of brakes.
Or is it a birth cry?
And here we are, hung out over the dead drop
Uncle, pants factory Fatso, millionaire.
And you out cold beside me in your chair.

The wheels, two rubber grubs, bite their sweet tails.
Is that Spain down there?
Red and yellow, two passionate hot metals
Writhing and sighing, what sort of a scenery is it?
It isn't England, it isn't France, it isn't Ireland.

It's violent. We're here on a visit,
With a goddam baby screaming off somewhere.
There's always a bloody baby in the air.
I'd call it a sunset, but
Whoever heard a sunset yowl like that?

You are sunk in your seven chins, still as a ham.
Who do you think I am,
Uncle, uncle?
Sad Hamlet, with a knife?
Where do you stash your life?

Is it a penny, a pearl—
Your soul, your soul?
I'll carry it off like a rich pretty girl,
Simply open the door and step out of the car
And live in Gibraltar on air, on air.

19 October 1962

Fever 103°

Pure? What does it mean?
The tongues of hell
Are dull, dull as the triple

Tongues of dull, fat Cerberus
Who wheezes at the gate. Incapable
Of licking clean

The aguey tendon, the sin, the sin.
The tinder cries.
The indelible smell

Of a snuffed candle!
Love, love, the low smokes roll
From me like Isadora's scarves, I'm in a fright

One scarf will catch and anchor in the wheel.
Such yellow sullen smokes
Make their own element. They will not rise,

But trundle round the globe
Choking the aged and the meek,
The weak

Hothouse baby in its crib,
The ghastly orchid
Hanging its hanging garden in the air,

Devilish leopard!
Radiation turned it white
And killed it in an hour.

Greasing the bodies of adulterers
Like Hiroshima ash and eating in.
The sin. The sin.

Darling, all night
I have been flickering, off, on, off, on.
The sheets grow heavy as a lecher's kiss.

Three days. Three nights.
Lemon water, chicken
Water, water make me retch.

I am too pure for you or anyone.
Your body
Hurts me as the world hurts God. I am a lantern——

My head a moon
Of Japanese paper, my gold beaten skin
Infinitely delicate and infinitely expensive.

Does not my heat astound you. And my light.
All by myself I am a huge camellia
Glowing and coming and going, flush on flush.

I think I am going up,
I think I may rise——
The beads of hot metal fly, and I, love, I

Am a pure acetylene
Virgin
Attended by roses,

By kisses, by cherubim,
By whatever these pink things mean.
Not you, nor him

Not him, nor him
(My selves dissolving, old whore petticoats)——
To Paradise.

20 October 1962

189   # Amnesiac

No use, no use, now, begging Recognize!
There is nothing to do with such a beautiful blank but smooth it.
Name, house, car keys,

The little toy wife—
Erased, sigh, sigh.
Four babies and a cooker!

Nurses the size of worms and a minute doctor
Tuck him in.
Old happenings

Peel from his skin.
Down the drain with all of it!
Hugging his pillow

Like the red-headed sister he never dared to touch,
He dreams of a new one—
Barren, the lot are barren!

And of another color.
How they'll travel, travel, travel, scenery
Sparking off their brother-sister rears

A comet tail!
And money the sperm fluid of it all.
One nurse brings in

A green drink, one a blue.
They rise on either side of him like stars.
The two drinks flame and foam.

O sister, mother, wife,
Sweet Lethe is my life.
I am never, never, never coming home!

21 October 1962

190   Lyonnesse

No use whistling for Lyonnesse!
Sea-cold, sea-cold it certainly is.
Take a look at the white, high berg on his forehead—

1962

There's where it sunk.
The blue, green,
Gray, indeterminate gilt

Sea of his eyes washing over it
And a round bubble
Popping upward from the mouths of bells

People and cows.
The Lyonians had always thought
Heaven would be something else,

But with the same faces,
The same places. . .
It was not a shock —

The clear, green, quite breathable atmosphere,
Cold grits underfoot,
And the spidery water-dazzle on field and street.

It never occurred that they had been forgot,
That the big God
Had lazily closed one eye and let them slip

Over the English cliff and under so much history!
They did not see him smile,
Turn, like an animal,

In his cage of ether, his cage of stars.
He'd had so many wars!
The white gape of his mind was the real Tabula Rasa.

21 October 1962

Cut

For Susan O'Neill Roe

What a thrill——
My thumb instead of an onion.
The top quite gone
Except for a sort of a hinge

Of skin,
A flap like a hat,
Dead white.
Then that red plush.

Little pilgrim,
The Indian's axed your scalp.
Your turkey wattle
Carpet rolls

Straight from the heart.
I step on it,
Clutching my bottle
Of pink fizz.

A celebration, this is.
Out of a gap
A million soldiers run,
Redcoats, every one.

Whose side are they on?
O my
Homunculus, I am ill.
I have taken a pill to kill

The thin
Papery feeling.
Saboteur,
Kamikaze man——

The stain on your
Gauze Ku Klux Klan

1962

Babushka
Darkens and tarnishes and when

The balled
Pulp of your heart
Confronts its small
Mill of silence

How you jump——
Trepanned veteran,
Dirty girl,
Thumb stump.

24 October 1962

By Candlelight

This is winter, this is night, small love—
A sort of black horsehair,
A rough, dumb country stuff
Steeled with the sheen
Of what green stars can make it to our gate.
I hold you on my arm.
It is very late.
The dull bells tongue the hour.
The mirror floats us at one candle power.

This is the fluid in which we meet each other,
This haloey radiance that seems to breathe
And lets our shadows wither
Only to blow
Them huge again, violent giants on the wall.
One match scratch makes you real.
At first the candle will not bloom at all—
It snuffs its bud
To almost nothing, to a dull blue dud.

I hold my breath until you creak to life,
Balled hedgehog,

1962

Small and cross. The yellow knife
Grows tall. You clutch your bars.
My singing makes you roar.
I rock you like a boat
Across the Indian carpet, the cold floor,
While the brass man
Kneels, back bent, as best he can

Hefting his white pillar with the light
That keeps the sky at bay,
The sack of black! It is everywhere, tight, tight!
He is yours, the little brassy Atlas—
Poor heirloom, all you have,
At his heels a pile of five brass cannonballs,
No child, no wife.
Five balls! Five bright brass balls!
To juggle with, my love, when the sky falls.

24 October 1962

The Tour

O maiden aunt, you have come to call.
Do step into the hall!
With your bold
Gecko, the little flick!
All cogs, weird sparkle and every cog solid gold.
And I in slippers and housedress with no lipstick!

And you want to be shown about!
Yes, yes, this is my address.
Not a patch on *your* place, I guess, with the Javanese
Geese and the monkey trees.
It's a bit burnt-out,
A bit of a wild machine, a bit of a mess!

O I shouldn't put my finger in *that*
Auntie, it might bite!
That's my frost box, no cat,
Though it *looks* like a cat, with its fluffy stuff, pure white.

1962

You should see the objects it makes!
Millions of needly glass cakes!

Fine for the migraine or the bellyache. And *this*
Is where I kept the furnace,
Each coal a hot cross-stitch—a *lovely* light!
It simply exploded one night,
It went up in smoke.
And that's why I have no hair, auntie, that's why I choke

Off and on, as if I just had to retch.
Coal gas is ghastly stuff.
Here's a spot I thought you'd love—
Morning Glory Pool!
The blue's a jewel.
It boils for forty hours at a stretch.

O I shouldn't dip my hankie in, it *hurts*!
Last summer, my God, last summer
It ate seven maids and a plumber
And returned them steamed and pressed and stiff as shirts.
I am bitter? I'm averse?
Here's your specs, dear, here's your purse.

Toddle on home to tea now in your flat hat.
It'll be *lemon* tea for me,
Lemon tea and earwig biscuits—creepy-creepy.
You'd not want that.
Toddle on home, before the weather's worse.
Toddle on home, and don't trip on the nurse!—

She may be bald, she may have no eyes,
But auntie, she's awfully nice.
She's pink, she's a born midwife—
She can bring the dead to life
With her wiggly fingers and for a very small fee.
Well I *hope* you've enjoyed it, auntie!

Toddle on home to tea!

25 October 1962

238

Ariel

Stasis in darkness.
Then the substanceless blue
Pour of tor and distances.

God's lioness,
How one we grow,
Pivot of heels and knees!—The furrow

Splits and passes, sister to
The brown arc
Of the neck I cannot catch,

Nigger-eye
Berries cast dark
Hooks——

Black sweet blood mouthfuls,
Shadows.
Something else

Hauls me through air——
Thighs, hair;
Flakes from my heels.

White
Godiva, I unpeel——
Dead hands, dead stringencies.

And now I
Foam to wheat, a glitter of seas.
The child's cry

Melts in the wall.
And I
Am the arrow,

The dew that flies
Suicidal, at one with the drive
Into the red

Eye, the cauldron of morning.

27 October 1962

Poppies in October

195

Even the sun-clouds this morning cannot manage such skirts.
Nor the woman in the ambulance
Whose red heart blooms through her coat so astoundingly——

A gift, a love gift
Utterly unasked for
By a sky

Palely and flamily
Igniting its carbon monoxides, by eyes
Dulled to a halt under bowlers.

O my God, what am I
That these late mouths should cry open
In a forest of frost, in a dawn of cornflowers.

27 October 1962

Nick and the Candlestick

196

I am a miner. The light burns blue.
Waxy stalactites
Drip and thicken, tears

The earthen womb
Exudes from its dead boredom.
Black bat airs

1962

Wrap me, raggy shawls,
Cold homicides.
They weld to me like plums.

Old cave of calcium
Icicles, old echoer.
Even the newts are white,

Those holy Joes.
And the fish, the fish——
Christ! they are panes of ice,

A vice of knives,
A piranha
Religion, drinking

Its first communion out of my live toes.
The candle
Gulps and recovers its small altitude,

Its yellows hearten.
O love, how did you get here?
O embryo

Remembering, even in sleep,
Your crossed position.
The blood blooms clean

In you, ruby.
The pain
You wake to is not yours.

Love, love,
I have hung our cave with roses,
With soft rugs——

The last of Victoriana.
Let the stars
Plummet to their dark address,

Let the mercuric
Atoms that cripple drip
Into the terrible well,

You are the one
Solid the spaces lean on, envious.
You are the baby in the barn.

29 October 1962

Purdah

Jade—
Stone of the side,
The agonized

Side of green Adam, I
Smile, cross-legged,
Enigmatical,

Shifting my clarities.
So valuable!
How the sun polishes this shoulder!

And should
The moon, my
Indefatigable cousin

Rise, with her cancerous pallors,
Dragging trees—
Little bushy polyps,

Little nets,
My visibilities hide.
I gleam like a mirror.

At this facet the bridegroom arrives
Lord of the mirrors!
It is himself he guides

1962

In among these silk
Screens, these rustling appurtenances.
I breathe, and the mouth

Veil stirs its curtain
My eye
Veil is

A concatenation of rainbows.
I am his.
Even in his

Absence, I
Revolve in my
Sheath of impossibles,

Priceless and quiet
Among these parakeets, macaws!
O chatterers

Attendants of the eyelash!
I shall unloose
One feather, like the peacock.

Attendants of the lip!
I shall unloose
One note

Shattering
The chandelier
Of air that all day flies

Its crystals
A million ignorants.
Attendants!

Attendants!
And at his next step
I shall unloose

1962

I shall unloose—
From the small jeweled
Doll he guards like a heart—

The lioness,
The shriek in the bath,
The cloak of holes.

29 October 1962

Lady Lazarus

I have done it again.
One year in every ten
I manage it——

A sort of walking miracle, my skin
Bright as a Nazi lampshade,
My right foot

A paperweight,
My face a featureless, fine
Jew linen.

Peel off the napkin
O my enemy.
Do I terrify?——

The nose, the eye pits, the full set of teeth?
The sour breath
Will vanish in a day.

Soon, soon the flesh
The grave cave ate will be
At home on me

And I a smiling woman.
I am only thirty.
And like the cat I have nine times to die.

1962

This is Number Three.
What a trash
To annihilate each decade.

What a million filaments.
The peanut-crunching crowd
Shoves in to see

Them unwrap me hand and foot——
The big strip tease.
Gentlemen, ladies

These are my hands
My knees.
I may be skin and bone,

Nevertheless, I am the same, identical woman.
The first time it happened I was ten.
It was an accident.

The second time I meant
To last it out and not come back at all.
I rocked shut

As a seashell.
They had to call and call
And pick the worms off me like sticky pearls.

Dying
Is an art, like everything else.
I do it exceptionally well.

I do it so it feels like hell.
I do it so it feels real.
I guess you could say I've a call.

It's easy enough to do it in a cell.
It's easy enough to do it and stay put.
It's the theatrical

1962

Comeback in broad day
To the same place, the same face, the same brute
Amused shout:

'A miracle!'
That knocks me out.
There is a charge

For the eyeing of my scars, there is a charge
For the hearing of my heart——
It really goes.

And there is a charge, a very large charge
For a word or a touch
Or a bit of blood

Or a piece of my hair or my clothes.
So, so, Herr Doktor.
So, Herr Enemy.

I am your opus,
I am your valuable,
The pure gold baby

That melts to a shriek.
I turn and burn.
Do not think I underestimate your great concern.

Ash, ash—
You poke and stir.
Flesh, bone, there is nothing there——

A cake of soap,
A wedding ring,
A gold filling.

Herr God, Herr Lucifer
Beware
Beware.

Out of the ash
I rise with my red hair
And I eat men like air.

23–29 October 1962

199   # The Couriers

The word of a snail on the plate of a leaf?
It is not mine. Do not accept it.

Acetic acid in a sealed tin?
Do not accept it. It is not genuine.

A ring of gold with the sun in it?
Lies. Lies and a grief.

Frost on a leaf, the immaculate
Cauldron, talking and crackling

All to itself on the top of each
Of nine black Alps.

A disturbance in mirrors,
The sea shattering its gray one——

Love, love, my season.

4 November 1962

200   # Getting There

How far is it?
How far is it now?
The gigantic gorilla interior

Of the wheels move, they appall me——
The terrible brains
Of Krupp, black muzzles
Revolving, the sound
Punching out Absence! like cannon.
It is Russia I have to get across, it is some war or other.
I am dragging my body
Quietly through the straw of the boxcars.
Now is the time for bribery.
What do wheels eat, these wheels
Fixed to their arcs like gods,
The silver leash of the will——
Inexorable. And their pride!
All the gods know is destinations.
I am a letter in this slot——
I fly to a name, two eyes.
Will there be fire, will there be bread?
Here there is such mud.
It is a trainstop, the nurses
Undergoing the faucet water, its veils, veils in a nunnery,
Touching their wounded,
The men the blood still pumps forward,
Legs, arms piled outside
The tent of unending cries——
A hospital of dolls.
And the men, what is left of the men
Pumped ahead by these pistons, this blood
Into the next mile,
The next hour——
Dynasty of broken arrows!

How far is it?
There is mud on my feet,
Thick, red and slipping. It is Adam's side,
This earth I rise from, and I in agony.
I cannot undo myself, and the train is steaming.
Steaming and breathing, its teeth
Ready to roll, like a devil's.
There is a minute at the end of it
A minute, a dewdrop.
How far is it?

It is so small
The place I am getting to, why are there these obstacles——
The body of this woman,
Charred skirts and deathmask
Mourned by religious figures, by garlanded children.
And now detonations——
Thunder and guns.
The fire's between us.
Is there no still place
Turning and turning in the middle air,
Untouched and untouchable.
The train is dragging itself, it is screaming——
An animal
Insane for the destination,
The bloodspot,
The face at the end of the flare.
I shall bury the wounded like pupas,
I shall count and bury the dead.
Let their souls writhe in a dew,
Incense in my track.
The carriages rock, they are cradles.
And I, stepping from this skin
Of old bandages, boredoms, old faces

Step to you from the black car of Lethe,
Pure as a baby.

6 November 1962

The Night Dances

201

A smile fell in the grass.
Irretrievable!

And how will your night dances
Lose themselves. In mathematics?

Such pure leaps and spirals——
Surely they travel

249

1962

The world forever, I shall not entirely
Sit emptied of beauties, the gift

Of your small breath, the drenched grass
Smell of your sleeps, lilies, lilies.

Their flesh bears no relation.
Cold folds of ego, the calla,

And the tiger, embellishing itself——
Spots, and a spread of hot petals.

The comets
Have such a space to cross,

Such coldness, forgetfulness.
So your gestures flake off——

Warm and human, then their pink light
Bleeding and peeling

Through the black amnesias of heaven.
Why am I given

These lamps, these planets
Falling like blessings, like flakes

Six-sided, white
On my eyes, my lips, my hair

Touching and melting.
Nowhere.

6 November 1962

Gulliver

Over your body the clouds go
High, high and icily
And a little flat, as if they

Floated on a glass that was invisible.
Unlike swans,
Having no reflections;

Unlike you,
With no strings attached.
All cool, all blue. Unlike you——

You, there on your back,
Eyes to the sky.
The spider-men have caught you,

Winding and twining their petty fetters,
Their bribes——
So many silks.

How they hate you.
They converse in the valley of your fingers, they are inchworms.
They would have you sleep in their cabinets,

This toe and that toe, a relic.
Step off!
Step off seven leagues, like those distances

That revolve in Crivelli, untouchable.
Let this eye be an eagle,
The shadow of this lip, an abyss.

6 November 1962

Thalidomide

O half moon—

Half-brain, luminosity—
Negro, masked like a white,

Your dark
Amputations crawl and appall—

Spidery, unsafe.
What glove

What leatheriness
Has protected

Me from that shadow—
The indelible buds,

Knuckles at shoulder-blades, the
Faces that

Shove into being, dragging
The lopped

Blood-caul of absences.
All night I carpenter

A space for the thing I am given,
A love

Of two wet eyes and a screech.
White spit

Of indifference!
The dark fruits revolve and fall.

The glass cracks across,
The image

Flees and aborts like dropped mercury.

8 November 1962

Letter in November

Love, the world
Suddenly turns, turns color. The streetlight
Splits through the rat's-tail
Pods of the laburnum at nine in the morning.
It is the Arctic,

This little black
Circle, with its tawn silk grasses—babies' hair.
There is a green in the air,
Soft, delectable.
It cushions me lovingly.

I am flushed and warm.
I think I may be enormous,
I am so stupidly happy,
My wellingtons
Squelching and squelching through the beautiful red.

This is my property.
Two times a day
I pace it, sniffing
The barbarous holly with its viridian
Scallops, pure iron,

And the wall of old corpses.
I love them.
I love them like history.
The apples are golden,
Imagine it——

My seventy trees
Holding their gold-ruddy balls
In a thick gray death-soup,
Their million
Gold leaves metal and breathless.

O love, O celibate.
Nobody but me
Walks the waist-high wet.
The irreplaceable
Golds bleed and deepen, the mouths of Thermopylae.

11 November 1962

Death & Co.

Two, of course there are two.
It seems perfectly natural now——
The one who never looks up, whose eyes are lidded
And balled, like Blake's,
Who exhibits

The birthmarks that are his trademark——
The scald scar of water,
The nude
Verdigris of the condor.
I am red meat. His beak

Claps sidewise: I am not his yet.
He tells me how badly I photograph.
He tells me how sweet
The babies look in their hospital
Icebox, a simple

Frill at the neck,
Then the flutings of their Ionian
Death-gowns,
Then two little feet.
He does not smile or smoke.

The other does that,
His hair long and plausive.
Bastard
Masturbating a glitter,
He wants to be loved.

1962

I do not stir.
The frost makes a flower,
The dew makes a star,
The dead bell,
The dead bell.

Somebody's done for.

14 November 1962

Years

They enter as animals from the outer
Space of holly where spikes
Are not the thoughts I turn on, like a Yogi,
But greenness, darkness so pure
They freeze and are.

O God, I am not like you
In your vacuous black,
Stars stuck all over, bright stupid confetti.
Eternity bores me,
I never wanted it.

What I love is
The piston in motion——
My soul dies before it.
And the hooves of the horses,
Their merciless churn.

And you, great Stasis——
What is so great in that!
Is it a tiger this year, this roar at the door?
Is it a Christus,
The awful

God-bit in him
Dying to fly and be done with it?
The blood berries are themselves, they are very still.

The hooves will not have it,
In blue distance the pistons hiss.

16 November 1962

The Fearful

This man makes a pseudonym
And crawls behind it like a worm.

This woman on the telephone
Says she is a man, not a woman.

The mask increases, eats the worm,
Stripes for mouth and eyes and nose,

The voice of the woman hollows—
More and more like a dead one,

Worms in the glottal stops.
She hates

The thought of a baby—
Stealer of cells, stealer of beauty—

She would rather be dead than fat,
Dead and perfect, like Nefertit,

Hearing the fierce mask magnify
The silver limbo of each eye

Where the child can never swim,
Where there is only him and him.

16 November 1962

Mary's Song

The Sunday lamb cracks in its fat.
The fat
Sacrifices its opacity. . . .

A window, holy gold.
The fire makes it precious,
The same fire

Melting the tallow heretics,
Ousting the Jews.
Their thick palls float

Over the cicatrix of Poland, burnt-out
Germany.
They do not die.

Gray birds obsess my heart,
Mouth-ash, ash of eye.
They settle. On the high

Precipice
That emptied one man into space
The ovens glowed like heavens, incandescent.

It is a heart,
This holocaust I walk in,
O golden child the world will kill and eat.

19 November 1962

Winter Trees

The wet dawn inks are doing their blue dissolve.
On their blotter of fog the trees
Seem a botanical drawing—
Memories growing, ring on ring,
A series of weddings.

1962

Knowing neither abortions nor bitchery,
Truer than women,
They seed so effortlessly!
Tasting the winds, that are footless,
Waist-deep in history —

Full of wings, otherworldliness.
In this, they are Ledas.
O mother of leaves and sweetness
Who are these pietàs?
The shadows of ringdoves chanting, but easing nothing.

26 November 1962

210

Brasilia

Will they occur,
These people with torsos of steel
Winged elbows and eyeholes

Awaiting masses
Of cloud to give them expression,
These super-people! —

And my baby a nail
Driven, driven in.
He shrieks in his grease

Bones nosing for distances.
And I, nearly extinct,
His three teeth cutting

Themselves on my thumb —
And the star,
The old story.

In the lane I meet sheep and wagons,
Red earth, motherly blood.
O You who eat

1962

People like light rays, leave
This one
Mirror safe, unredeemed

By the dove's annihilation,
The glory
The power, the glory.

1 December 1962

Childless Woman

The womb
Rattles its pod, the moon
Discharges itself from the tree with nowhere to go.

My landscape is a hand with no lines,
The roads bunched to a knot,
The knot myself,

Myself the rose you achieve—
This body,
This ivory

Ungodly as a child's shriek.
Spiderlike, I spin mirrors,
Loyal to my image,

Uttering nothing but blood—
Taste it, dark red!
And my forest

My funeral,
And this hill and this
Gleaming with the mouths of corpses.

1 December 1962

Eavesdropper

Your brother will trim my hedges!
They darken your house,
Nosy grower,
Mole on my shoulder,
To be scratched absently,
To bleed, if it comes to that.
The stain of the tropics
Still urinous on you, a sin.
A kind of bush-stink.

You may be local,
But that yellow!
Godawful!
Your body one
Long nicotine-finger
On which I,
White cigarette,
Burn, for your inhalation,
Driving the dull cells wild.

Let me roost in you!
My distractions, my pallors.
Let them start the queer alchemy
That melts the skin
Gray tallow, from bone and bone.
So I saw your much sicker
Predecessor wrapped up,
A six and a half foot wedding-cake.
And he was not even malicious.

Do not think I don't notice your curtain—
Midnight, four o'clock,
Lit (you are reading),
Tarting with the drafts that pass,
Little whore tongue,
Chenille beckoner,
Beckoning my words in—
The zoo yowl, the mad soft
Mirror talk you love to catch me at.

1962

How you jumped when I jumped on *you*!
Arms folded, ear cocked,
Toad-yellow under the drop
That would not, would not drop
In a desert of cow people
Trundling their udders home
To the electric milker, the wifey, the big blue eye
That watches, like God, or the sky
The ciphers that watch it.

I called.
You crawled out,
A weather figure, boggling,
Belge troll, the low
Church smile
Spreading itself, like butter.
This is what I am in for—
Flea body!
Eyes like mice

Flicking over my property,
Levering letter flaps,
Scrutinizing the fly
Of the man's pants
Dead on the chair back,
Opening the fat smiles, the eyes
Of two babies
Just to make sure—
Toad-stone! Sister-bitch! Sweet neighbor!

15 October 1962, 31 December 1962

1963

Sheep in Fog

The hills step off into whiteness.
People or stars
Regard me sadly, I disappoint them.

The train leaves a line of breath.
O slow
Horse the color of rust,

Hooves, dolorous bells——
All morning the
Morning has been blackening,

A flower left out.
My bones hold a stillness, the far
Fields melt my heart.

They threaten
To let me through to a heaven
Starless and fatherless, a dark water.

2 December 1962, 28 January 1963

The Munich Mannequins

Perfection is terrible, it cannot have children.
Cold as snow breath, it tamps the womb

Where the yew trees blow like hydras,
The tree of life and the tree of life

1963

Unloosing their moons, month after month, to no purpose.
The blood flood is the flood of love,

The absolute sacrifice.
It means: no more idols but me,

Me and you.
So, in their sulfur loveliness, in their smiles

These mannequins lean tonight
In Munich, morgue between Paris and Rome,

Naked and bald in their furs,
Orange lollies on silver sticks,

Intolerable, without mind.
The snow drops its pieces of darkness,

Nobody's about. In the hotels
Hands will be opening doors and setting

Down shoes for a polish of carbon
Into which broad toes will go tomorrow.

O the domesticity of these windows,
The baby lace, the green-leaved confectionery,

The thick Germans slumbering in their bottomless Stolz.
And the black phones on hooks

Glittering
Glittering and digesting

Voicelessness. The snow has no voice.

28 January 1963

Totem

The engine is killing the track, the track is silver,
It stretches into the distance. It will be eaten nevertheless.

Its running is useless.
At nightfall there is the beauty of drowned fields,

Dawn gilds the farmers like pigs,
Swaying slightly in their thick suits,

White towers of Smithfield ahead,
Fat haunches and blood on their minds.

There is no mercy in the glitter of cleavers,
The butcher's guillotine that whispers: 'How's this, how's this?'

In the bowl the hare is aborted,
Its baby head out of the way, embalmed in spice,

Flayed of fur and humanity.
Let us eat it like Plato's afterbirth,

Let us eat it like Christ.
These are the people that were important——

Their round eyes, their teeth, their grimaces
On a stick that rattles and clicks, a counterfeit snake.

Shall the hood of the cobra appall me——
The loneliness of its eye, the eye of the mountains

Through which the sky eternally threads itself?
The world is blood-hot and personal

Dawn says, with its blood-flush.
There is no terminus, only suitcases

Out of which the same self unfolds like a suit
Bald and shiny, with pockets of wishes,

1963

Notions and tickets, short circuits and folding mirrors.
I am mad, calls the spider, waving its many arms.

And in truth it is terrible,
Multiplied in the eyes of the flies.

They buzz like blue children
In nets of the infinite,

Roped in at the end by the one
Death with its many sticks.

28 January 1963

Child

Your clear eye is the one absolutely beautiful thing.
I want to fill it with color and ducks,
The zoo of the new

Whose names you meditate—
April snowdrop, Indian pipe,
Little

Stalk without wrinkle,
Pool in which images
Should be grand and classical

Not this troublous
Wringing of hands, this dark
Ceiling without a star.

28 January 1963

Paralytic

It happens. Will it go on?——
My mind a rock,
No fingers to grip, no tongue,
My god the iron lung

That loves me, pumps
My two
Dust bags in and out,
Will not

Let me relapse
While the day outside glides by like ticker tape.
The night brings violets,
Tapestries of eyes,

Lights,
The soft anonymous
Talkers: 'You all right?'
The starched, inaccessible breast.

Dead egg, I lie
Whole
On a whole world I cannot touch,
At the white, tight

Drum of my sleeping couch
Photographs visit me——
My wife, dead and flat, in 1920 furs,
Mouth full of pearls,

Two girls
As flat as she, who whisper 'We're your daughters.'
The still waters
Wrap my lips,

Eyes, nose and ears,
A clear
Cellophane I cannot crack.
On my bare back

1963

I smile, a buddha, all
Wants, desire
Falling from me like rings
Hugging their lights.

The claw
Of the magnolia,
Drunk on its own scents,
Asks nothing of life.

29 January 1963

Gigolo

Pocket watch, I tick well.
The streets are lizardy crevices
Sheer-sided, with holes where to hide.
It is best to meet in a cul-de-sac,

A palace of velvet
With windows of mirrors.
There one is safe,
There are no family photographs,

No rings through the nose, no cries.
Bright fish hooks, the smiles of women
Gulp at my bulk
And I, in my snazzy blacks,

Mill a litter of breasts like jellyfish.
To nourish
The cellos of moans I eat eggs —
Eggs and fish, the essentials,

The aphrodisiac squid.
My mouth sags,
The mouth of Christ
When my engine reaches the end of it.

The tattle of my
Gold joints, my way of turning
Bitches to ripples of silver
Rolls out a carpet, a hush.

And there is no end, no end of it.
I shall never grow old. New oysters
Shriek in the sea and I
Glitter like Fontainebleau

Gratified,
All the fall of water an eye
Over whose pool I tenderly
Lean and see me.

29 January 1963

Mystic

The air is a mill of hooks—
Questions without answer,
Glittering and drunk as flies
Whose kiss stings unbearably
In the fetid wombs of black air under pines in summer.

I remember
The dead smell of sun on wood cabins,
The stiffness of sails, the long salt winding sheets.
Once one has seen God, what is the remedy?
Once one has been seized up

Without a part left over,
Not a toe, not a finger, and used,
Used utterly, in the sun's conflagrations, the stains
That lengthen from ancient cathedrals
What is the remedy?

The pill of the Communion tablet,
The walking beside still water? Memory?

Or picking up the bright pieces
Of Christ in the faces of rodents,
The tame flower-nibblers, the ones

Whose hopes are so low they are comfortable—
The humpback in his small, washed cottage
Under the spokes of the clematis.
Is there no great love, only tenderness?
Does the sea

Remember the walker upon it?
Meaning leaks from the molecules.
The chimneys of the city breathe, the window sweats,
The children leap in their cots.
The sun blooms, it is a geranium.

The heart has not stopped.

1 February 1963

220

Kindness

Kindness glides about my house.
Dame Kindness, she is so nice!
The blue and red jewels of her rings smoke
In the windows, the mirrors
Are filling with smiles.

What is so real as the cry of a child?
A rabbit's cry may be wilder
But it has no soul.
Sugar can cure everything, so Kindness says.
Sugar is a necessary fluid,

Its crystals a little poultice.
O kindness, kindness
Sweetly picking up pieces!
My Japanese silks, desperate butterflies,
May be pinned any minute, anesthetized.

And here you come, with a cup of tea
Wreathed in steam.
The blood jet is poetry,
There is no stopping it.
You hand me two children, two roses.

1 February 1963

Words

Axes
After whose stroke the wood rings,
And the echoes!
Echoes traveling
Off from the center like horses.

The sap
Wells like tears, like the
Water striving
To re-establish its mirror
Over the rock

That drops and turns,
A white skull,
Eaten by weedy greens.
Years later I
Encounter them on the road——

Words dry and riderless,
The indefatigable hoof-taps.
While
From the bottom of the pool, fixed stars
Govern a life.

1 February 1963

Contusion

Color floods to the spot, dull purple.
The rest of the body is all washed out,
The color of pearl.

In a pit of rock
The sea sucks obsessively,
One hollow the whole sea's pivot.

The size of a fly,
The doom mark
Crawls down the wall.

The heart shuts,
The sea slides back,
The mirrors are sheeted.

4 February 1963

Balloons

Since Christmas they have lived with us,
Guileless and clear,
Oval soul-animals,
Taking up half the space,
Moving and rubbing on the silk

Invisible air drifts,
Giving a shriek and pop
When attacked, then scooting to rest, barely trembling.
Yellow cathead, blue fish——
Such queer moons we live with

Instead of dead furniture!
Straw mats, white walls
And these traveling
Globes of thin air, red, green,
Delighting

The heart like wishes or free
Peacocks blessing
Old ground with a feather
Beaten in starry metals.
Your small

Brother is making
His balloon squeak like a cat.
Seeming to see
A funny pink world he might eat on the other side of it,
He bites,

Then sits
Back, fat jug
Contemplating a world clear as water.
A red
Shred in his little fist.

5 February 1963

224

Edge

The woman is perfected.
Her dead

Body wears the smile of accomplishment,
The illusion of a Greek necessity

Flows in the scrolls of her toga,
Her bare

Feet seem to be saying:
We have come so far, it is over.

Each dead child coiled, a white serpent,
One at each little

Pitcher of milk, now empty.
She has folded

1963

Them back into her body as petals
Of a rose close when the garden

Stiffens and odors bleed
From the sweet, deep throats of the night flower.

The moon has nothing to be sad about,
Staring from her hood of bone.

She is used to this sort of thing.
Her blacks crackle and drag.

5 February 1963

Notes on Poems 1956–1963

1956

In this year, Sylvia Plath (SP) began to write the poems of her first published collection.

At the beginning of the year she was in England, at Cambridge University, reading English on a Fulbright Fellowship and living in Whitstead, an annexe of Newnham College. In February she met her future husband, Ted Hughes (TH). In April, she was in Rome and Paris, touring alone.

On 16 June she married, and lived until September in Spain, mainly in the fishing village of Benidorm (at that time still undeveloped as a tourist resort).

Through September she was in West Yorkshire with her husband, returning to Cambridge in October to live again in Whitstead until December, when she and TH moved into a flat in the town. At Christmas they returned to West Yorkshire.

1   CONVERSATION AMONG THE RUINS. On the painting by Giorgio de Chirico, a postcard reproduction of which was pinned to the door of the poet's room.

2   WINTER LANDSCAPE, WITH ROOKS. On 20 February 1956, SP noted: 'Wrote one good poem: "Winter Landscape, with Rooks": it moves, and is athletic: a psychic landscape.'

5   TALE OF A TUB. On 20 February 1956, she had written: 'Began another big one, more abstract [than 'Winter Landscape, with Rooks'; cf. note on No. 2], written from the bathtub: take care it doesn't get too general.'

34   SPIDER. Anansi is the famous spider trickster hero of West African and Caribbean folklore. Towards the end of this year SP became interested in African folklore in general, with results that can be detected throughout the rest of her work.

43   NOVEMBER GRAVEYARD. At Heptonstall, West Yorkshire, where the poet is buried.

1957

In this year SP completed her M.A. degree at Cambridge University.

In June, she and her husband moved to the United States, where she had been invited to teach at her old college, Smith, in Northampton, Massachusetts. They spent the summer on Cape Cod.

In October she took up her teaching post at Smith College.

48   THE EVERLASTING MONDAY. Monday held an ominous symbolic significance for SP (cf. the poem 'An Appearance' [No. 159], and elsewhere).

49   HARDCASTLE CRAGS. Valley of the Hebden River, a deep wooded gorge lying below the high road in the West Yorkshire moorland.

54   THE LADY AND THE EARTHENWARE HEAD. The 'head' in question was lodged in a

willow, on the banks of the Cam, and never reclaimed. (Cf. her later opinion of this poem, quoted in the Introduction, p. 13.)

57 TWO VIEWS OF WITHENS. Top Withens is a ruinous farmhouse under the moor's edge above Haworth, West Yorkshire—allegedly the model for Emily Brontë's Wuthering Heights. SP approached it from the south, over some miles of moorland, on her first visit.

58 THE GREAT CARBUNCLE. On an odd phenomenon sometimes observed on high moorland for half an hour or so at evening, when the hands and faces of people seem to become luminous.

60 THE DISQUIETING MUSES. Reading this poem on a BBC radio programme, SP commented: 'It borrows its title from the painting by Giorgio de Chirico—*The Disquieting Muses*. All through the poem I have in mind the enigmatic figures in this painting—three terrible faceless dressmaker's dummies in classical gowns, seated and standing in a weird, clear light that casts the long strong shadows characteristic of de Chirico's early work. The dummies suggest a twentieth-century version of other sinister trios of women—the Three Fates, the witches in *Macbeth*, de Quincey's sisters of madness.'

62 OUIJA. SP occasionally amused herself, with one or two others, by holding her finger on an upturned glass, in a ring of letters laid out on a smooth table, and questioning the 'spirits'.

The following 'Dialogue Over a Ouija Board', which she never showed, though it must have been written some time in 1957–8, used the actual 'spirit' text of one of the ouija sessions. The spirit named here was the one regularly applied to. His news could be accurate. (The first time he was guided through Littlewood's football coupon, he predicted all thirteen of the draws made on the following Saturday—but anticipated them, throughout, by just one match. The first dividend at that time, in 1956, was £75,000. The spirit's later attempts were progressively less accurate and very soon no better than anyone else's.) Usually his communications were gloomy and macabre, though not without wit.

DIALOGUE OVER A OUIJA BOARD

A VERSE DIALOGUE

Characters: SIBYL
LEROY

SIBYL:
Go get the glass, then. But I know tonight will be
In every respect like every other night:
While we're sitting, face to face across the coffee-
Table, trying our luck, index fingers set
On the round base of the inverted wine-glass here,
They'll go by, trundling like marble statues way out
In the wings somewhere, or like heirloom furniture

Moving, being moved. And we'll imagine
A great frieze, Egyptian, perhaps, or Greek,
And their eyes looking out of it: keen,
With the cold burn dry ice has. Yet the clock
Has never failed to see our fabling sheared
Down to a circle of letters: twenty-six
In all. Plus Yes. Plus No. And this bare board.

LEROY:
That's how you always talk before we start.
But I've brought brandy and built the fire up
So the artful glass won't change its chill for heart's
Blood and bank wrist, elbow, shoulder, lip
With winter as you claim it does. The coal
Cracks red.
SYBIL: Nothing happens.
LEROY: Wait. Its trip
Begins. A jerk. And now the first slow ramble

Around the ring. I think it must be making sure
The letters live in the same place. Or else
Each time must learn the letters new. Are
You to ask who's home, or I?
SYBIL: I will.
Is anybody there? It goes. It goes
Direct to Yes. I bet it's Pan. Who'll
Come on call like that but Pan? He's

Signing in. Just P this time. And off,
And back to P, as if he knew us well
Enough for nicknames.
LEROY: *How are you, Pan?*
SIBYL: F-
I-N-E, he says. You feel him pull
Under your finger? I mean, you don't push
Even a little?
LEROY: You know I don't, and still . . .
SIBYL: And still I'm skeptic. I know. I'm being foolish

I suppose. If I didn't trust you at this
I wouldn't trust myself. The fault's my faith
In Pan: it's been ebbing ever since the mess
He made of the football pools—teasing us with
Near wins, week by week, waiting until
We thought we'd trained him, before going haywire. Truth
Isn't in him.
LEROY: Maybe. But maybe the pools

Bored him. He's more philosopher, it seems,
Than financier.
SIBYL: What good is he, if not
For fortune-telling? And where is it fortune comes
From, if not the pools?
LEROY: Oh, from a lot
Of places: the oil well my uncle owns, for one;
Or your white-haired benefactress, who may see fit
To alter her will our way. Shall we go on

Asking about money?
SIBYL: I'm sick of that.

LEROY:
Well what, then?
SIBYL: That's the trouble. Let's say he
Really can see into the future. What,
Pools aside, wills aside, do we
Really want to know about?
LEROY: Everything.
Our work. Love. The after-life . . .
SIBYL: Do you
Honestly want to find if you'll have a fling

At fame or not? As for love, I figure when we're
Out of it will be time and plenty for us
To court remorse. Or someone else. I'd rather
Sift him about the after-life than this:
It's not so imminent. At least I feel
Less dread of the world beyond than ours.
LEROY: That's because
You don't quite believe in it. You're deaf to real

Dangers, but don't mind hearing about the ones
In hell, since hell's a fairytale.
SIBYL: I would
Believe, if they could manage to convince
Me.
LEROY: Ask, anyhow.
SIBYL: I admit it: I'm afraid,
Always, the glass will blurt what I don't want
To know at all. And yet I go ahead.
Pan, are you still there?
LEROY: See, his sprint

To Yes says he is ready.
SIBYL: *Pan, is there*
A life after this life? He shoots so swift
To Yes, his sureness must be his, not ours.
Do you know how my father is?
LEROY: He's left
For Yes, dragging our fingers after.
SIBYL: *How*
Is he, then? He spells. I-N. He'll lift
The glass yet as he glides. P-L-U-

M-A-G-E. In plumage. I'd never have thought
To say that. That must be his: his word.
LEROY: You see,
You're melting now, because you think he's hit
An original note. If he'd said, however, merely:
Dead, you'd swear him a victim of our own vain
Ventriloquy. But wings neither you nor I
Would traffic in.
SIBYL: Let him finish what he began.

Plumage of what, Pan? P . . . He starts again,
Tugging us through plumage. I almost feel
Feathers winnowing the room. A thin
Column of dazzle draws my eyes to the wall
As if the air were laboring to produce
An angel. Plumage. O-F-R. He'll
Jog off in jabberwocky now and lose us,

Lapsing into Russian or Serbo-Croat.
A-W-W. He's gone off: what English
Word wears two W's? O-R. Or what?
M-S. Manuscript? He stops. I wish
Those letters separated into sense
Instead of brewing us such a balderdash
Of half-hints.
LEROY: You persist in spelling half-hints

Out of a wholeness. Worms, not wings is what
Pan said. A plumage of raw worms.
SIBYL: How
Tedious. That's what we'd say. About rot
Feeding at the root of things. He stole that, too,
As he stole our perplexities about the pools
And tricked us to trust his vision, while night after night he
Palmed off our own hunches as oracles.

I was perfectly right: Pan's a mere puppet
Of our two intuitions.
LEROY: And if he is?
That's something to study even if it's not
The Faith-Maker, fisted in his cloud, or the chorus
Of mandatory voices you half expect
To fracture these four walls. Your faith flies
Like an olive-beaked dove above the engulfing fact:

Tables and chairs can elbow us with ease
Out of our very countenance by simply
Bulking more real than we think we are: we face
Obliteration hourly unless our eye
Can whipcrack the tables into tigers and foist
Castles upon the smug-shaped chairs.
SIBYL: All this I
Know: which is why I, when the wondrous fist

Fails to appear, turn, and, turning, shrink
The size of my demand to magic: no more
Than against gravity's grip, tables rising; the drink
Drunk, and tea-leaves candid; the clairvoyant seizure
Predicting three boys an hour hence will play
Some paltry scene on the soup-kitchen stair:
These gifts are given.
LEROY: And when withheld, you'll say

279

Gods grow too proud to practice doorman duties
At the whim of a wine-glass and let us into worlds
Saved for the acorn-stomached saint or eyes
Burning like knotholes from a nun's shroud–circled
Smirk.
SIBYL: Saints' door apart, backdoor's a door,
And I'd sooner be staked for a witch, kindled, and curled
To a cinder, than meet a poor upstart of our nether

Selves posing as prophet and slyly poaching
Pebbles we preserve in our own cupboards
To build his canting towers. While you, you long
To view how versatile we are: you've pampered
Pan as if he were our first-breached brat
Fusing two talents, a sort of psychic bastard
Sprung to being on our wedding night

Nine months too soon for comfort, but a bright
Boy, prone to compose queer poetry
In apt iambics, if prodded to recite
By scoldings, or by subtle praise. Only I,
Even if you seem pacified, prefer
To picture some other party speaking through
Our separate veins and this glass mouth.
LEROY: Oh you're

Going to get Gabriel's thumb into the pie
If you must butcher Mother Goose to do it.
Gabriel or Beelzebub: I see,
Now, you really don't much care which, or what
Minor imps pipe up, so long as each
May testify to drive your doubting out.
I never knew such credulity to pitch

Such skeptic cracks. With sense sealed watertight
So, you'll scoff, and yet you'd drop to kneel
If that elderberry bush beside the gate
Belched into blaze and, though red–hot, kept whole
And hale its green latticework of leaves. You need
Nothing short of a miracle to nail
Faith fast: a miracle and the smell of blood

To prove it genuine.
SIBYL: You'd kneel, too,
If a bush borrowed tongues and spoke to you. You'd kneel
Until it finished, and then look furtively
For loudspeaker wires running like a logical
Argument to the house next door. Or if
Your Sherlock Holmesing steered to a blank wall
You'd presume your inner voice god-plumed enough

To people the boughs with talking birds.
LEROY: I'd plant
Gods and rear them like beanstalks from out these ribs

Before one heaved himself through heaven's tent
To contradict me.
SIBYL: Your shouldering words outstrip
The stint of Sisyphus.
LEROY: Ask Pan, then, where
He lives. His answer will put an end to gibes
And get us clear of this.
SIBYL: Oh, he'll go clever

Like all the others and swear that he's a puma
In Tibet, or a llama in Zanzibar
As if tempting our gross gullibility
To give another inch.
LEROY: If you prefer,
I'll ask.
SIBYL: Do. We've kept him waiting long
Enough. But be polite. You're too severe
On him sometimes.
LEROY: He's lazy. Like any young

Boy, he needs a beating now and then
To quicken his sluggard's blood.
SIBYL: But he needn't come
To collect his beatings. And if he's a go-between
Our world and theirs we'd best play safe and groom
Our questions in humble habit to gain grace
And chance of a true answer.
LEROY: You waste no time
Eating your words: you'll revoke his godhood soon as

His drift endorses your inklings of a doom
Descended on your favorites, and yet
You'll issue him his pass to angeldom
Before he spells again, should his next writ
Warrant him whelped in the wake of two shooting
Stars, not our cheeseparing psyches.
SIBYL: It
Pays to be politic. Oh, I'm not one to hang

Bled white with briars by a busy conscience
If nothing comes of it. On the other hand,
What greenhorn vents his venom against giants
Outside the cave whose contours most remind
One of a giant's ear?
LEROY: I guess this glass
Might do as a god's mouthpiece if a whirlwind
Did. It's small, but the volume of the voice

Is small these days.
SIBYL: Don't be so smart.
LEROY: I'll ask,
And we'll see who's smartest. *Pan, tell us now:
Where do you live?*

SIBYL: He moves.
LEROY: He's moving brisk
Like a good boy.
SIBYL: Be careful. I'm not sure that he
Can spell sarcasm through our fingertips.
LEROY:
He goes . . .
SIBYL: I-N-G-O-D-P-I-
E.
LEROY:
    Godpie! That's rich. The jackanapes

Is joking at the pie-in-the-sky mirage
Which props you through this desert like a dream
Of water.
SIBYL: Wait.
LEROY: Godpie I don't begrudge
You: a priest-baked pasty stuffed to the brim
With blackbirds—twenty-four, and every one
A devil.
SIBYL: Wait: he shifts. He hasn't come
To the end of it. He starts again: I-N-

G-O-D-H-E-A-D. There, see!
I knew he'd got it mixed before: visions
Aren't vouchsafed to antique virgins only:
It takes patience. If veronicas and fountains
Can once in a blue moon catch the shadows of
Their passing on a perishable screen
Of cambric or waterdrops, who knows what belief

Might work on this glass medium.
LEROY: Belief, yes,
If either of us had it: but not the half-
Hearted gambling-game you warily practice
Under the guise of nonchalance. Pan's laugh
Is on the two of us for lending heat
To propel his playfulness, but on you, above
All, if you'll hide hopes of heaven in a hat

Of formal scorn, until the first sign of an
Angel's eye in the audience, then whisk them out
Like live white rabbits, ready to begin
Running neck and neck with the most devout
Rabbits in the lot.
SIBYL: You're in a huff
Because Pan bluntly spelt out god's head, not
Your head after all. It seems his laugh

Is on you now, for planning to dredge up
Pools, prophecies and such from the unfathomed
Bottom of your brain. By some mishap,
Instead of fat fish on the line, you've plumbed

Deeper than your own ocean floor, and got
A barnacle-pated, moss-wigged, lobster-limbed
Chimera on the hook, who claims he's late

Of Davy's locker, and the lord's to home,
And not extinct, as everyone supposed.
LEROY:
If you can hang religion on the rim
Of one wine-glass, you'll pin it like a prize
Tail on each toy donkey that will bray
God-pie.
SIBYL: Why, then, did you deign to introduce
Pan as our evening guest if he's so free

With fibs?
LEROY: The fibs are ours, not his. Pan's fine
For sounding syllables we haven't yet
Surfaced in ourselves: he'll spell a line
Of poetry from these letters, but the beat
Will be our beat, just as the gift is ours,
And tongue, and thought, as well as the blood-heat
He leeches by our lenience.
SIBYL: He still bores

You to taunts though, when he reflects a face
Other than your own.
LEROY: As he bores you
When he recites one of my similes
For rot.
SIBYL: Don't think you had me fooled. I knew
Where those worms came from.
LEROY: I swear I didn't expect
Them any more than you did.
SIBYL: Oh, let it go.
You say he's told two lies . . .
LEROY: Call them two plucked

Fruits of your willful tree: god-head, god-pie
Feed your own wishful thinking.
SIBYL: Try asking him
To name his home a third time. Give your will three
Chances to master mine. They say the third time
Counts.
LEROY: Such duels infect best friendships.
SIBYL: *Pan*
Tell us the truth this time: tell us the kingdom
You inhabit.
LEROY: *Plainly as you can,*

Tell us the truth.
SIBYL: *Where do you live?*
LEROY: He starts
As if bloodhounds bore him down.

SIBYL: I-N-C-O . . .
Does he write C for G?
LEROY: No. He darts
To R now. E.
SIBYL: In core . . .
LEROY: O-F-N-E-
R-V-E.
SIBYL:
          In core of nerve! I hope
You're satisfied. My will has evidently
Curtseyed to yours.
LEROY: Too bad you called Pan up

A third time.
SIBYL: Don't gloat. Your will misfired twice
Before it made the bull's-eye.
LEROY: Do we have to battle
Like rival parents over a precocious
Child to see which one of us can call
Pan's prowess our own creation, and not the other's
Work at all?
SIBYL: How can we help but battle
If our nerves are the sole nourishers

Of Pan's pronouncements, and our nerves are strung
To such cross-purposes?
LEROY: At last you glimpse
Some light.
SIBYL: I glimpse no light at all as long
As we two glower from our separate camps,
This board our battlefield. Let's give Pan up
As a bad job.
LEROY: Wait.
SIBYL: He stirs.
LEROY: He romps
Round to earn his pay: he'll have us keep

Him yet, and give us good reason.
SIBYL: No, he's on
A binge of jeers. Look. He's running through
His book of insults.
LEROY: Nerve or noumenon,
His manners are atrocious.
SIBYL: A-P-E-
S.
LEROY:
    He calls us apes.
SIBYL: I'll settle him!
(*Breaking glass*)
There! That shuts him up!
LEROY: So. Better so,
My wish one with your aim.

SIBYL: Once, in a dream,
I smashed a glass, and ever since that dream
I've dreamed of doing it again. And now
It's done.
LEROY: It's done, and there's no mending him.
SIBYL:
It was his tongue that wanted mending.
LEROY: You know,
Those glass bits in the grate strike me chill:
As if I'd half-believed in him, and he,
Being not you, nor I, nor us at all,

Must have been wholly someone else.
SIBYL: It's absurd,
But now that anger cools, I've a sense of sorrow
Adrift in the guise of some great-taloned bird
Over my mind, casting a shadow. Sorrow
Settles in the room now. Its wings blacken the table.
The chairs belong to its darkness. I smell decay
Like the underside of mushrooms. Do you feel

Wiser for tonight's wise words?
LEROY: I felt drawn
Deeper within the dark, and as I pitched further
Into myself and into my conviction
A rigor seized me: I saw cracks appear,
Dilating to craters in this livingroom,
And you, shackled ashen across the rift, a specter
Of one I loved.
SIBYL: I saw division bloom

On darkness, more vivid and unnatural
Than any orchid.
LEROY: You broke him then.
SIBYL: I broke
The image of you, transfixed by roots, wax-pale,
Under a stone.
LEROY: Those two dreamed deaths took
Us in a third undid them.
SIBYL: And we grew one
As the glass flew to its fragments.
LEROY: Let us stake
Death's two dreams down with the body that bled the vein,

As is the use with vampires, and resign our stand
At the unreal frontier.
SIBYL: Let our backs, now bold,
Oppose what we faced earlier. Feel my hand.
LEROY:
Why, your hand's cold as ice!
SIBYL: Then chafe the cold
Out of it. There. The room returns

To normal. Let's close the curtains.
LEROY: It looks wild
Beyond the window-frame tonight.
SIBYL: Wind warns

November's done with. The blown leaves make bat-shapes,
Web-winged and furious.
LEROY: The full moonlight
Strikes the tiles of the neighbors' gable-tops
Blue as lizard-scales.
SIBYL: Frost sheens the street.
LEROY:
I am resolved. No reason could untwist
That skein of voices.
SIBYL: We promised to forget
The labyrinth and ignore what manner of beast

Might range in it.
LEROY: I only shut the door
And bolt it up by taking oath no guess
Could grope its way to gospel through that welter
Of contending words.
SIBYL: Some pythoness
In her prophetic fit heard what we heard,
Stuck to her tripod, over the fuming crevice,
Breathing the god's word, or the devil's word,

Or her own word, ambushed in an equivocal
Thicket of words.
LEROY: The curtain's drawn on that.
SIBYL:
The table looks as if it would stay a table
All night long, even should our eyes shut
In sleep.
LEROY: The chairs won't vanish or become
Castles when we glance aside.
SIBYL: That's that.
As sure as those coals burn, the livingroom

Is itself again, and ours.
LEROY: The dream
Of dreamers is dispelled. Once more we cut
A solid shape on air.
SIBYL: May the decorum
Of our days sustain us.
LEROY: May each thought
And act bear witness, in the crux of time,
To our meaning well.
BOTH: When lights go out
May two real people breathe in a real room.

ON THE DECLINE OF ORACLES. SP frequently mentioned flashes of prescience —always about something unimportant.

l. 5 *Old Böcklin*: Arnold Böcklin, Swiss late-Romantic painter.

1958

In the early months of this year SP continued to teach at Smith College, while her husband taught at the University of Massachusetts. Some time in the spring they made the decision to leave teaching and attempt to live on their earnings as writers.

During the summer they were again on Cape Cod, and returned to a flat in Boston, at 9 Willow Street, where they remained until the following June.

Throughout this time SP found writing difficult. She resorted to set themes, and deliberate exercises in style, in her efforts to find release.

66–8, 73   *Art News* had asked SP for poems based on paintings VIRGIN IN A TREE (No. 66) is on a drawing by Paul Klee, as is PERSEUS (No. 67); BATTLE-SCENE . . .(No. 68) and THE GHOST'S LEAVETAKING (No. 73) are on paintings by Klee.

69   YADWIGHA, ON A RED COUCH, AMONG LILIES. On a painting, *The Dream*, by the Douanier Rousseau. SP wrote of it, on 27 March 1958, 'my first and only good sestina'.

74   SCULPTOR. Bronze dead men lay in numbers around the house and studio of the sculptor Leonard Baskin.

75   FULL FATHOM FIVE. Her first poem about her father in his mythic role as 'father-sea god-muse' (cf. Introduction, p. 13). She composed the poem while reading one of Cousteau's books about the submarine world, alternating reading and writing without moving her position.

76   LORELEI. On 3 July, SP and TH had a session with the ouija oracle (cf. note on No. 62), 'for the first time in America'. She noted at the time: 'Among other penetrating observations, Pan said I should write on the poem-subject "Lorelei" because they are "my own kin". So today [4 July], for fun, I did so, remembering the plaintive German song Mother used to play and sing to us beginning "Ich weiss nicht was soll es bedeuten . . .". The subject appealed to me doubly (or triply): the German legend of the Rhine Sirens, the sea–childhood symbol, and the death-wish involved in the song's beauty. The poem devoured my day, but I feel it is a book poem and am pleased with it.'

l. 32   *Drunkenness of the great depths*: a phrase from the book of Cousteau's she was reading as she wrote 'Full Fathom Five' (No. 75) some time earlier. It describes the euphoric visionary state of acute oxygen shortage in which divers blissfully forget all precautions and danger.

77   MUSSEL HUNTER AT ROCK HARBOR. Rock Harbor on Cape Cod. On 4 July 1958 SP noted: 'I suppose now my star piece is "Mussel Hunter at Rock Harbor".'

82   CHILD'S PARK STONES. Child's Park, the setting of several poems from this period, lay next door to the house where SP lived in Elm Street, Northampton, Massachusetts. She wrote on 11 June 1958: 'I have just written a good syllabic poem on the Child's Park Stones as juxtaposed to the ephemeral orange and fuchsia azaleas and feel the park is my favorite place in America.'

83   OWL. On 26 June 1958, she noted: 'Wrote a brief poem this morning —"Owl over Main Street" —in "syllabic" verse. Could be better. The beginning is a bit lyrical for the subject and the last verse might be expanded.' This poem eventually became 'Owl', and in Boston on 23 April 1959, looking back over her poems, she wrote: 'I have forty

unattackable poems. I think. And a joy about them of sorts. Although I would love more potent ones. All the Smith ones are miserable death-wishes. The ones here, however gray ("Companionable Ills" [No. 87], "Owl"), have a verve and life-joy.'

84   WHITENESS I REMEMBER. On 9 July 1958, she noted: 'I wrote what I consider a "book poem" about my runaway ride in Cambridge on the horse Sam: a "hard" subject for me, horses alien to me, yet the daredevil change in Sam and my hanging on God knows how is a kind of revelation: it worked well.'

87   GREEN ROCK, WINTHROP BAY. SP spent her first years on the Winthrop peninsula, where her grandparents lived.

1959

SP and her husband lived in Boston until June 1959. During this period she worked as a secretary in the records office at the Massachusetts General Hospital. She also began to see her old psychiatrist Ruth Beutscher (cf. note on No. 101), and attended—along with Anne Sexton and George Starbuck—a writing course given by Robert Lowell.

Setting off in July, she and TH drove around the United States, from Canada to San Francisco to New Orleans and back, camping on the way—a journey of about nine weeks. In September they accepted an invitation to Yaddo, the artists' colony near Saratoga Springs, in upstate New York.

In this year TH had received a Guggenheim Foundation award, and adding this cash to what they had saved from their teaching and other work, they sailed for Europe in December.

92   THE BULL OF BENDYLAW. Cf. *English and Scottish Popular Ballads*, edited by F. J. Child (1883), where the following occurs as a 'fragment':

> The great bull of Bendy-law
> Has broken his band and run awa
> And the King and a his court
> Canna turn that bull about

94   POINT SHIRLEY. The end of the Winthrop peninsula; cf. note on No. 86. On 20 January 1959 SP wrote: 'Finished a poem this weekend, "Point Shirley", revisited, on my grandmother. Oddly powerful and moving to me in spite of rigid formal structure. Evocative. Not so one-dimensional.'

95   GOATSUCKER. Nightjar, fern-owl, etc.—nocturnal bird of many names. Esther Baskin was collecting material for a book about night creatures, and this poem was SP's contribution. On 20 January she noted: 'Spent a really pleasant afternoon, rainy, in the library looking up goatsuckers for a poem for Esther's night creature book. Much more than on frogs and a much more congenial subject. I have eight lines of a sonnet on the bird, very alliterative and colored.' She collected several pages of detailed notes.

96   WATERCOLOR OF GRANTCHESTER MEADOWS. On 19 February, she noted: 'Wrote a Grantchester poem of pure description . . . a fury of frustration. Some inhibition keeping me from writing what I really feel.' Grantchester meadows lie along the river Cam, towards Grantchester, near Cambridge.

99   TWO VIEWS OF A CADAVER ROOM. The Brueghel painting is *The Triumph of Death*.

101 THE RAVAGED FACE. On 9 March, she wrote: 'After a lugubrious session with RB [Ruth Beutscher, her psychiatrist] much freed. Good weather, good bits of news. If I don't stop crying she'll have me tied up. Got idea on trolley for a poem because of my ravaged face: called "The Ravaged Face". A line came, too. Wrote it down and then

the [other] five lines of a sestet. Wrote the first eight lines after coming back from a fine day in Winthrop yesterday. I rather like it—it has all the forthrightness of "Suicide off Egg Rock".' From her earlier suicide attempt SP carried a broad patch of scar tissue across her cheek.

103   ELECTRA ON AZALEA PATH. Azalea Path was the name of the cemetery path beside which SP's father's grave lies. On 9 March she wrote: 'A clear blue day in Winthrop. Went to my father's grave, a very depressing sight. Three graveyards separated by streets, all made within the last fifty years or so, ugly crude black stones, headstones together, as if the dead were sleeping head to head in a poorhouse. In the third yard, on a flat grassy area looking across a sallow barren stretch to rows of wooden tenements I found the flat stone: *Otto E. Plath: 1885–1940*. Right beside the path, where it would be walked over. Felt cheated. My temptation to dig him up. To prove he existed and really was dead. How far gone would he be? No trees, no peace, his headstone jammed up against the body on the other side. Left shortly. It is good to have the place in mind.'

On 20 March she wrote: 'Finished . . . "Electra on Azalea Path". They are never perfect but I think have goodnesses.' And on 23 April: 'Must do justice to my father's grave. Have rejected the Electra poem from my book. Too forced and rhetorical.'

104   THE BEEKEEPER'S DAUGHTER. The detail in the last verse is mentioned in her father's book *Bumblebees and Their Ways*, and had been demonstrated to her by him.

105   THE HERMIT AT OUTERMOST HOUSE. *The Outermost House*: a popular classic about Cape Cod.

113   THE MANOR GARDEN. The setting is the gardens of the manor at Yaddo. SP called this a poem 'for Nicholas', but her first child, born five months later, was a girl.

119   POEM FOR A BIRTHDAY. In Boston, earlier in the year, she had tried for a way out through Robert Lowell's earlier manner of writing (as in 'Point Shirley'). She had always responded strongly to Theodore Roethke's poems, but it was only at Yaddo, in October, that she realized how he could help her. This sequence began as a deliberate Roethke pastiche, a series of exercises which would be light and throwaway to begin with, but might lead to something else. On 22 October she wrote: 'Ambitious seeds of a long poem made up of separate sections. Poem on her Birthday. [Her own birthday fell on 27 October.] To be a dwelling on madhouse, nature: meanings of tools, greenhouses, florists' shops, tunnels vivid and disjointed. An adventure. Never over. Developing. Rebirth. Despair. Old women. Block it out.' And then on 4 November: 'Miraculously I wrote seven poems in my "Poem for a Birthday" sequence. . . .'

120   THE BURNT-OUT SPA. The old health spa at Saratoga Springs remained only as a burned-out ruin.

121   MUSHROOMS. On 14 November: 'Wrote an exercise on Mushrooms yesterday which Ted likes. And I do too. My absolute lack of judgment when I've written something: whether it's trash or genius.'

1960

Back in England before Christmas 1959, the poet and her husband found a flat at 3 Chalcot Square, near Primrose Hill, in London.

In February she signed a contract with Heinemann for the publication of her first collection of poems, *The Colossus*. On 1 April, her daughter Frieda was born at home. In October *The Colossus* was published in London.

130   MAGI. 'Abstractions, by definition, are withdrawn from life and formulated in despite

of life's minute and vital complexities. In this poem, "Magi", I imagine the great
absolutes of the philosophers gathered around the crib of a newborn baby girl who is
nothing *but* life.' So SP introduced this poem in a BBC radio broadcast reading.

133 WAKING IN WINTER. This poem has been extracted from a tangle of heavily corrected
manuscript lines, and must be regarded as unfinished.

Another poem from this same period which she seems to have finished but which
she never included in her own file is the following:

QUEEN MARY'S ROSE GARDEN

In this day before the day nobody is about.
A sea of dreams washes the edge of my green island
In the center of the garden named after Queen Mary.
The great roses, many of them scentless,
Rule their beds like beheaded and resurrected and all silent royalty,
The only fare on my bare breakfast plate.

Such a waste of brightness I can't understand.
It is six in the morning and finer than any Sunday —
Yet there is no walker and looker but myself.
The sky of the city is white; the light from the country.
Some ducks step down off their green-reeded shelf
And into the silver element of the pond.

I see them start to cruise and dip for food
Under the bell-jar of a wonderland.
Hedged in and evidently inviolate
Though hundreds of Londoners know it like the palm of their hand.
The roses are named after queens and people of note
Or after gay days, or colors the grower found good.

And I have no intention of disparaging them
For being too well-bred and smelless and liking the city.
I enjoy petticoats and velvets and gossip of court,
And a titled lady may frequently be a beauty.
A Devon meadow might offer a simpler sort
Of personage — single-skirted, perfumed, a gem —
But I am content with this more pompous lot.

1961

In the spring and early summer of this year SP wrote her autobiographical novel *The Bell Jar*.
During the summer, after a visit to the Dordogne, she and TH bought a house in a small
town in Devon, and moved there in September.

134 PARLIAMENT HILL FIELDS. Part of Hampstead Heath, in north London. Introducing
this poem in a BBC broadcast, SP said: 'This poem is a monologue. I imagine the
landscape of Parliament Hill Fields in London seen by a person overwhelmed by an
emotion so powerful as to color and distort the scenery. The speaker here is caught
between the old and the new year, between the grief caused by the loss of a child

(miscarriage) and the joy aroused by the knowledge of an older child safe at home. Gradually the first images of blankness and silence give way to images of convalescence and healing as the woman turns, a bit stiffly and with difficulty, from her sense of bereavement to the vital and demanding part of her world which still survives.'

136 ZOO KEEPER'S WIFE. Chalcot Square is close to Regent's Park Zoo, which she visited regularly.

137 FACE LIFT. The experience of an acquaintance, requisitioned for the poet's myth of self-renewal.

141 IN PLASTER. In March of this year SP spent a week in hospital undergoing an appendectomy. The patient in complete plaster lay on a neighbouring bed. This and the next poem, 'Tulips' (No. 142), were written during this week.

147 THE RIVAL. This poem originally had two further sections, as follows:

(2)

Compared to you, I am corruptible as a loaf of bread.
While I sleep, the black spores nod
Their magnified heads and plan to kill me as soon as possible.

The wrinkles creep up like waves,
One camouflaging itself behind another.
I should have a steel complexion like yours
In which the minutes could admire their reflections and forget about me.

(3)

I try to think of a place to hide you
As a desk drawer hides a poison pen letter,
But there is no drawer to hold you.
Blue sky or black
You preoccupy my horizon.
What good is all that space if it can't draw you off?
You are the one eye out there.

The sea, also, is ineffectual.
It keeps washing you up like an old bone.
And I, on the sky-mirroring, bland sands
Find you over and over, lipped like a skate and smiling,
With the sound of the sea in your mouth.
Angel of coldness,
Surely it is not I you want so badly.

I thought Earth might use you.
She has a terrible way with minerals,
But even her tonnage doesn't impress a diamond.
Your facets are indestructible;
Their lights whiten my heart.
Toad-stone! I see I must wear you in the centre of my forehead
And let the dead sleep as they deserve.

149 BLACKBERRYING. In a cliff cove looking out on to the Atlantic.

150 FINISTERRE. The westernmost tip of Brittany: the same outlook as 'Blackberrying' (No. 149), but a different country.

153 THE MOON AND THE YEW TREE. The yew tree stands in a churchyard to the west of the house in Devon, and visible from SP's bedroom window. On this occasion, the full moon, just before dawn, was setting behind this yew tree and her husband assigned her to write a verse 'exercise' about it.

Speaking about this poem in a BBC radio broadcast, she said: 'I do not like to think of all the things, familiar, useful and worthy things, I have never put into a poem. I did, once, put a yew tree in. And that yew tree began, with astounding egotism, to manage and order the whole affair. It was not a yew tree by a church on a road past a house in a town where a certain woman lived . . . and so on, as it might have been in a novel. Oh no. It stood squarely in the middle of my poem, manipulating its dark shades, the voices in the churchyard, the clouds, the birds, the tender melancholy with which I contemplated it—everything! I couldn't subdue it. And, in the end, my poem was a poem about a yew tree. The yew tree was just too proud to be a passing black mark in a novel.'

1962

On 17 January, SP's second child, a son, Nicholas, was born. In May *The Colossus* was published in the U.S. by Knopf.

In this year she signed a contract with Heinemann for the publication in England of her novel *The Bell Jar*. Both Harpers and Knopf in the U.S. rejected the novel.

She and her husband separated in October. Thereafter she was dependent on home help. In December she moved with her two children to London, to a flat at 23 Fitzroy Road, N.W.3, close to Chalcot Square.

156 NEW YEAR ON DARTMOOR. A fragment extracted from a tangle of corrected manuscript, this poem must be regarded as unfinished.

157 THREE WOMEN. This piece was written for radio at the invitation of Douglas Cleverdon, who produced it with great effect on the BBC's Third Programme, on 19 August 1962. The text was published by Turret Books in 1968, in a limited edition of 180 copies.

158 LITTLE FUGUE. Although never until now showing more than a general interest in music, about this time SP became keenly interested in Beethoven's late quartets, the Grosse Fuge in particular.

161 AMONG THE NARCISSI. Percy Key was the next-door neighbour whose eventual death is commemorated in 'Berck-Plage' (No. 167). The orchard in Devon was thick with daffodils and narcissi.

163 ELM. The house in Devon was overshadowed by a giant wych-elm, flanked by two others in a single mass, growing on the shoulder of a moated prehistoric mound.

This poem grew (21 sheets of working drafts) from a slightly earlier fragment:

> She is not easy, she is not peaceful;
> She pulses like a heart on my hill.
> The moon snags in her intricate nervous system.
> I am excited, seeing it there.
> It is like something she has caught for me.
>
> The night is a blue pool; she is very still.
> At the center she is still, very still with wisdom.
> The moon is let go, like a dead thing.
> Now she herself is darkening
> Into a dark world I cannot see at all.

These lines were a premature crystallization out of four densely crowded pages of manuscript. In her next attempt, some days later, she took them up and developed out of them the final poem 'Elm'.

167   BERCK-PLAGE. A beach on the coast of Normandy, which SP visited in June 1961. Overlooking the sea there was a large hospital for mutilated war veterans and accident victims—who took their exercise along the sands. The funeral in the poem is that of Percy Key (cf. note on No. 161), who died in June 1962, exactly a year after her visit to Berck-Plage.

     st. 7, l. 7   *flowery cart*: The old-fashioned funeral hand-cart on which the coffin, piled with wreaths, was wheeled through the town, ahead of the mourning cars.

     st. 7, l. 16   *mouth, red and awkward*: The soil and subsoil of the graveyard is red.

176   THE BEE MEETING. SP kept one hive of bees, and attended meetings of the local Beekeepers Association. This poem draws on her experience of the first meeting she attended.

178   STINGS. The first stirring of this sequence of poems appeared on 2 August, when SP attempted to write a poem, which she never finalized in any way, titled 'Stings'. The following can be extracted from a mass of corrected manuscript:

> What honey summons these animalcules?
> What fear? It has set them zinging
> On envious strings, and you are the center.
> They are assailing your brain like numerals,
> They contort your hair
>
> Beneath the flat handkerchief you wear instead of a hat.
> They are making a cat's cradle, they are suicidal.
> Their death-pegs stud your gloves, it is no use running.
> The black veil molds to your lips:
> They are fools.
>
> After, they stagger and weave, under no banner.
> After, they crawl
> Dispatched, into trenches of grass.
> Ossifying like junked statues—
> Gelded and wingless. Not heroes. Not heroes.

179   THE SWARM. When bees swarm, they sometimes cluster in a ball high in a tree, while they make up their minds where to go. Any loud sudden noise, such as gunfire, can make them come down to a much lower level where the beekeeper can reach them, and collect them into a box or skip. He then shakes the whole lot out on to a broad surface that slopes up into a fresh empty hive. The bees obediently march up into the hive, as described towards the end of this poem.

     The poet uses an incident she watched in a neighbouring beekeeper's garden.

182   THE APPLICANT. Introducing this poem in a reading prepared for BBC radio, SP commented: 'In this poem, . . . the speaker is an executive, a sort of exacting super-salesman. He wants to be sure the applicant for his marvelous product really needs it and will treat it right.'

183   DADDY. In a reading prepared for BBC radio, she said of this poem: 'Here is a poem spoken by a girl with an Electra complex. Her father died while she thought he was God. Her case is complicated by the fact that her father was also a Nazi and her mother very possibly part Jewish. In the daughter the two strains marry and paralyse each other—she has to act out the awful little allegory once over before she is free of it.'

188   FEVER 103°. In a BBC radio reading she prepared, SP introduced this poem as follows: '[It] is about two kinds of fire—the fires of hell, which merely agonize, and the fires of heaven, which purify. During the poem, the first sort of fire suffers itself into the second.'

She had made a somewhat earlier (but undated) attempt to break through to the substance of this poem. After several pages of what looks like feverish exploration of the theme, her earlier controls took over, and reduced the confusion to the following, which she left in manùscript, unfinalized:

> Four o'clock, and the fever soaks from me like honey.
> O ignorant heart!
> All night I have heard
>
> The meaningless cry of babies. Such a sea
> Broods in the newsprint!
> Fish-grease, fish-bones, refuse of atrocities.
>
> Bleached and finished, I surface
> Among the blanched, boiled instruments, the virginal curtains.
> Here is a white sky. Here is the beauty
>
> Of cool mouths and hands open and natural as roses.
> My glass of water refracts the morning.
> My baby is sleeping.

192 BY CANDLELIGHT. The candlestick was a small brass image of Hercules, in his lion's pelt, kneeling under the candle. Behind his heels, five brass balls completed the design. (Cf. the poem 'Nick and the Candlestick', No. 196.)

194 ARIEL. The name of a horse which she rode, at a riding school on Dartmoor, in Devonshire.

196 NICK AND THE CANDLESTICK. 'In this poem,' she said in a reading prepared for BBC radio, '. . . a mother nurses her baby son by candlelight and finds in him a beauty which, while it may not ward off the world's ill, does redeem her share of it.'

198 LADY LAZARUS. In a reading prepared for BBC radio, SP introduced this poem: 'The speaker is a woman who has the great and terrible gift of being reborn. The only trouble is, she has to die first. She is the Phoenix, the libertarian spirit, what you will. She is also just a good, plain, very resourceful woman.'

201 THE NIGHT DANCES. A revolving dance which her baby son performed at night in his crib.

203 THALIDOMIDE. By the time this poem was written, the connection between the tranquillizing drug thalidomide and the 1960–1 crop of deformed babies was well established.

205 DEATH & CO. Introducing this poem in a reading prepared for BBC radio, she said: 'This poem is about the double or schizophrenic nature of death—the marmoreal coldness of Blake's death mask, say, hand in glove with the fearful softness of worms, water and other katabolists. I imagine these two aspects of death as two men, two business friends, who have come to call.'

 The actual occasion was a visit by two well-meaning men who invited TH to live abroad at a tempting salary, and whom she therefore resented.

208 MARY'S SONG.

 l. 10 *Over the cicatrix of Poland*: In one of the final typescripts of this poem (a carbon), this line is corrected, in SP's hand, to:

> Over scoured Poland, burnt-out
> Germany.

The earlier reading has been kept, as in all published versions.

212 EAVESDROPPER. This poem was written in slightly longer form on 15 October 1962, but reduced to its present length, by simple deletions, on 31 December. No final copy was made.

1963

From the beginning of this year, in what was to be the coldest winter in England since 1947, SP lived at 23 Fitzroy Road.

On 23 January her novel *The Bell Jar*, published under the pseudonym Victoria Lucas, came out in London.

On 11 February she died by her own hand.

213   SHEEP IN FOG. Introducing this poem in a reading prepared for BBC radio, SP said: 'In this poem, the speaker's horse is proceeding at a slow, cold walk down a hill of macadam to the stable at the bottom. It is December. It is foggy. In the fog there are sheep.'

It was first written on 2 December 1962. The last three lines of the original version were replaced by the present final three-line verse on 28 January 1963.

215   TOTEM. She explained this poem in conversation as 'a pile of interconnected images, like a totem pole'.

l.5   *Dawn gilds the farmers . . .*: She imagines the West country farmers in the early morning train, on their way up to London to the great meat market at Smithfield, whose 'white towers' she had been able to see from Primrose Hill during her first residence in London.

l. 11   *In the bowl . . .*: A pyrex bowl, used on different occasions both for her son's afterbirth and the cleaned body of a hare.

l. 18   *a counterfeit snake*: an articulated toy snake of scorch-patterned bamboo joints.

The 'Ariel' Poems

Sylvia Plath's own prepared collection of poems, titled *Ariel*, was ordered as follows:

1	Morning Song	22	The Courage of Shutting-Up
2	The Couriers	23	Nick and the Candlestick
3	The Rabbit Catcher	24	Berck-Plage
4	Thalidomide	25	Gulliver
5	The Applicant	26	Getting There
6	Barren Woman	27	Medusa
7	Lady Lazarus	28	Purdah
8	Tulips	29	The Moon and the Yew Tree
9	A Secret	30	A Birthday Present
10	The Jailer	31	Letter in November
11	Cut	32	Amnesiac
12	Elm	33	The Rival
13	The Night Dances	34	Daddy
14	The Detective	35	You're
15	Ariel	36	Fever 103°
16	Death & Co.	37	The Bee Meeting
17	Magi	38	The Arrival of the Bee Box
18	Lesbos	39	Stings
19	The Other	40	The Swarm
20	Stopped Dead	41	Wintering
21	Poppies in October		

Notes
Translation

The only translations by Sylvia Plath that survive are four sonnets of Ronsard and one poem by Rilke, made in the course of studying French and German literature. Following is her literal rendering of Rilke's 'A Prophet', made about 1954:

Dilated by immense visions
bright with the firelight from the outcome
of judgments, which never destroy him,
are his eyes, gazing out from under thick
brows. And in his inmost soul
already words are raising themselves again.

Not his words (for what would his be
and how indulgently would they be lavished?)
but others, severe: pieces of iron, stones,
which he must dissolve like a volcano

in order to cast them forth in the outburst
from his mouth, which curses and damns;
while his forehead, like the face of a hound
seeks to transmit that

which the Master chooses within his mind:
this One, this One, whom they all might find
if they followed the great pointing hand
which reveals him as he is: enraged.

A Concordance with Published Volumes

Following are the contents of the four previously published volumes of Sylvia Plath's poetry, with the poems listed according to the numbers they have been given in the present collected edition:

The Colossus (London, 1960; New York, 1962): Nos. 13, 15, 17, 35, 37, 38, 44, 47, 49, 50, 55, 59, 60, 61, 63, 72, 73, 74, 75, 76, 77, 78, 87, 89, 91, 92, 93, 94, 96, 97, 98, 99, 100, 102, 104, 105, 106, 112, 113, 114, 117, 119, 120, 121
Ariel (London and New York, 1965): Nos. 122, 123, 138, 142, 147, 153, 158, 163, 167, 170, 173, 176, 177, 178, 180, 182, 183, 184, 188, 191, 194, 195, 196, 198, 199, 200, 201, 202, 204, 205, 206, 213, 214, 215, 217, 220, 221, 222, 223, 224
Crossing the Water (London and New York, 1971): Nos. 124, 125, 126, 127, 128, 129, 130, 131, 132, 134, 135, 136, 137, 140, 141, 143, 144, 145, 148, 149, 150, 151, 152, 154, 155, 159, 160, 161, 162, 165, 166, 193
Winter Trees (London, 1971; New York, 1972): Nos. 157, 164, 168, 172, 175, 179, 186, 187, 190, 192, 197, 203, 208, 209, 210, 211, 216, 218, 219

JUVENILIA

A Selection of Fifty Early Poems

The fifty poems printed here are a selection from Sylvia Plath's work produced mainly in the three or four years preceding 1956. Many of them were written as class assignments for her English professor at Smith College, Alfred Young Fisher, and the typescripts bear his profuse and detailed comments. In most cases, she seems to have followed his textual suggestions.

Bitter Strawberries

All that morning in the strawberry field
They talked about the Russians.
Squatted down between the rows
We listened.
We heard the head woman say,
'Bomb them off the map.'

Horseflies buzzed, paused and stung.
And the taste of strawberries
Turned thick and sour.

Mary said slowly, 'I've got a fella
Old enough to go.
If anything should happen . . .'

The sky was high and blue.
Two children laughed at tag
In the tall grass,
Leaping awkward and long-legged
Across the rutted road.
The fields were full of bronzed young men
Hoeing lettuce, weeding celery.

'The draft is passed,' the woman said.
'We ought to have bombed them long ago.'
'Don't,' pleaded the little girl
With blond braids.

Her blue eyes swam with vague terror.
She added pettishly, 'I can't see why
You're always talking this way . . .'
'Oh, stop worrying, Nelda,'
Snapped the woman sharply.
She stood up, a thin commanding figure
In faded dungarees.
Businesslike she asked us, 'How many quarts?'
She recorded the total in her notebook,
And we all turned back to picking.

Kneeling over the rows,
We reached among the leaves
With quick practiced hands,
Cupping the berry protectively before
Snapping off the stem
Between thumb and forefinger.

Family Reunion

Outside in the street I hear
A car door slam; voices coming near;
Incoherent scraps of talk
And high heels clicking up the walk;
The doorbell rends the noonday heat
With copper claws;
A second's pause.
  The dull drums of my pulses beat
Against a silence wearing thin.
The door now opens from within.
Oh, hear the clash of people meeting—
The laughter and the screams of greeting:

Fat always, and out of breath,
A greasy smack on every cheek
From Aunt Elizabeth;
There, that's the pink, pleased squeak
Of Cousin Jane, our spinster with
The faded eyes
And hands like nervous butterflies;
While rough as splintered wood
  Across them all
Rasps the jarring baritone of Uncle Paul;

300

Juvenilia

The youngest nephew gives a fretful whine
And drools at the reception line.

Like a diver on a lofty spar of land
Atop the flight of stairs I stand.
A whirlpool leers at me,
Absorbent as a sponge;
I cast off my identity
And make the fatal plunge.

Female Author

All day she plays at chess with the bones of the world:
Favored (while suddenly the rains begin
Beyond the window) she lies on cushions curled
And nibbles an occasional bonbon of sin.

Prim, pink-breasted, feminine, she nurses
Chocolate fancies in rose-papered rooms
Where polished highboys whisper creaking curses
And hothouse roses shed immoral blooms.

The garnets on her fingers twinkle quick
And blood reflects across the manuscript;
She muses on the odor, sweet and sick,
Of festering gardenias in a crypt,

And lost in subtle metaphor, retreats
From gray child faces crying in the streets.

April 18

the slime of all my yesterdays
rots in the hollow of my skull

and if my stomach would contract
because of some explicable phenomenon
such as pregnancy or constipation

I would not remember you

or that because of sleep
infrequent as a moon of greencheese
that because of food
nourishing as violet leaves
that because of these

and in a few fatal yards of grass
in a few spaces of sky and treetops

a future was lost yesterday
as easily and irretrievably
as a tennis ball at twilight

Gold mouths cry

Gold mouths cry with the green young
certainty of the bronze boy
remembering a thousand autumns
and how a hundred thousand leaves
came sliding down his shoulderblades
persuaded by his bronze heroic reason.
We ignore the coming doom of gold
and we are glad in this bright metal season.
Even the dead laugh among the goldenrod.

The bronze boy stands kneedeep in centuries,
and never grieves,
remembering a thousand autumns,
with sunlight of a thousand years upon his lips
and his eyes gone blind with leaves.

Dirge for a Joker

Always in the middle of a kiss
Came the profane stimulus to cough;
Always from the pulpit during service
Leaned the devil prompting you to laugh.

Behind mock-ceremony of your grief
Lurked the burlesque instinct of the ham;
You never altered your amused belief
That life was a mere monumental sham.

Juvenilia

From the comic accident of birth
To the final grotesque joke of death
Your malady of sacrilegious mirth
Spread gay contagion with each clever breath.

Now you must play the straight man for a term
And tolerate the humor of the worm.

To Eva Descending the Stair
A Villanelle

Clocks cry: stillness is a lie, my dear;
The wheels revolve, the universe keeps running.
(Proud you halt upon the spiral stair.)

The asteroids turn traitor in the air,
And planets plot with old elliptic cunning;
Clocks cry: stillness is a lie, my dear.

Red the unraveled rose sings in your hair:
Blood springs eternal if the heart be burning.
(Proud you halt upon the spiral stair.)

Cryptic stars wind up the atmosphere,
In solar schemes the tilted suns go turning;
Clocks cry: stillness is a lie, my dear.

Loud the immortal nightingales declare:
Love flames forever if the flesh be yearning.
(Proud you halt upon the spiral stair.)

Circling zodiac compels the year.
Intolerant beauty never will be learning.
Clocks cry: stillness is a lie, my dear.
(Proud you halt upon the spiral stair.)

Cinderella

The prince leans to the girl in scarlet heels,
Her green eyes slant, hair flaring in a fan
Of silver as the rondo slows; now reels
Begin on tilted violins to span

Juvenilia

The whole revolving tall glass palace hall,
Where guests slide gliding into light like wine;
Rose candles flicker on the lilac wall
Reflecting in a million flagons' shine,

And gilded couples all in whirling trance
Follow holiday revel begun long since,
Until near twelve the strange girl all at once
Guilt-stricken halts, pales, clings to the prince

As amid the hectic music and cocktail talk
She hears the caustic ticking of the clock.

Jilted

My thoughts are crabbed and sallow,
  My tears like vinegar,
Or the bitter blinking yellow
  Of an acetic star.

Tonight the caustic wind, love,
  Gossips late and soon,
And I wear the wry-faced pucker of
  The sour lemon moon.

While like an early summer plum,
  Puny, green, and tart,
Droops upon its wizened stem
  My lean, unripened heart.

Sonnet: To Eva

All right, let's say you could take a skull and break it
The way you'd crack a clock; you'd crush the bone
Between steel palms of inclination, take it,
Observing the wreck of metal and rare stone.

This was a woman: her loves and stratagems
Betrayed in mute geometry of broken
Cogs and disks, inane mechanic whims,
And idle coils of jargon yet unspoken.

Juvenilia

Not man nor demigod could put together
The scraps of rusted reverie, the wheels
Of notched tin platitudes concerning weather,
Perfume, politics, and fixed ideals.

The idiot bird leaps up and drunken leans
To chirp the hour in lunatic thirteens.

Bluebeard

I am sending back the key
that let me into bluebeard's study;
because he would make love to me
I am sending back the key;
in his eye's darkroom I can see
my X-rayed heart, dissected body:
I am sending back the key
that let me into bluebeard's study.

Aquatic Nocturne

deep in liquid indigo
turquoise slivers
of dilute light

quiver in thin streaks
of bright tinfoil
on mobile jet:

pale flounder
waver by
tilting silver:

in the shallows
agile minnows
flicker gilt:

grapeblue mussels
dilate lithe and
pliant valves:

305

Juvenilia

dull lunar globes
  of bulbous jellyfish
    glow milkgreen:

eels twirl
  in wily spirals
    on elusive tails:

adroit lobsters
  amble darkly olive
    on shrewd claws:

down where sound
  comes blunt and wan
    like the bronze tone
      of a sunken gong.

Notes to a Neophyte

Take the general mumble,
blunt as the faceless gut
of an anonymous clam,
vernacular as the strut
of a slug or small preamble
by snail under hump of home:

metamorphose the mollusk
of vague vocabulary
with structural discipline:
stiffen the ordinary
malleable mask
to the granite grin of bone.

For such a tempering task,
heat furnace of paradox
in an artifice of ice;
make love and logic mix,
and remember, if tedious risk
seems to jeopardize this:

it was a solar turbine
gave molten earth a frame,

and it took the diamond stone
a weight of world and time
being crystallized from carbon
to the hardest substance known.

Metamorphoses of the Moon

Cold moons withdraw, refusing to come to terms
with the pilot who dares all heaven's harms
  to raid the zone where fate begins,
flings silver gauntlet of his plane at space,
demanding satisfaction; no duel takes place:
  the mute air merely thins and thins.

Sky won't be drawn closer: absolute,
it holds aloof, a shrouded parachute
  always the same distance from
the falling man who never will abstain
from asking, but inventive, hopes; in vain
  challenges the silent dome.

No violation but gives dividends
of slow disaster: the bitten apple ends
  the eden of bucolic eve:
understanding breaks through the skull's shell
and like a cuckoo in the nest makes hell
  for naïve larks who starve and grieve.

What prince has ever seized the shining grail
but that it turned into a milking pail?
  It's likely that each secret sought
will prove to be some common parlor fake:
a craft with paint and powder that can make
  cleopatra from a slut.

For most exquisite truths are artifice
framed in disciplines of fire and ice
  which conceal incongruous
elements like dirty socks and scraps
of day-old bread and egg-stained plates; perhaps
  such sophistry can placate us.

Juvenilia

But yet the perverse imp within will probe
beneath the fringes of forbidden robe,
  seduced by curiosity,
until in disenchantment our eyes glut
themselves on the clay toes and short clubfoot
  which mar the idol's sanctity.

The choice between the mica mystery
of moonlight or the pockmarked face we see
  through the scrupulous telescope
is always to be made: innocence
is a fairy-tale; intelligence
  hangs itself on its own rope.

Either way we choose, the angry witch
will punish us for saying which is which;
  in fatal equilibrium
we poise on perilous poles that freeze us in
a cross of contradiction, racked between
  the fact of doubt, the faith of dream.

Dialogue *En Route*

'If only something would happen!'
sighed Eve, the elevator-girl ace,
to Adam the arrogant matador
as they shot past the forty-ninth floor
in a rocketing vertical clockcase,
fast as a fallible falcon.

'I wish millionaire uncles and aunts
would umbrella like liberal toadstools
in a shower of Chanel, Dior gowns,
filet mignon and walloping wines,
a pack of philanthropical fools
to indulge my extravagant wants.'

Erect in his folderol cloak
sham Adam the matador cried:
'O may G-men all die of the choler,
and my every chimerical dollar
breed innumerable bills, bona fide:
a hot hyperbolical joke!'

Juvenilia

Said Eve: 'I wish venomous nematodes
were bewitched to assiduous lovers,
each one an inveterate gallant
with Valentino's crack technical talent
for recreation down under the covers:
erotic and elegant episodes.'

Added Adam, that simian swell,
with his modish opposable thumb:
'O for ubiquitous free aphrodisiacs,
and for pumpkins to purr into Cadillacs
and voluptuous Venus to come
waltzing up to me out of her cockle-shell.'

Breaking through gravity's garrison,
Eve, the elevator-girl ace,
and Adam the arrogant matador
shot past the ninety-fourth floor
to corral the conundrum of space
at its cryptic celestial origin.

They both watched the barometer sink
as the world swiveled round in its orbit
and thousands were born and dropped dead,
when, from the inane overhead
(too quick for the pair to absorb it),
came a gargantuan galactic wink.

To a Jilted Lover

Cold on my narrow cot I lie
  and in sorrow look
through my window-square of black:

figured in the midnight sky,
  a mosaic of stars
diagrams the falling years,

while from the moon, my lover's eye
  chills me to death
with radiance of his frozen faith.

Juvenilia

Once I wounded him with so
  small a thorn
I never thought his flesh would burn

or that the heat within would grow
  until he stood
incandescent as a god;

now there is nowhere I can go
  to hide from him:
moon and sun reflect his flame.

In the morning all shall be
  the same again:
stars pale before the angry dawn;

the gilded cock will turn for me
  the rack of time
until the peak of noon has come

and by that glare, my love will see
  how I am still
blazing in my golden hell.

The Dream

'Last night,' he said, 'I slept well
except for two uncanny dreams
that came before the change of weather
when I rose and opened all
the shutters to let warm wind feather
with wet plumage through my rooms.

'In the first dream I was driving
down the dark in a black hearse
with many men until I crashed
a light, and right away a raving
woman followed us and rushed
to halt our car in headlong course.

'Crying, she came to the island
where we stopped, and with a curse
demanded that I pay a fine
for being such a rude assailant
and damaging the whole unseen
lighting plant of the universe.

'Behind me then I heard a voice
warning me to hold her hand
and kiss her on the mouth for she
loved me and a brave embrace
would avoid all penalty.
"I know, I know," I told my friend.

'But yet I waited to be fined
and took the woman's bright subpoena
(while she washed the way with tears),
then drove to you upon the wind. . . .
I do not tell you the nightmare
which occurred to me in China.'

Sonnet: To Time

Today we move in jade and cease with garnet
Amid the ticking jeweled clocks that mark
Our years. Death comes in a casual steel car, yet
We vaunt our days in neon and scorn the dark.

But outside the diabolic steel of this
Most plastic-windowed city, I can hear
The lone wind raving in the gutter, his
Voice crying exclusion in my ear.

So cry for the pagan girl left picking olives
Beside a sunblue sea, and mourn the flagon
Raised to toast a thousand kings, for all gives
Sorrow; weep for the legendary dragon.

Time is a great machine of iron bars
That drains eternally the milk of stars.

The Trial of Man

The ordinary milkman brought that dawn
  Of destiny, delivered to the door
In square hermetic bottles, while the sun
  Ruled decree of doomsday on the floor.

The morning paper clocked the headline hour
  You drank your coffee like original sin,
And at the jet-plane anger of God's roar
  Got up to let the suave blue policeman in.

Impaled upon a stern angelic stare
  You were condemned to serve the legal limit
And burn to death within your neon hell.

Now, disciplined in the strict ancestral chair,
  You sit, solemn-eyed, about to vomit,
The future an electrode in your skull.

April Aubade

Worship this world of watercolor mood
in glass pagodas hung with veils of green
where diamonds jangle hymns within the blood
and sap ascends the steeple of the vein.

A saintly sparrow jargons madrigals
to waken dreamers in the milky dawn,
while tulips bow like a college of cardinals
before that papal paragon, the sun.

Christened in a spindrift of snowdrop stars,
where on pink-fluted feet the pigeons pass
and jonquils sprout like solomon's metaphors,
my love and I go garlanded with grass.

Again we are deluded and infer
that somehow we are younger than we were.

Go get the goodly squab

Go get the goodly squab in gold-lobed corn
And pluck the droll-flecked quail where thick they lie;
Reap the round blue pigeon from roof ridge,
But let the fast-feathered eagle fly.

Let the fast-feathered eagle fly
And the skies crack through with thunder;
Hide, hide, in the deep nest
Lest the lightning strike you to cinder.

Go snare the sleeping bear in leaf-lined den
And trap the muskrat napping in slack sun;
Dupe the dull sow lounging snout in mud,
But let the galloping antelope run.

Let the galloping antelope run
And the snow blow up behind;
Hide, hide, in the safe cave
Lest the blizzard drive you blind.

Go cull the purple snails from slothful shells
And bait the drowsing trout by the brook's brim;
Gather idle oysters from green shoals,
But let the quicksilver mackerel swim.

Let the quicksilver mackerel swim
Where the black wave topples down;
Hide, hide, in the warm port
Lest the water drag you to drown.

Trio of Love Songs

(*1*)

Major faults in granite
mark a mortal lack,
yet individual planet
directs all zodiac.

Diagram of mountains
graphs a fever chart,

Juvenilia

yet astronomic fountains
  exit from the heart.

Tempo of strict ocean
  metronomes the blood,
yet ordered lunar motion
  proceeds from private flood.

Drama of each season
  plots doom from above,
yet all angelic reason
  moves to our minor love.

(2)

My love for you is more
  athletic than a verb,
agile as a star
  the tents of sun absorb.

Treading circus tightropes
  of each syllable,
the brazen jackanapes
  would fracture if he fell.

Acrobat of space,
  the daring adjective
plunges for a phrase
  describing arcs of love.

Nimble as a noun,
  he catapults in air;
a planetary swoon
  could climax his career,

but adroit conjunction
  eloquently shall
link to his lyric action
  a periodic goal.

Juvenilia

(3)

If you dissect a bird
   to diagram the tongue,
you'll cut the chord
   articulating song.

If you flay a beast
   to marvel at the mane,
you'll wreck the rest
   from which the fur began.

If you assault a fish
   to analyse the fin,
your hands will crush
   the generating bone.

If you pluck out my heart
   to find what makes it move,
you'll halt the clock
   that syncopates our love.

Lament
A Villanelle

The sting of bees took away my father
  who walked in a swarming shroud of wings
and scorned the tick of the falling weather.

Lightning licked in a yellow lather
  but missed the mark with snaking fangs:
the sting of bees took away my father.

Trouncing the sea like a raging bather,
  he rode the flood in a pride of prongs
and scorned the tick of the falling weather.

A scowl of sun struck down my mother,
  tolling her grave with golden gongs,
but the sting of bees took away my father.

He counted the guns of god a bother,
  laughed at the ambush of angels' tongues,
and scorned the tick of the falling weather.

Juvenilia

O ransack the four winds and find another
  man who can mangle the grin of kings:
the sting of bees took away my father
who scorned the tick of the falling weather.

Doomsday

The idiot bird leaps out and drunken leans
  Atop the broken universal clock:
The hour is crowed in lunatic thirteens.

Our painted stages fall apart by scenes
  While all the actors halt in mortal shock:
The idiot bird leaps out and drunken leans.

Streets crack through in havoc-split ravines
  As the doomstruck city crumbles block by block:
The hour is crowed in lunatic thirteens.

Fractured glass flies down in smithereens;
  Our lucky relics have been put in hock:
The idiot bird leaps out and drunken leans.

God's monkey wrench has blasted all machines;
  We never thought to hear the holy cock:
The hour is crowed in lunatic thirteens.

Too late to ask if end was worth the means,
  Too late to calculate the toppling stock:
The idiot bird leaps out and drunken leans,
The hour is crowed in lunatic thirteens.

Moonsong at Morning

O moon of illusion,
  enchanting men
with tinsel vision
  along the vein,

cocks crow up a rival
  to mock your face

Juvenilia

and eclipse that oval
  which conjured us

to leave our reason
  and come to this
fabled horizon
  of caprice.

Dawn shall dissever
  your silver veil
which let lover think lover
  beautiful;

the light of logic
  will show us that
all moonstruck magic
  is dissolute:

no sweet disguises
  withstand that stare
whose candor exposes
  love's paling sphere.

In gardens of squalor
  the sleepers wake
as their golden jailer
  turns the rack;

each sacred body
  night yielded up
is mangled by study
  of microscope:

facts have blasted
  the angel's frame
and stern truth twisted
  the radiant limb.

Reflect in terror
  the scorching sun:
dive at your mirror
  and drown within.

Juvenilia

Doom of Exiles

Now we, returning from the vaulted domes
Of our colossal sleep, come home to find
A tall metropolis of catacombs
Erected down the gangways of our mind.

Green alleys where we reveled have become
The infernal haunt of demon dangers;
Both seraph song and violins are dumb;
Each clock tick consecrates the death of strangers.

Backward we traveled to reclaim the day
Before we fell, like Icarus, undone;
All we find are altars in decay
And profane words scrawled black across the sun.

Still, stubbornly we try to crack the nut
In which the riddle of our race is shut.

16 April 1954

The Dispossessed

The enormous mortgage must be paid somehow,
  so if you can dream up any saving plan
tell me quick, darling, tell me now.

An odd disease has hit our holy cow,
  no milk or honey fills the empty can;
the enormous mortgage must be paid somehow.

If you've a plot to halt the lethal flow
  of weevil tribe and locust caravan
tell me quick, darling, tell me now.

Our creditor advances with a bow
  to cast lock, stock and barrel under ban;
the enormous mortgage must be paid somehow.

If you can think of means to mend the vow
  we broke the minute that the world began
tell me quick, darling, tell me now.

Juvenilia

We've squandered all the banker will allow
  and mislaid every vital talisman;
the enormous mortgage must be paid somehow:
tell me quick, darling, tell me now!

Admonitions

Oh never try to knock on rotten wood
  or play another card game when you've won;
never try to know more than you should.

The magic golden apples all look good
  although the wicked witch has poisoned one.
oh never try to knock on rotten wood.

From here the moon seems smooth as angel-food,
  from here you can't see spots upon the sun;
never try to know more than you should.

The suave dissembling cobra wears a hood
  and swaggers like a proper gentleman;
oh never try to knock on rotten wood.

While angels wear a wakeful attitude
  disguise beguiles and mortal mischief's done:
never try to know more than you should.

For deadly secrets strike when understood
  and lucky stars all exit on the run:
never try to knock on rotten wood,
never try to know more than you should.

Never try to trick me with a kiss

Never try to trick me with a kiss
Pretending that the birds are here to stay;
The dying man will scoff in scorn at this.

A stone can masquerade where no heart is
And virgins rise where lustful Venus lay:
Never try to trick me with a kiss.

319

Juvenilia

Our noble doctor claims the pain is his,
While stricken patients let him have his say;
The dying man will scoff in scorn at this.

Each virile bachelor dreads paralysis,
The old maid in the gable cries all day:
Never try to trick me with a kiss.

The suave eternal serpents promise bliss
To mortal children longing to be gay;
The dying man will scoff in scorn at this.

Sooner or later something goes amiss;
The singing birds pack up and fly away;
So never try to trick me with a kiss:
The dying man will scoff in scorn at this.

The Dead

Revolving in oval loops of solar speed,
Couched in cauls of clay as in holy robes,
Dead men render love and war no heed,
Lulled in the ample womb of the full-tilt globe.

No spiritual Caesars are these dead;
They want no proud paternal kingdom come;
And when at last they blunder into bed
World-wrecked, they seek only oblivion.

Rolled round with goodly loam and cradled deep,
These bone shanks will not wake immaculate
To trumpet-toppling dawn of doomstruck day:
They loll forever in colossal sleep;
Nor can God's stern, shocked angels cry them up
From their fond, final, infamous decay.

Danse macabre

Down among strict roots and rocks,
    eclipsed beneath blind lid of land
goes the grass-embroidered box.

Juvenilia

Arranged in sheets of ice, the fond
    skeleton still craves to have
fever from the world behind.

Hands reach back to relics of
    nippled moons, extinct and cold,
frozen in designs of love.

At twelve, each skull is aureoled
    with recollection's ticking thorns
winding up the raveled mold.

Needles nag like unicorns,
    assault a sleeping virgin's shroud
till her stubborn body burns.

Lured by brigands in the blood,
    shanks of bone now resurrect,
inveigled to forsake the sod.

Eloping from their slabs, abstract
    couples court by milk of moon:
sheer silver blurs their phantom act.

Luminous, the town of stone
    anticipates the warning sound
of cockcrow crying up the dawn.

With kiss of cinders, ghosts descend,
compelled to deadlock underground.

Circus in Three Rings

In the circus tent of a hurricane
designed by a drunken god
my extravagant heart blows up again
in a rampage of champagne-colored rain
and the fragments whir like a weather vane
while the angels all applaud.

Daring as death and debonair
I invade my lion's den;
a rose of jeopardy flames in my hair

yet I flourish my whip with a fatal flair
defending my perilous wounds with a chair
while the gnawings of love begin.

Mocking as Mephistopheles,
eclipsed by magician's disguise,
my demon of doom tilts on a trapeze,
winged rabbits revolving about his knees,
only to vanish with devilish ease
in a smoke that sears my eyes.

Prologue to Spring

The winter landscape hangs in balance now,
   Transfixed by glare of blue from gorgon's eye;
The skaters freeze within a stone tableau.

Air alters into glass and the whole sky
   Grows brittle as a tilted china bowl;
Hill and valley stiffen row on row.

Each fallen leaf is trapped by spell of steel,
   Crimped like fern in the quartz atmosphere;
Repose of sculpture holds the country still.

What countermagic can undo the snare
   Which has stopped the season in its tracks
And suspended all that might occur?

Locked in crystal caskets are the lakes,
   Yet as we wonder what can come of ice
Green-singing birds explode from all the rocks.

Song for a Revolutionary Love

O throw it away, throw it all away on the wind:
   first let the heavenly foliage go,
   and page by pride the good books blow;
scatter smug angels with your hand.

Undo the doings of the fathering age:
  chuck the broken acropolis out,
  fling the seven wonders after that
with struts and props of the holy stage.

Disrupt the calendars next; send the duteous
  packing without a compass or scale
  to chart the measure of fortune's wheel;
let nothing be left to swaddle us.

Unravel antique samplers, unwind the clocks,
  till unruly children stream down the sky
  and old maids on impromptu petticoats fly
with begonia and building blocks.

Now empty boxes of the hoodwinked dead
  upon the pouring air until
  god hears from his great sunstruck hell
the chittering crackpots that he made.

Then hurl the bare world like a bluegreen ball
  back into the holocaust
  to burn away the humbug rust
and again together begin it all.

Sonnet to Satan

In darkroom of your eye the moonly mind
somersaults to counterfeit eclipse:
bright angels black out over logic's land
under shutter of their handicaps.

Commanding that corkscrew comet jet forth ink
to pitch the white world down in swiveling flood,
you overcast all order's noonday rank
and turn god's radiant photograph to shade.

Steepling snake in that contrary light
invades the dilate lens of genesis
to print your flaming image in birthspot
with characters no cockcrow can deface.

O maker of proud planet's negative,
obscure the scalding sun till no clocks move.

A Sorcerer Bids Farewell to Seem

I'm through with this grand looking-glass hotel
where adjectives play croquet with flamingo nouns;
methinks I shall absent me for a while
from rhetoric of these rococo queens.
Item: chuck out royal rigmarole of props
and auction off each rare white-rabbit verb;
send my muse Alice packing with gaudy scraps
of mushroom simile and gryphon garb.

My native sleight-of-hand is wearing out:
mad hatter's hat yields no new metaphor,
the jabberwock will not translate his songs:
it's time to vanish like the cheshire cat
alone to that authentic island where
cabbages are cabbages; kings: kings.

Midsummer Mobile

Begin by dipping your brush into clear light.
Then syncopate a sky of Dufy-blue
With tilted spars of sloops revolved by white
Gulls in a feathered fugue of wings. Outdo

Seurat: fleck schooner flanks with sun and set
A tremolo of turquoise quivering in
The tessellated wave. Now nimbly let
A tinsel pizzicato on fish fin

Be plucked from caves of dappled amber where
A mermaid odalisque lolls at her ease
With orange scallops tangled in wet hair,
Fresh from the mellow palette of Matisse:

Suspend this day, so singularly designed,
Like a rare Calder mobile in your mind.

324

On Looking into the Eyes of a Demon Lover

Here are two pupils
  whose moons of black
transform to cripples
  all who look:

each lovely lady
  who peers inside
takes on the body
  of a toad.

Within these mirrors
  the world inverts:
the fond admirer's
  burning darts

turn back to injure
  the thrusting hand
and inflame to danger
  the scarlet wound.

I sought my image
  in the scorching glass,
for what fire could damage
  a witch's face?

So I stared in that furnace
  where beauties char
but found radiant Venus
  reflected there.

Insolent storm strikes at the skull

Insolent storm strikes at the skull,
assaults the sleeping citadel,
knocking the warden to his knees
in impotence, to sue for peace,
while wantonly amused by this,
wind wakes the whole metropolis.
Skeptic cyclones try the bone
of strict and sacred skeleton;
polemic gales prove point by point

325

how flesh cleaves fast to frozen joint,
and a hurricane headache rocks
the temples of the orthodox.

Abracadabra of the rain
drowns Noah's prayers with distain,
drives priest and prostitute in doorways,
bereft of Moses and of mores;
no ancient blueprint builds an ark
to navigate this final dark.
River floods transcend the level
demarcating good from evil,
and casuist arguments run riot
inundating Eden's quiet:
all absolutes that angels give
flounder in the relative.

Lightning conjures God's globe off its
orbit; neither law nor prophets
can rectify truant intent
to doublecross the firmament.
Now earth rejects communication
with heaven's autocratic station,
and violates celestial custom
by seceding from the solar system.
Scintillant irony inspires
independent rebel fires
till the Announcer's voice is lost
in heresies of holocaust.

Denouement

The telegram says you have gone away
And left our bankrupt circus on its own;
There is nothing more for me to say.

The maestro gives the singing birds their pay
And they buy tickets for the tropic zone;
The telegram says you have gone away.

The clever woolly dogs have had their day
They shoot the dice for one remaining bone;
There is nothing more for me to say.

Juvenilia

The lion and the tigers turn to clay
And Jumbo sadly trumpets into stone;
The telegram says you have gone away.

The morbid cobra's wits have run astray;
He rents his poisons out by telephone;
There is nothing more for me to say.

The colored tents all topple in the bay;
The magic sawdust writes: address unknown.
The telegram says you have gone away;
There is nothing more for me to say.

Two Lovers and a Beachcomber by the Real Sea

Cold and final, the imagination
  Shuts down its fabled summer house;
Blue views are boarded up; our sweet vacation
  Dwindles in the hour-glass.

Thoughts that found a maze of mermaid hair
  Tangling in the tide's green fall
Now fold their wings like bats and disappear
  Into the attic of the skull.

We are not what we might be; what we are
  Outlaws all extrapolation
Beyond the interval of now and here:
  White whales are gone with the white ocean.

A lone beachcomber squats among the wrack
  Of kaleidoscopic shells
Probing fractured Venus with a stick
  Under a tent of taunting gulls.

No sea-change decks the sunken shank of bone
  That chuckles in backtrack of the wave;
Though the mind like an oyster labors on and on,
  A grain of sand is all we have.

Water will run by rule; the actual sun
  Will scrupulously rise and set;
No little man lives in the exacting moon
  And that is that, is that, is that.

Juvenilia

Black Pine Tree in an Orange Light

Tell me what you see in it:
  the pine tree like a Rorschach-blot
black against the orange light:

Plant an orange pumpkin patch
  which at twelve will quaintly hatch
nine black mice with ebon coach,

or walk into the orange and make
  a devil's cataract of black
obscure god's eye with corkscrew fleck;

put orange mistress half in sun,
  half in shade, until her skin
tattoos black leaves on tangerine.

Read black magic or holy book
  or lyric of love in the orange and black
till dark is conquered by orange cock,

but more pragmatic than all of this,
  say how crafty the painter was
to make orange and black ambiguous.

Terminal

Riding home from credulous blue domes,
the dreamer reins his waking appetite
in panic at the crop of catacombs
sprung up like plague of toadstools overnight:
refectories where he reveled have become
the hostelry of worms, rapacious blades
who weave within the skeleton's white womb
a caviare decay of rich brocades.

Turning the tables of this grave gourmet,
the fiendish butler saunters in and serves
for feast the sweetest meat of hell's chef d'œuvres:
his own pale bride upon a flaming tray:
parsleyed with elegies, she lies in state
waiting for his grace to consecrate.

Love Is a Parallax

'Perspective betrays with its dichotomy:
train tracks always meet, not here, but only
  in the impossible mind's eye;
horizons beat a retreat as we embark
on sophist seas to overtake that mark
  where wave pretends to drench real sky.'

'Well then, if we agree, it is not odd
that one man's devil is another's god
  or that the solar spectrum is
a multitude of shaded grays; suspense
on the quicksands of ambivalence
  is our life's whole nemesis.'

So we could rave on, darling, you and I,
until the stars tick out a lullaby
  about each cosmic pro and con;
nothing changes, for all the blazing of
our drastic jargon, but clock hands that move
  implacably from twelve to one.

We raise our arguments like sitting ducks
to knock them down with logic or with luck
  and contradict ourselves for fun;
the waitress holds our coats and we put on
the raw wind like a scarf; love is a faun
  who insists his playmates run.

Now you, my intellectual leprechaun,
would have me swallow the entire sun
  like an enormous oyster, down
the ocean in one gulp: you say a mark
of comet hara-kiri through the dark
  should inflame the sleeping town.

So kiss: the drunks upon the curb and dames
in dubious doorways forget their monday names,
  caper with candles in their heads;
the leaves applaud, and santa claus flies in
scattering candy from a zeppelin,
  playing his prodigal charades.

Juvenilia

The moon leans down to look; the tilting fish
in the rare river wink and laugh; we lavish
    blessings right and left and cry
hello, and then hello again in deaf
churchyard ears until the starlit stiff
    graves all carol in reply.

Now kiss again: till our strict father leans
to call for curtain on our thousand scenes;
    brazen actors mock at him,
multiply pink harlequins and sing
in gay ventriloquy from wing to wing
    while footlights flare and houselights dim.

Tell now, we taunt, where black or white begins
and separate the flutes from violins:
    the algebra of absolutes
explodes in a kaleidoscope of shapes
that jar, while each polemic jackanapes
    joins his enemies' recruits.

The paradox is that 'the play's the thing':
though prima donna pouts and critic stings,
    there burns throughout the line of words,
the cultivated act, a fierce brief fusion
which dreamers call real, and realists, illusion:
    an insight like the flight of birds:

Arrows that lacerate the sky, while knowing
the secret of their ecstasy's in going;
    some day, moving, one will drop,
and, dropping, die, to trace a wound that heals
only to reopen as flesh congeals:
    cycling phoenix never stops.

So we shall walk barefoot on walnut shells
of withered worlds, and stamp out puny hells
    and heavens till the spirits squeak
surrender: to build our bed as high as jack's
bold beanstalk; lie and love till sharp scythe hacks
    away our rationed days and weeks.

Then let the blue tent topple, stars rain down,
and god or void appall us till we drown
    in our own tears: today we start

to pay the piper with each breath, yet love
knows not of death nor calculus above
  the simple sum of heart plus heart.

Aerialist

Each night, this adroit young lady
Lies among sheets
Shredded fine as snowflakes
Until dream takes her body
From bed to strict tryouts
In tightrope acrobatics.

Nightly she balances
Cat-clever on perilous wire
In a gigantic hall,
Footing her delicate dances
To whipcrack and roar
Which speak her maestro's will.

Gilded, coming correct
Across that sultry air,
She steps, halts, hung
In dead center of her act
As great weights drop all about her
And commence to swing.

Lessoned thus, the girl
Parries the lunge and menace
Of every pendulum;
By deft duck and twirl
She draws applause; bright harness
Bites keen into each brave limb

Then, this tough stint done, she curtsies
And serenely plummets down
To traverse glass floor
And get safe home; but, turning with trained eyes,
Tiger-tamer and grinning clown
Squat, bowling black balls at her.

Tall trucks roll in
With a thunder like lions; all aims
And lumbering moves

To trap this outrageous nimble queen
And shatter to atoms
Her nine so slippery lives.

Sighting the stratagem
Of black weight, black ball, black truck,
With a last artful dodge she leaps
Through hoop of that hazardous dream
To sit up stark awake
As the loud alarmclock stops.

Now as penalty for her skill,
By day she must walk in dread
Steel gauntlets of traffic, terror-struck
Lest, out of spite, the whole
Elaborate scaffold of sky overhead
Fall racketing finale on her luck.

Morning in the Hospital Solarium

Sunlight strikes a glass of grapefruit juice,
flaring green through philodendron leaves
in this surrealistic house
of pink and beige, impeccable bamboo,
patronized by convalescent wives;
heat shadows waver noiseless in
bright window-squares until the women seem
to float like dream-fish in the languid limbo
of an undulant aquarium.

Morning: another day, and talk
taxis indolent on whispered wheels;
the starched white coat, the cat's paw walk,
herald distraction: a flock of pastel pills,
turquoise, rose, sierra mauve; needles
that sting no more than love: a room where time
ticks tempo to the casual climb
of mercury in graded tubes, where ills
slowly concede to sun and serum.

Like petulant parakeets corked up in cages
of intricate spunglass routine,
the women wait, fluttering, turning pages
of magazines in elegant ennui,

332

hoping for some incredible dark man
to assault the scene and make some
gaudy miracle occur, to come
and like a burglar steal their fancy:
at noon, anemic husbands visit them.

The Princess and the Goblins

(1)

From fabrication springs the spiral stair
  up which the wakeful princess climbs to find
the source of blanching light that conjured her

to leave her bed of fever and ascend
  a visionary ladder toward the moon
whose holy blue anoints her injured hand.

With finger bandaged where the waspish pin
  flew from the intricate embroidery
and stung according to the witch's plan,

she mounts through malice of the needle's eye,
  trailing her scrupulously simple gown
along bright asterisks by milky way.

Colonnades of angels nod her in
  where ancient, infinite, and beautiful,
her legendary godmother leans down,

spinning a single stubborn thread of wool
  which all the artful wizards cannot crimp
to keep the young girl from her crowning goal.

Initiated by the lunar lamp,
  kindling her within a steepled flame,
the princess hears the thunder and the pomp

of squadrons underground abducting him
  who is the destination of the cord
now bound around her wrist till she redeem
  this miner's boy from goblin bodyguard.

Juvenilia

Guided only by the tug and twitch
  of that mercurial strand, the girl goes down
the darkening stair, undoes the palace latch

and slips unseen past watchmen on the lawn
  dozing around their silvered sentry box.
Across the frosted grass she marks the sheen

of thread conducting her to the worn tracks
  made by miners up the mountainside
among the jagged mazes of the rocks.

Laboring on the tilt of that steep grade
  behind which the declining moon has set,
she recalls queer stories her nurse read

about a goblin raid on miner's hut
  because new excavations came too near
the chambers where their fiendish queen would sit.

Hearing a weird cackle from afar,
  she clutches at the talismanic cord
and confronts a cairn of iron ore.

Suddenly a brazen song is heard
  from the pragmatic boy confined within,
gaily cursing the whole goblin horde.

Inviolate in the circle of that skein,
  looping like faith about her bleeding feet,
the princess frees the miner, stone by stone,
  and leads him home to be her chosen knight.

(3)

The princess coaxes the incredulous boy
  through candid kitchens in the rising sun
to seek the staircase by the glare of day.

Hand in hand, they scale meridian,
  clambering up the creaking heights of heat
until she hears the twittering machine

334

which quaintly wove the fabric of her fate
  behind the zodiac on attic door
with abracadabra from the alphabet.

Pointing toward the spindle's cryptic whir,
  she tells the greenhorn miner to bow down
and honor the great goddess of the air

suspended aloft within her planet-shine.
  Laughing aloud, the dazzled boy demands
why he should kneel before a silly scene

where pigeons promenade the gable-ends
  and coo quadrilles about the blighted core
in a batch of raveled apple rinds.

At his words, the indignant godmother
  vanishes in a labyrinth of hay
while sunlight winds its yarn upon the floor.

O never again will the extravagant straw
  knit up a gilded fable for the child
who weeps before the desolate tableau
  of clockwork that makes the royal blood run cold.

Touch-and-Go

Sing praise for statuary:
For those anchored attitudes
And staunch stone eyes that stare
Through lichen-lid and passing bird-foot
At some steadfast mark
Beyond the inconstant green
Gallop and flick of light
In this precarious park

Where vivid children twirl
Like colored tops through time
Nor stop to understand
How all their play is touch-and-go:
But, Go! they cry, and the swing
Arcs up to the tall tree tip;
Go! and the merry-go-round
Hauls them round with it.

Juvenilia

And I, like the children, caught
In the mortal active verb,
Let my transient eye break a tear
For each quick, flaring game
Of child, leaf and cloud,
While on this same fugue, unmoved,
Those stonier eyes look,
Safe-socketed in rock.

Temper of Time

An ill wind is stalking
  While evil stars whir
And all the gold apples
  Go bad to the core.

Black birds of omen
  Now prowl on the bough;
With a hiss of disaster
  Sibyl's leaves blow.

Through closets of copses
  Tall skeletons walk;
Nightshade and nettles
  Tangle the track.

In the ramshackle meadow
  Where Kilroy would pass
Lurks the sickle-shaped shadow
  Of snake in the grass.

Approaching his cottage
  By crooked detour,
He hears the gruff knocking
  Of the wolf at the door.

His wife and his children
  Hang riddled with shot,
There's a hex on the cradle
  And death in the pot.

Juvenilia

Epitaph in Three Parts

(1)

Rocking across the lapis lazuli sea
   comes a flock of bottle battleships
each with a telegram addressed to me.

'Destroy your mirror and avoid mishaps,'
   chirps the first; 'live on a silent island
where the water blots out all footsteps.'

The second sings: 'Receive no roving gallant
   who seeks to dally in the port till dawn,
for your fate involves a dark assailant.'

The third cries out as all the ships go down:
'There is more than one good way to drown.'

(2)

In the air above my island flies
   a crowd of shining gulls that plunge to launch
an accurate assault upon the eyes

of the bold sailor falling under drench
   and hunger of the surf that plucks the land,
devouring green gardens inch by inch.

Blood runs in a glissando from the hand
   that lifts to consecrate the sunken man.
Aloft, a lone gull halts upon the wind,

announcing after glutted birds have flown:
'There is more than one good way to drown.'

(3)

Grasshopper goblins with green pointed ears
   caper on leafstalk legs across my doorsill,
and mock the jangling rain of splintered stars.

My room is a twittering gray box with a wall
   there and there and there again, and then
a window which proves the sky sheer rigmarole

that happens to conceal the lid of one
  enormous box of gray where god has gone
and hidden all the bright angelic men.

A wave of grass engraves upon the stone:
'There is more than one good way to drown.'

Uncollected Juvenilia

A complete list of poems composed before 1956

This alphabetical list includes all the poems Sylvia Plath composed before 1956. The texts of all but half a dozen of these early pieces are in the Sylvia Plath Archive of juvenilia in the Lilly Library at Indiana University. The rest are with the Sylvia Plath Estate. The bracketed date following certain titles indicates the year of composition, where it is known. An asterisk before a title indicates that it is included in the selection of fifty early poems printed above, p. 299.

*Admonitions
Adolescence (1949)
Advice for an Artificer
*Aerialist
All I Can Tell You Is About the Fog
Alone and Alone in the Woods Was
   I (1948)
Among the Tall Deep-rooted
   Grasses
Apology for an April Satyr
Apparel for April (1953)
Apple Blossom (1943)
*April Aubade
*April 18
*Aquatic Nocturne
August Night
Autumn Portrait

A Ballad
Ballade banale
Bereft (1947)
*Bitter Strawberries
*Black Pine Tree in an Orange Light
Blue-shingled Rooftops (1947)
*Bluebeard
The Bronze Boy

Camp Helen Storrow (1945)
Carnival (1948)
Carnival Nocturne (1953)
Checkmate (1948)
Chef d' œuvre
*Cinderella
*Circus in Three Rings
City Streets
City Wife
Class Song (1950)
Closet Drama
Complaint
The Complex Couch
Crime Doesn't Pay
Crossing the Equator

Danse macabre
The Dark River (1949)
*The Dead
*Denouement
Desert Song
The Desperate Hours
*Dialogue *En Route*
Dirge
*Dirge for a Joker
Dirge for Abigail

339

Obsession (1948)
October (1946)
Ode to a Bitten Plum (1950)
*On Looking into the Eyes of a
  Demon Lover
On the Futility of a Lexicon

P.N.
Paradox
Patience (1948)
Pearls of Dew (1940)
Pigeon Post
Portrait (1948)
Portrait d'une jeune fille
*The Princess and the Goblins
*Prologue to Spring

Question (1949)

The Rain (1945)
Recognition (1948)
Reflection (1948)
Reflections at Twelve
Reverie (1947)
Riddle (1948)
Riverside Reverie (1952)
Rondeau
Rondeau redoublé

The Scarlet Beacon (1946)
Sea Symphony (1947)
Second Winter
Sleepers
Slow, Slow the Rhythm of the Moon
  (1950)
The Snowflake Star (1946)
Solo
*Song for a Revolutionary Love
Song for a Thaw
Song of Eve
Song of the Daydreamer (1948)
Song of the Superfluous Spring
Sonnet for a Green-eyed Sailor
Sonnet: The Suitcases Are Packed
  Again
Sonnet: To a Shade

*Sonnet: To Eva
*Sonnet to Satan
*Sonnet: To Time
*A Sorcerer Bids Farewell to Seem
  Sorrow (1947)
Spring Again (1947)
The Spring Parade (1945)
Spring Sacrament
Spring Song to a Housewife
Steely Blue Crags (1947)
The Stoic
The Stranger (1947)
The Stream
Summer Street (1948)

*Temper of Time
*Terminal
Thy Kingdom Come
To a Dissembling Spring
*To a Jilted Lover
To Ariadne
To Eva
*To Eva Descending the Stair
To Miss Cox
To the Boy Inscrutable as God
To Time
Torch Song
*Touch-and-Go
The Traveller (1948)
*The Trial of Man
*Trio of Love Songs
Triolet frivole
Tulips at Dawn (1948)
Twilight
*Two Lovers and a Beachcomber by
  the Real Sea

Valentine: Lines to a Rich Bachelor
Van Winkle's Village
Virus T.V.
Voices

Wallflower
Warning
Wayfaring at the Whitney
Wellfleet Beach Plums

Juvenilia

When the Stars Are Pale and Cool
White Girl Between Yellow Curtains
White Phlox (1950)
Why Must the Slim Spring Rains Fall
   Now
Wild Geese (1948)
A Winter Sunset (1946)
Winter Words

A Wish Upon a Star (1944)
Words Fall to Winter
Words of Advice to an English Prof

Youth (1947)
Youth's Appeal for Peace (1948)

Zeitgeist at the Zoo

Index of Titles and First Lines

Poems 1956–1963

Index

344

Index

Index

Index

Index

Fifty Early Poems

Index

Index